The ABCs of
Windows 95

The ABCs of
Windows® 95

Sharon Crawford

SYBEX®

San Francisco - Paris - Düsseldorf - Soest

Associate Publisher: Carrie Lavine
Acquisitions Manager: Kristine Plachy
Developmental Editor: Richard Mills
Editor: Vivian Perry
Project Editor: Maureen Adams
Technical Editor: Dean Denno
Desktop Publisher: Get Set! Prepress
Production Coordinator: Nathan Johanson
Indexer: Ted Laux
Cover Designer: Design Site
Cover Photographer: Mark Johann

Library of Congress Card Number: 95-72870
ISBN: 0-7821-1878-X

Manufactured in the United States of America

10 9 8 7

Dedication

For the brave, funny, smart, and enduring women I'm fortunate enough to know. Special thanks to Barbara, Brenda, Chris, Jan, Janna, Jovita, Lana, Linda, Mary Ann, Ruth, Savitha, Vicky, Veronica, and others, past and future. I'm lucky to know you all.

Acknowledgments

Thanks are due to all the wonderful people who helped me in the process of writing this book. Particular thanks go to Eric Belko, Boyd Gilbert, Leland Dumas, Bill (Spongemeister) Karow, Susan Hennessey, John Woram, Barbara Bowman, Jeff Pulver, John Toennies, and the many members of ClubWin (and other fellow beta testers), whose knowledge of Windows 95 is amazing and only surpassed by their generosity in sharing that information with others.

Of course, the fine people at Sybex are the ones responsible for shaping my efforts into a real book: Richard Mills, whose general advice and specific suggestions were invaluable, as always; Vivian Perry, a sensitive and tactful editor; Maureen Adams, who kept the project organized and moving forward; Dean Denno, who reviewed every word of the manuscript for technical accuracy and found every ambiguity; and much deserved thanks to production coordinator, Nathan Johanson; indexer first class, Ted Laux; and the desktop publishing specialists at Get Set! Prepress. This book is greatly enhanced by Cuong Le's drawings, which combine much artistry with technical accuracy.

Lastly, ongoing thanks to Dianne King and Rudy Langer who took a chance on me long ago. And to Charlie, who is everything a partner should be.

Contents at a Glance

Table of Contents

Chapter 16: A Bushel of Applets 251

Introduction

The phenomenon known as Windows 95 has arrived on the scene with more publicity and hype than any software product in history. Part of that is because so many more of us now own computers that the launching of a new operating system is of interest to more people. Another factor is that Windows 95 is genuinely something new on the scene—a real technological step forward. (Microsoft's $400 million advertising budget for Windows 95 didn't hurt, either.)

If you're now confronted (voluntarily or involuntarily) with learning to use Windows 95, this book is all you need to get started. Windows 95 is designed to be explored—that is, given enough time, you can learn all there is to learn all by yourself. But how many of us have unlimited time to learn a new system? Not many.

This book will guide you quickly through the elements of Windows 95 and point you to where all the time-saving and cool stuff can be found.

Who Is This Book For?

This book is written for the person coming to Windows 95 for the first time. There are occasional references to earlier versions of Windows, but previous knowledge of Windows is definitely *not* required.

I assume that you are a reasonably intelligent person so I don't talk to you as if you're a dummy. On the other hand, lots of smart people don't know much about computers, so everything is explained with the absolute minimum of techie talk or jargon. And if a bit of jargon is necessary, it'll be defined in clear terms.

Also assumed is that you want to get going with Windows 95 as soon as possible. You can read just the chapters about subjects that interest you and come back to the others when you're ready, though I recommend not skipping Chapters 1 and 2 because they give you some basic facts about Windows 95 that'll help make you Windows 95-competent that much more quickly.

What's in This Book?

Inside you'll see 17 chapters plus an appendix. I have arranged the chapters so the first seven or eight are the basic stuff that you'll need to move around in Windows 95. The rest of the chapters are also basic, but some will interest you more than others, so feel free to dip into them as questions come up. Here's how the chapters break down:

Chapter 1: What's New about Windows 95?

A short chapter on the things that make Windows 95 different from what has come before. Includes simple definitions of the terms you've heard tossed around at the local computer store like multitasking and virtual memory, plus a summation of the new features that make Windows 95 useful and efficient.

Chapter 2: First Things First (or Second in This Case)

A chapter you shouldn't skip because it includes tips and instructions on using two key elements of Windows 95: shortcuts and the new powers of the mouse. Once you get the hang of using these, you're well on your way to understanding much of Windows 95 on your own.

Chapter 3: Looking at the New Environment

Deals with the Desktop you see on first entering Windows 95. What the elements are and how to make them work for you. Using the Start button and setting the look of your Desktop's colors, display resolution, and fonts.

Chapter 4: Making and Taking Shortcuts

More on those wonderful tools: shortcuts. In fact, everything you'll probably ever need to know about making and using them.

Chapter 5: New Mouse Powers

Details of what the mouse can do now and how you can configure it to do even more. Settings for your mouse and using mouse pointers of many types, including animated ones!

Chapter 6: Exploring

The abilities of the Explorer are described here. Plus how to change window views and navigate through your hard drive's contents. If you're a former user of Windows 3.1, this chapter also explains how to find and use the old File Manager.

Chapter 7: Files and Folders

Here's where you'll find out about moving, copying, renaming, and deleting files and folders. There's also a section on the great search tool called Find and how to use long file names.

Chapter 8: Running Programs

An introduction to all the ways you can run programs so you can set up all your Desktop operations in a way that makes sense to you.

Chapter 9: The Recycle Bin

Another new tool in Windows 95, the Recycle Bin lets you decide the exact margin of safety you want for deleted files. This chapter tells you the easy way to approach setting up the Recycle Bin.

Chapter 10: Using DOS

Windows 95 will run all your DOS programs *better* and *faster* than old DOS. Even the most aggressive games can be tamed and this chapter tells you how.

Chapter 11: Hardware Made Easy

The adoption of the Plug-and-Play standard by an operating system makes hardware installation and configuration positively easy. But even for older hardware, changing hardware can be a simple prospect if you read this chapter.

Chapter 12: Sights and Sounds

This chapter describes all the really cool multimedia features that come with Windows 95, including new sound and video capabilities. You'll see how easy it is to record and play back your own sound files and use the CD player to listen to your favorite music.

Chapter 13: In the Control Panel

Here's where you'll find explanations for all the icons in the Control Panel. Find out what they mean and how to make them work.

Chapter 14: Making Your Own Network

This may not seem like a beginner's topic, but with Windows 95 it can be. This chapter tells everything you need to know to make a simple network of a few computers. Included are explanations of some basic networking terms and step-by-step instructions on buying and installing hardware, plus getting the network running.

Chapter 15: Connecting to the Outside World

More on the neat and useful communications programs built into Windows 95. You'll find easy, step-by-step directions on how to use Exchange, one tool in Windows 95 that is unnecessarily complicated to set up. There's also a section on the Microsoft Network, the online capability that's included in Windows 95.

Chapter 16: A Bushel of Applets

This chapter has simple instructions on how to extract the maximum in benefit from the many included programs such as the calculator, HyperTerminal, Paint, and more.

Chapter 17: Tools to Keep Your System Healthy

Fortunately, Windows 95 comes with a number of system utilities that are handy and, in some cases, essential for keeping your computer happy. This chapter tells you which ones are essential and how to use them.

Appendix

The easiest installation is, of course, the one someone else does for you! But if you need to do your own installation of Windows 95, read this appendix to see how to do it painlessly.

Glossary

A glossary of useful computer terms is included. Some of these words are not discussed in the book but they do float around any environment where you find computers. Knowing what they mean can be helpful.

TIP
You'll see a lot of these—quicker and smarter ways to accomplish a task, based on many, many months spent testing and using Windows 95.

NOTE
You'll see these Notes too. They usually represent alternate ways to accomplish a task or some additional information that needs to be highlighted.

WARNING
In a very few places you'll see a Warning like this one. There are few because it's hard to do irrevocable things in Windows 95 unless you work very hard at it. But when you see a warning, do pay attention to it.

Getting Going

Now it's time to flip the page and get started. I'd be delighted to hear from you if you find the book useful or even if you find it missing something you'd like to see included in a future edition. My e-mail address is **authors@scribes.com.** And don't hesitate—I love getting e-mail.

Hope you enjoy the book—I'm *sure* you'll enjoy Windows 95.

Chapter

1

WHAT'S NEW ABOUT WINDOWS 95?

- **Memory: past and present**
- **Multitasking in Windows**
- **All the new features**

As an operating system, Windows 95 is designed to be "discoverable." This means that as you potter about, you can find many of the features and shortcuts all by yourself. However, most of us have work to do and lives to live, so we don't have endless hours in which to discover the best, shortest, easiest way to do things. This book will give you a quick start on how to use the features of Windows 95 to your best advantage.

In this chapter we'll talk a little about what's different about Windows 95. It's not at all necessary to learn a bunch of technical stuff to use Windows 95 but a little information about the basics goes a long way toward making the whole system more understandable and accessible.

A Little History

Every computer requires an operating system. This, at a minimum, is a set of instructions for setting up a file system and for launching programs. DOS (for Disk Operating System) has been the dominant system for PCs since the first PC in 1981. At first DOS was perfectly adequate for the hardware that existed. DOS could only use a limited amount of memory but that didn't matter because computers didn't *have* much memory.

With DOS, you could only run one program or process at a time. So once you'd finished writing your document, you had to cool your heels waiting for it to print. If your letter needed numbers from your spreadsheet program, you had to close the word processor, open the spreadsheet, get the numbers, close the spreadsheet, open the word processor—you get the picture.

Over time though, programs got bigger and computers got faster but we were still using DOS. Many jury-rigged solutions (including every version of Windows through version 3.11) have been devised to fool DOS into being faster and to even do two tasks at once. All of the "solutions" were based on smoke and mirrors and various types of hocus pocus. And none of them worked very well. The fact is that a system bound to DOS has serious problems doing high-powered work.

Windows 95 is the first system that breaks free from the restrictions imposed by DOS and yet can still run existing DOS and Windows programs. It's a transitional system, in effect, one that advances into the future without leaving all of the past behind.

Memory As It Was Done

Memory has always been a tricky matter on PCs. Back in the earliest days of these machines, the designers of DOS thought that 640,000 bytes (640K) of memory would be the absolute most any program would need to run in. In their defense, let me add that they were working at a time when the latest, greatest desktop machine had maybe 64K total memory!

> **NOTE**
>
> Programs run in memory (random access memory or RAM). RAM is where things happen in your computer. The processor does the work but it can only hold so much information at a time (not a lot), so both the document you are working on and the program instructions for how to work on it are kept in RAM.

So why wouldn't they assume that 640K would be *plenty*? Unfortunately, this turned into a notorious miscalculation right up there with New Coke and over the years many, many people labored long and hard to figure out ways to fool the system. Suffice it to say that many ways were devised and all of them, sooner or later, no matter how elegantly engineered, ended up delivering a message to your Desktop:

> Out of Memory

Another artifact from the age of Windows 3.1 is the "Out of Resources" message—which is just as fatal. And you could run out of resources even when you had massive amounts of memory available.

Memory As It Is Now

In the past, memory was like money. When you ran out, you were busted. But these days if you run out of money in your wallet, you have access to virtual money in the form of a credit card. It's not exactly the same as cash and there is some overhead you have to pay for using it (such as interest charges), but when you're buying stuff it works just like real money.

Windows 95 plays a similar sort of trick when it comes to memory so Windows applications have access to as much memory as they need, no matter how much memory you have actually installed. When you run one or more big memory-hog applications in Windows 95, your actual RAM (whatever amount) is used first. If, for some reason, the program or programs need more memory, Windows 95 is capable of virtualizing as much memory as needed.

This is wonderful stuff because it enables your system to keep plugging along without crashing. The bad news is that after using up your actual RAM, the system has to start using free space on your hard drive. Hard drives are always much slower than RAM so when this happens, you're bound to notice that just about everything on your computer gets a lot slower.

That's why it pays to have as much memory as you can afford (or a little more) to keep processing time down. However, even if you can't afford massive amounts of RAM, you'll still be able to run Windows 95 safely.

Resources are still a matter separate from memory except now they are much harder to deplete. You can open multiple instances of multiple programs and not run out of resources. And unlike previous versions of Windows, if you somehow manage to open enough programs to deplete the resources in Windows 95 (and believe me, it's not easy), you'll be admonished to close some programs before anything else can be opened. What you won't get is a crash.

In addition, if a program crashes in Windows 95, you can close the program and not have the entire system crash and require a reboot. If you ever used Windows 3.0 or 3.1, you know that a crash of your program always brought Windows to a halt as well. Windows 95 has a much smarter way of dealing with resources. If a program crashes, you can close it and get on with other work.

Multitasking As It Was Done

Multitasking is the running of more than one program (or "task") at the same time, requiring that the processor's time be shared among the programs. On a typical desktop PC running typical programs, the operating system gives each process a slice of the processor's time. This time slicing is handled in such a way that each application or process thinks it's the only process running. At least it's supposed to work that way.

Windows 3.1 tries to do *cooperative* multitasking, which requires the willingness of applications to share processor time with one another. Unfortunately, the standard Windows application is no better at sharing than the average three-year-old.

As a result, one was often left staring at the eternal hourglass. The next step: the three-finger salute (Ctrl-Alt-Del) while hoping not too much work would be lost.

Multitasking As It Is Now

With Windows 95, the operating system at last has the authority to tell an application to make way for another process. This is crucial if you want to make sure that no single application can bring the whole system to a halt. This is called *preemptive* multitasking and it's impossible to implement in Windows 3.1 because the underlying system there is still DOS.

Without the necessity of going to DOS for certain file operations, Windows 95 allows you to format a floppy disk, download e-mail, print a document, and enter data in your spreadsheet all at the same time.

So What Else Is New?

Aside from the technical wizardry of multitasking and virtual memory, Windows 95 offers many new features. Some are merely cosmetic while others truly add a new and improved degree of functionality. Which ones are seen as cosmetic and which ones as major improvements depends, of course, on the individual. As with many things in life, one person's indispensable item is another's frippery.

There are enough of these new features, however, so that everyone will be able to find some that are very handy or even essential.

Simple User Interface: The Desktop that greets you when Windows 95 starts is free of clutter and has an obvious entry point, the Start button. The Desktop is an actual working area that you can customize to your heart's content. Chapter 3 provides a quick start on the Desktop elements and how to use them.

A Smarter Mouse: The mouse in Windows 95 is more than a handy point-and-click device. Not only is Windows 95 noticeably more "mousy" than previous operating systems, the mouse has many more functions. For those who've wondered why their mouse has two (or even three) buttons, Chapters 2 and 5 have answers.

Long File Names: You can give your files names up to 255 characters because Windows 95 and all the programs that come with it allow the use of these names. When you give a file a long name, the system also creates a shorter eight-character name so your pre-Windows 95 applications and DOS applications can recognize and deal with it. Chapter 7 covers the use of long file names, including both their advantages and their limitations.

Taskbar: Part of the clean and efficient look of the Desktop is the Taskbar, where the Start button rests. The Taskbar is the home for icons representing all your open programs. A single click on a program icon will bring that program to the top of your display so no matter how many programs you have running, the one you need is immediately at hand. Chapter 3 has more on using the Taskbar.

Almost Infinite Configurability: The organization of your Desktop and menus can, within some limits, be designed and arranged to suit your preferences. Chapters 2 and 4 tell you more about shortcuts, one of the really valuable tools you'll use to customize your setup.

Run Any DOS Program: Almost any DOS program can be run while you're still running Windows 95. And even the most resource-hungry DOS program can be set up to run without having to reboot your machine. Chapter 10 explains the relationship of forces between DOS and Windows 95 and why Windows 95 wins every battle.

Plug and Play: Windows 95 presents the first step toward hardware installation without tears. But even hardware *not* built to the new Plug-and-Play standard is much more likely to be installed and configured without trouble. Installing new hardware is covered in Chapter 11.

Sight and Sound: Multimedia capabilities of considerable power are also included in Windows 95. Want to play music CDs, view video clips, or record your own sound files? All are possible with the right equipment and Windows 95. See Chapter 12 for more information.

Mail and Fax Service: If you have a fax modem, the software necessary to send and receive faxes is built in. E-mail accounts can be easily added to the Microsoft Exchange in Windows 95 so you can centralize all your messaging. Chapter 15 tells you how to set this up.

Next Step

And these are only a few of the features that make Windows 95 special and that you'll find easy to master with the help of this book. In the next chapter, we cut straight to the chase and tell you a couple of important skills and concepts that will give you a head start on using Windows 95. In fact, it's not too much of an exaggeration to say that after Chapter 2, you'll be well equipped to start your own explorations. However, if you also read the rest of the book, you can save yourself some considerable discovery time.

Chapter 2

FIRST THINGS FIRST (OR SECOND IN THIS CASE)

FEATURING

- **New powers for your mouse**
- **What is document-centric?**
- **A short look at shortcuts**

We're going to break with tradition and tell you some very important skills up front and not dole it out in dribs and drabs in a dozen places in the back of the book. Of course, this isn't everything that's important—there's lots more than can fit in a single chapter. That's why there's a whole book. But if you read no more than this chapter, you'll still have a head start on making Windows 95 work for you.

The Newly Talented Mouse

The first thing to understand is that the key to using Windows 95 efficiently is right there on your Desktop—namely, your mouse or trackball. Windows 95 is very mousy compared to any other operating system. In fact, you scarcely have to touch the keyboard at all for most basic operations.

NOTE You *can* still use the keyboard if you like. A list of keyboard commands and shortcuts is included in Chapter 4.

But your old familiar mouse works quite differently now in two important ways.

Mouse Trick #1: First, the right mouse button is used *everywhere.* In fact it's not too much of an exaggeration to say that you can place the pointer almost anywhere, press the right mouse button and something will happen. Usually, you'll see a pop-up menu like one of these:

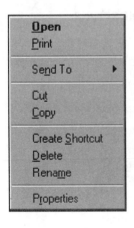

The contents of the menu will vary depending on whether you're pointing at a file, a folder (Windows 95's term for a directory), a Windows 95 element, or an icon representing hardware of some type.

Then there are those occasions when you're looking at a dialog box full of settings—most of which you don't understand. Place your pointer on the text and click the right mouse button. If you see a "What's This?" box like the one shown here you can click on it and get a window of explanation. Usually good information too, so always try that first.

Mouse Trick #2: Here's another way the mouse behaves differently. To open a menu, you click only once on the menu title. Slide the mouse pointer to the item you want to select and (only then) click one more time.

Holding the mouse button down as you move the pointer is limited to those times you're actually dragging and dropping an object. However, there's different behavior depending on whether you're using the left or right mouse button.

Click and Drag Object with	Location	Result
Left mouse button	Within a drive	Object is moved
Left mouse button	Across drives	Object is copied
Right mouse button	Anywhere	Menu allowing choice between moving the object, copying the object, or creating a shortcut

As you can see from the above list, the right mouse button is by far the easiest to use. The left mouse button requires you to remember where the object is relative to your hard drive(s). If you get in the habit of using the right mouse button, you can be saved from that silliness.

Throughout this book a click refers to pressing the left mouse button and right-click means pressing the right button. (Unless you're using a left-handed mouse in which case everything is reversed!)

You'll be using the mouse a lot in Windows 95 so you might as well start practicing now.

NOTE   In Windows 95, the mouse has even more skills that you can read about in Chapter 5.

Document-Centric

In Windows 3.1 or DOS, you used applications to get at your work. For example, to write a letter, you open the word processor and choose New from the File menu. When you want to read or change that letter, you again open the program and use it to get at your letter.

You can still do that in Windows 95. However, Windows 95 also lets you work *another* way. This new way is called the document-centric approach. That is, documents—not the applications that made the documents—are at the center of your work.

With the document-centric approach, your Desktop is an actual workspace. You put folders on the Desktop and inside the folders you put documents (or applications or whatever). When you open the folder, a double-click on the document causes the document to open in whatever application created it.

> **NOTE** It may or may not interest you to know that folders are in fact directories and the Desktop itself is a sort of super-folder. You can use Windows 95 successfully whether you know this or not.

If you've used Windows 3.1, you'll undoubtedly work in ways you always have when you first start using Windows 95. However, over time you'll probably start seeing the usefulness of Desktop folders for shortcuts (see below) to applications and documents of various types. A nice thing about Windows 95 is that it doesn't force you into new ways of working with files until you're ready.

Shortcuts

Shortcuts are necessary to the above-mentioned document-centricity (now *there's* a word!). If you're to use your Desktop as a workplace, you want to be able to organize everything you need in one place and be able to access it instantly. And even when documents aren't involved—as in, say, using a calculator or phone dialer—you'd like to have immediate access to necessary programs without searching for them.

Shortcuts are one of the leading benefits of Windows 95 and yet they're not an *obvious* feature like multitasking or long file names. That's why shortcuts are mentioned here, so you can learn a little about what they are and the part they play in Windows 95.

A shortcut is a little file that acts as a pointer to a file or a folder or a program. For example, a shortcut lets you have as many "copies" of your printer as you want—in as many locations as you want. Of course, a shortcut to the printer isn't really a copy of the printer, just a pointer. With shortcuts you can have your word processor in as many locations as necessary and only use a little hard disk space for each instance. Another advantage of shortcuts is that when you're done with one, you can delete it with impunity. Deleting the shortcut has no effect on the original object.

Shortcuts are identifiable by the little arrow in the lower-left corner of the icon. When created they'll also have a label: "Shortcut to..." followed by the name of the object. Shortcuts can be renamed to make the label more manageable.

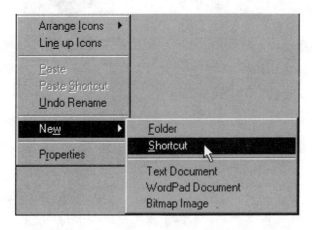

The Create Shortcut option is available:

- On objects' pop-up menus
- From various drop-down menus
- On the Desktop (see Figure 2.1)

FIGURE 2.1:
The Create Shortcut command can be found on many menus.

For more on shortcuts and their many talents, see Chapter 4, where you'll find information on how to make the most of these useful tools.

Next Step

Now that you've been introduced to the basic concepts that make a difference from day one, in the next chapter you'll get an introduction to the Desktop elements you first see when Windows 95 boots up.

Chapter 3

LOOKING AT THE NEW ENVIRONMENT

F E A T U R I N G

- **Using the Start button**
- **Getting help when you need it**
- **Main features of the Desktop**
- **Setting the Desktop's look**

In this chapter, we'll do a quick tour of the screen you see when you first start Windows 95. There'll be a description of what you see and how to get more information on each item. Of course, everything can't be covered in detail here so there are frequent references to later chapters—but we'll try not to bounce around any more than necessary.

Start Button

The opening screen in Windows 95 is a mostly blank Desktop with a Taskbar at the bottom of the screen and two or more icons in the upper-left corner. Fortunately, there's a clear signal where to begin in the form of the Start button in the lower-left corner.

Click once on the Start button to open a menu of choices. Initially there will be only a few basic items but they're enough to get you going. Starting from the top, here's what you'll see.

Programs: Slide the mouse pointer to Programs and you'll get a cascading menu that includes all the programs currently installed plus access to a DOS prompt (more in Chapter 10), the Exchange (that's the mail and fax stuff described in Chapter 15), and the Explorer (talked about here and in Chapter 6 among other places).

You can add programs to the Start menu and change what's on the Programs menu quite easily. Take a look at Chapter 8 for the steps to do just that.

Documents: Windows 95 remembers the files you recently worked on and puts them on this menu. To clear the Documents menu:

1. Right-click on the Taskbar and select Properties.
2. Select Start Menu Programs.
3. Under the Documents menu, click on the Clear button.

There's no way to clear this menu selectively. It's all or nothing.

Settings: Branching off this item, you'll find the Control Panel, the Printers folder, and another way to get at the Taskbar settings. The Control Panel is similar to the one in Windows 3.1. For information on elements in the Control Panel, look them up individually. Printers and their settings are covered in Chapter 11.

Find: This is a neat little program that will let you search for files or even a particular piece of text. Chapter 7 has more on using Find to search for almost anything. You can search your whole computer or just a particular drive. If you're on a network, you can search for a particular computer by name. (There's also the ability to search for something on the Microsoft Network—see Chapter 15 for more on the MSN.)

Select Find and then Files or Folders to open this window.

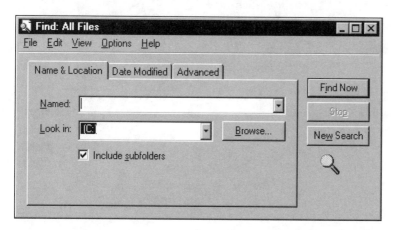

As you can see from the tabs, you can search by name and location and by the date modified. The Advanced tab has an option for searching for a particular word or phrase. The menus include options to make your search case sensitive or to save the results of a search.

The really nice thing about Find is that once you locate the file you want, you can just double-click on the file to open it or you can drag it to another location. In other words, the file or list of files displayed at the end of a search is "live" and you can act on it accordingly.

| **TIP** | **To launch a search of the current file or folder, press the F3 key.** |

Help: The Help files in Windows 95 are much improved over those in the past. They're a lot more searchable, for one thing. When you first select Help you'll a get a window like the one shown in Figure 3.1.

The Contents and Index tabs are pretty straightforward. However, a nice new feature is on the Find tab. Using Find you can search all or part of the help files for a particular word or phrase. This can be really nice when you know the term you want but haven't a clue as to what the authors of the documentation might have filed it under. The first time you use

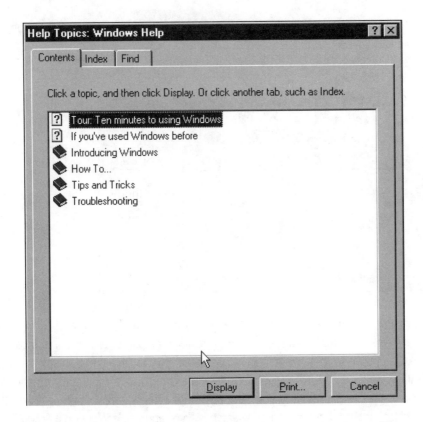

FIGURE 3.1:
Looking for Help in all the right places

this tool, Windows 95 builds a database of help files for future searching. You choose from one of three options:

Minimize database size With this option you don't get every single help file but all the ones likely to have useful information.

Maximize search capabilities This means every help file is included. It's the most thorough approach but may make searches a little slower depending on the speed of your processor and hard drive.

Customize search capabilities Select this option and you can decide which help files go into the database.

After the database is built you can use the Find tab to make very sophisticated searches.

Run: Those who love the command line will find succor here. Select Run and you can type in the name of any program you want to launch. You'll have to include the path but if you like this kind of hands-on operation, you won't mind at all.

TIP

You can also use the Browse button to look around for the program you want. And if you click on the downward arrow, you get a drop-down list of all the recent programs you've run from this box.

Taskbar

The Taskbar starts out at the bottom of your screen. It's the replacement for the sadly under-appreciated Task List in Windows 3.1. Every open program (or folder) will have a button on the Taskbar. This is extremely handy because it means you don't have to close windows or move them aside to find other ones. Click on the button and the corresponding open item will become active.

You can change the Taskbar's location. Just click on it and drag it to the top of the screen or to either side. To make it wider, position the mouse pointer at the edge of the Taskbar and when you see a double-headed arrow, click and drag the border to where you want it.

Make the Taskbar Disappear

If you have a smallish monitor, you may want the Taskbar to disappear except when you need it. To try this look, take these steps:

1. Click on the Start button and select Settings ➣ Taskbar.
2. On the Taskbar Option page put a check mark next to Auto hide.
3. If you want to be able to get at the Taskbar even when you're running a program full-screen, select Always on top as well.

Now when you move the mouse pointer away from the Taskbar, the Taskbar will fade away. Move the mouse pointer back and the Taskbar pops up.

Also on the Taskbar

The right corner of the Taskbar is interesting as well. That's where you'll find active bits of hardware. If you have a sound card and it's working, there'll be a little speaker icon on the Taskbar. Also, when you're printing or faxing, a miniature printer appears in the same area. Position the mouse pointer over the time display and a box showing the day and date will pop open.

If you have an internal modem, sometimes it's hard to tell if the modem is still connected to the phone line. Just look at the Taskbar and if you see this icon next to the time display, the modem is still operating (it may not be operating *correctly*, but that's another matter).

My Computer

This icon is on every Windows 95 Desktop. Double-click on it to see icons for all your drives, plus a folder for the Control Panel and a Printers folder. This isn't the only way to get at your drives—maybe not even the easiest way but some people definitely prefer it to using Explorer.

My Computer and the Explorer are essentially the same thing. (Chapter 6 is all about the Explorer.) This may not be apparent at first because My Computer opens as a single pane with the Large Icons view selected. But if you right-click on the My Computer icon and select Explore from the pop-up menu, you'll see that the two are the same.

One important difference is that My Computer cannot be deleted or even removed from your Desktop. So it's always handy for making changes to settings:

- Right-click on the My Computer icon and select Properties for a look at your hardware. (Chapter 11 has more on using this access to get reluctant hardware to work properly.)
- Double-click on the My Computer icon and select Options from the View menu. On the Folder tab you can select whether you want single-window or separate-window browsing. Single window means that as you go from folder to subfolder to sub-subfolder, only one window is open at a time. Separate window means that the parent folders also stay open.

Single-window browsing is probably to be preferred unless you have a very large monitor. On the average monitor, having every click open a new window (with all the old ones remaining) can turn your Desktop into a crowded mess very quickly.

The My Computer folder is discussed again in Chapter 6.

Recycle Bin

Recycle Bin

The Recycle Bin, as you might imagine, is where old deleted files go to die.

Despite the name, the deleted files aren't recycled unless you rescue them from the bin before they're deleted permanently. Nevertheless, the Recycle Bin gives you a nice margin of safety that wasn't available in Windows 3.1 (unless you had another program that provided it). Now when you delete a file you have days or even weeks (depending on how you set things up) to change your mind and retrieve it.

Chapter 9 is all about the Recycle Bin, how to configure and use it to your best advantage. In the meantime, here are two important facts about the Recycle Bin:

- The Recycle Bin icon cannot be renamed or deleted.
- Files that are deleted using DOS programs or any program that's not part of Windows 95 are not sent to the Recycle Bin. They're just deleted. Be careful.

NOTE Other icons that may be on your desktop, depending on the installation, may include the Inbox, Microsoft Network, and a globe labeled The Internet. Use of these is covered in Chapter 15.

Properties Sheets

In Windows 3.1 it's a real pain sometimes to find out how to change the settings for something. Depending on whether it was a file or a program or a piece of hardware, you had to memorize where critical settings were found. This is all changed in Windows 95 so now there's only one rule to remember:

- Right-click on the object and select Properties.

When you select Properties, you open what's called a Properties sheet. Properties sheets vary, of course. Some types of files will have multiple pages in the Properties sheet, others will have only one page and very few options. Figure 3.2 shows a Properties sheet for a simple text file.

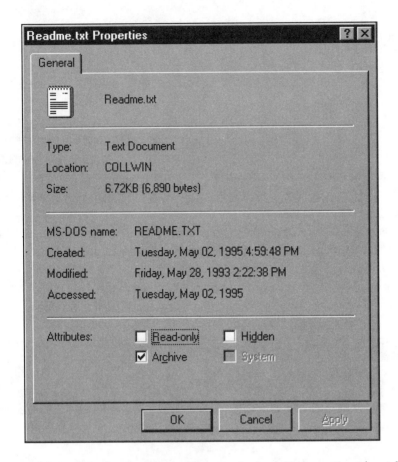

FIGURE 3.2:
A Properties sheet
for a text file

Properties sheets are valuable repositories of information about files, programs, and devices. So when you find yourself with a program or a piece of hardware that isn't working the way you want it to, refer to the rule above. As a matter of fact, you might apply that rule to just about every aspect of Windows 95. When you want to know more about *any-thing* in Windows 95, right-click on it and see what appears.

How to use Properties sheets is discussed in later chapters. For example, the Properties sheets for DOS programs are covered in Chapter 10, the Properties sheets for printers are covered in Chapter 11, and so forth.

Desktop Settings

The default Windows 95 screen is not one likely to induce little cries of joy unless you're a total neat freak, and then you won't want to change a thing. However, most of us will find it a tad boring. But you can have it as plain or fancy as you want.

Remember that you can use the entire area of your monitor's screen in Windows 95. You can have many folders, a few, or none. You can have all your programs on menus that fold out of the Start button's menus or you can have program icons on the Desktop where you can open them with a double-click.

Even better, you can have colors, fonts, and Desktop wallpaper of many types. Here's how to get at all the settings that affect the Desktop.

Move the pointer to a blank spot (of which there's a muchness) and click the right mouse button. Select Properties from the pop-up menu and you're there (see Figure 3.3).

Each tab covers one aspect of the display. Next, we'll explore the contents of individual pages.

Background

Here you set the wallpaper and background pattern much like the Desktop settings in Windows 3.1. Use the Browse button to locate files you can use as wallpaper.

Any files that are bitmaps (.BMP) or device-independent bitmaps (.DIB) can be used as wallpaper.

TIP The Apply button lets you see how a setting will work without having to close the Display Properties box.

Screen Saver

If you installed screen savers—either the ones that come with Windows 95 or some other package—you can adjust the settings on this page. All the installed screen savers are in the Screen Saver drop-down list.

Click on the Preview button to get a full-screen view of the selected screen saver. Move your mouse or press any key on the keyboard to return to the display properties.

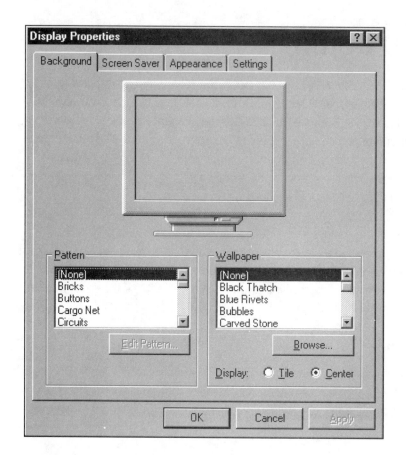

FIGURE 3.3:
The Properties sheets for display

Appearance

This page is also similar to Desktop settings in Windows 3.1. Use one of the many color combinations listed under Schemes or make your own.

Click on any of the elements in the window at the top of the Appearance page and a description appears in the Item box. Change the size or color, or both. If there's a font that can be changed, the current one will show in the Font box.

Settings

Of all the pages in the Display properties, this page has the most going on (see Figure 3.4). Here's where you can change how your screen actually looks (as well as what Windows 95 knows about your display hardware).

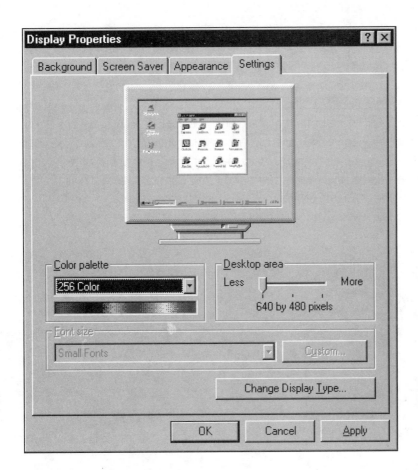

FIGURE 3.4:
The page for changing display settings

Changing Resolutions

Displays are described in terms of their resolution—that's the number of dots on the screen and the number of colors that can be displayed at the same time. The resolutions you can choose using the slider under Desktop Area are determined by the hardware you have. You can't make your monitor and video card display more than is built into them.

Here are the most likely possibilities:

- 640x480 A standard VGA display that's 640 pixels wide by 480 pixels high.
- 800x600 A typical SVGA display (super VGA).
- 1024x768 This is the upper limit of SVGA and the beginning of more advanced systems such as 8514/A and XGA. This is a very fine (that is, non-grainy) resolution but if your monitor is 15 inches or smaller, you'd better have very good eyes.
- 1280x1024 A very fine resolution but one that requires a large monitor. Even with a 17-inch screen, you'll need good eyes.

You'll notice as you move the slider toward higher resolutions that the number of colors displayed in the Color Palette box changes. As resolution numbers go up, color numbers have to go down because they're both competing for the same video memory. That's why, if you want the most realistic color represented on your screen, you'll need a video card (also called a display adapter) with 2, 4, or more megabytes of its own memory.

Resolution choices are based on what you like to look at—constrained by the capabilities of your monitor and video card. At the lowest resolution, you may not be able to see all the elements of some programs, so try the next higher resolution. At the highest resolutions, screen elements are very small, so you may want to try Large Fonts from the Font Size box. That will make the captions on the Desktop easier to see.

Most of the time you'll have to reboot to see the effect of these changes.

NOTE   If you change your screen resolution, you may end up with some very peculiar arrangements of your icons. They may be way too far apart or so close together that they're difficult to use. The Appearance page has controls for the spacing of icons. Pull down the Item drop-down list and select one of the Icon Spacing choices. You can also select Icon and change both the size of your icons and their font. However, I strongly recommend that you make note of the original settings because it's fairly easy to make a hash of your Desktop and not remember where you started.

Changing the Display Type: Also on the Settings tab is a button labeled Change Display Type. This is used when you're changing either your display adapter (video card) or monitor. (Or if you want to use a different video driver beside the one Windows 95 is currently using.)

Click on the Change Display Type button and you'll see a window like the one in Figure 3.5. To change either the adapter or the monitor, click on the Change button and follow the instructions.

NOTE   If you have the Plus! for Windows 95 package, there will also be a property sheet tab for Plus! which lists various visual enhancements that Plus! provides. Choices that are grayed-out are not available because your hardware can't deliver them. To configure Desktop themes using Plus! use the Themes icon in the Control Panel.

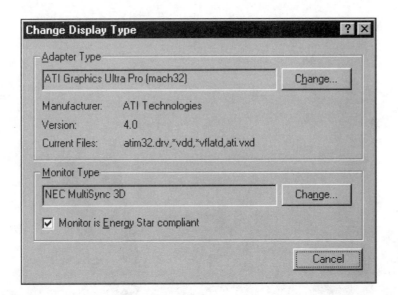

FIGURE 3.5:
Information about
your video system

Next Step

Now that you've been at least casually introduced to Windows 95, we'll move to specifics. In the next chapter you'll find everything you need to know about the tools known as *shortcuts*—which will probably become indispensable very quickly.

Chapter 4

MAKING AND TAKING SHORTCUTS

Shortcuts introduce a new level of convenience and customization to Windows. They're meant to be convenient ways to get at all the things on your computer or network: documents, applications, folders, printers, and so on. So they're most likely to be placed on your desktop, on the Start menu or in the Send To folder. In this chapter, we'll cover all the ways to make and modify a shortcut and how to place the shortcuts you want in the places you want them to be.

A shortcut is identified by the small arrow in the lower-left corner of the icon (see Figure 4.1).

The arrow isn't just there to be cute. It's important to know (particularly before a deletion) whether something is a shortcut or a real object. You can delete shortcuts at will. You're not deleting anything that you can't recreate in a second or two. But if you delete an actual program or other file, you'll have to rummage around in the Recycle Bin to retrieve it. (And if it's a while before you notice it's missing, the Recycle Bin may have been emptied in the meantime and the object is *gone*.)

NOTE Configuring and using the Recycle Bin is covered in Chapter 9.

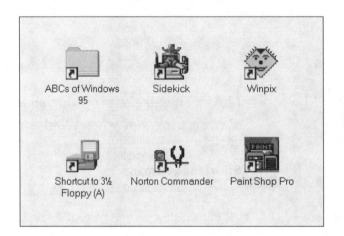

FIGURE 4.1:
All shortcut icons have an arrow in the lower-left corner.

Here's an example. I have a folder on my hard drive called *ABCs of Windows 95*. On my Desktop, I have a shortcut to that folder. If I delete the shortcut folder on my Desktop, the folder on the hard drive remains untouched. If I delete the folder on the hard drive, the shortcut is still there but there's nothing for it to point to. And when I click on the shortcut, I get a dialog box like the one shown in Figure 4.2.

FIGURE 4.2:
If you delete or move the original object, you'll see this window when you try to open the shortcut.

You'll find the Create Shortcut option in a lot of places, including:

- On objects' pop-up menus (see Figure 4.3)
- From various drop-down menus
- On the desktop pop-up menu as New ➢ Shortcut

FIGURE 4.3:
Create Shortcut is an option almost every time you use the right mouse button to click on an object.

Shortcuts are an excellent tool for configuring your Desktop to suit you. You can make shortcuts to folders, to programs, and to individual files. Arrange them any way you want on the Desktop, inside other folders, or on menus.

NOTE   Until Windows 95, the term shortcut always referred to a keyboard shortcut—in other words, a combination of keys that would produce some action on screen. But now we have shortcuts meaning pointers. In this book, "shortcut" will always mean a pointer and "keyboard shortcut" will be used when a key combination is meant.

How to Make a Shortcut

Shortcuts are pointers to objects. So you need to either find the object you want to point to or be able to tell the system where the original object is located. The easiest way to make a shortcut to a program is to right-click on the Start button and select Explore. The contents of your Start menu, including the Programs folder, will be in the right pane of the window that opens. Click your way down through the tree until you find the program you want.

You can also open Explorer and similarly find the program. Explorer (or My Computer) is where you'll need to look to find drives, printers, or folders when you want to make shortcuts to them. Explorer (or My Computer) will also be needed for a DOS program or any other program that doesn't manage to install itself off the Start menu.

With the Original in View

To make a shortcut when you have the original object in view inside the Explorer or My Computer, follow these steps:

1. Point to the object and click on it once with the right mouse button.
2. Holding the button down, drag the object to the Desktop.

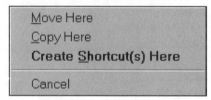

3. When you release the mouse button, you'll see a menu like the one at the left.
4. Select Create Shortcut(s) here.

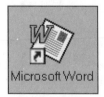

Here's a shortcut to the Word for Windows program on the Desktop. This shortcut, when double-clicked, will open the Word for Windows program.

> **TIP**
>
> If you use the method of right-clicking on the Start button described above, you'll be using a shortcut to make another shortcut, without having to go back to the original object. Just right-click on the shortcut and select Make Shortcut from the menu that opens.

Cut and Paste a Shortcut

Another way to make a shortcut is to right-click on the program or file, and select Create Shortcut from the pop-up menu. A shortcut to the object you clicked on will appear in the same folder. You can then move the shortcut by right-clicking on it and using Cut from the menu. Then right-click where you want the shortcut to be and choose Paste. (Or you can drag it from the folder and drop it in a new location.)

To Objects You Don't See

If the original object isn't handy or you don't want to go find it, you can still create a shortcut as follows:

1. Right-click on the Desktop and select New ➤ Shortcut.
2. In the dialog box that opens, type in the location and name of the original object. If you don't know the path (and who ever does?), click on the Browse button.
3. Using the Browse window, mouse around until you find the file or object you want to link to. You may have to change the Files of Type item in the Browse window to read All Files. Highlight the file with the mouse (the name will appear in the File name box) and click on Open.
4. The Command line box will now contain the name and location of the object. Click on Next and accept or change the name for the shortcut.
5. Click on Finish and the shortcut appears on your Desktop.

Renaming a Shortcut

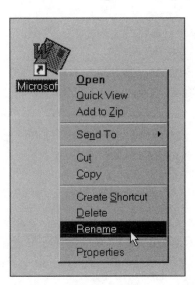

When you create a shortcut, the system always gives it a name that starts with "Shortcut to" and then names the object the shortcut is pointing to. To rename the shortcut, you can right-click on the icon and select Rename from the menu that opens.

Type in the name you want. Click on a blank spot on the Desktop when you're through.

You can also rename a shortcut (or most other icons for that matter) by clicking once on the name, waiting a second or two, and clicking again. That'll highlight the name and you can edit it as you wish.

Choosing a Name

When you rename a shortcut, take full advantage of long file names to give it a name that's meaningful to you. No need to get carried away, but you might as well call a folder March Budget Reports rather than MARBUDGT, as you might have previously. Certain characters aren't allowed in shortcut names: / \ < > | : " ? * but you ought to be able to live without those few.

Starting a Program When Windows Starts

You may have programs you want to have started and ready to run when you start Windows—for example, your calendar or other application that you want to be able to launch immediately. Windows 95 includes a startup folder for such programs. To put a shortcut in the startup folder, follow these steps:

1. Right-click on the Start button and select Open or Explore from the pop-up menu.
2. Double-click on Programs and then Startup.
3. Drag shortcuts to the programs you want launched into the Startup folder. If you want to leave the original shortcut where it is, drag with the right mouse button and choose Copy Here from the menu that pops up when you release the button.

To specify how you want the programs to look when Windows 95 starts:

1. Right-click on the shortcut and select Properties.
2. Click on the Shortcut tab.
3. In the Run window select Minimized (or Normal or Maximized).
4. Click on OK when you're done.

A minimized program will be on the Taskbar after the system starts. A Maximized selection will cause the program to appear full-screen. Normal will be whatever the normal-sized window is for that program.

Putting Shortcuts Where You Want Them

Obviously, the point of shortcuts is to save time and energy. Merely placing a bunch of shortcuts on your desktop may help you or it may not. So here are a number of other ways shortcuts can be made useful.

Putting a Start Menu Item on the Desktop

As you've seen, when you click on the Start menu and follow the Programs arrow, you get a hierarchical display of all the programs installed on your system. All those menu items are just representations of shortcuts. To find them and put the ones you want on your Desktop, you'll need to (if you'll pardon the expression) go Exploring.

1. Right-click on the Start button and select Open or Explore.
2. Double-click on the Programs icon.
3. Find the programs you want here or you may have to go down another level by clicking on one of the folders.
4. Right-click on the shortcut you want and drag it to the Desktop, selecting Create Shortcut Here from the menu that opens when you release the mouse button.

Adding a Program to the Start Menu

You undoubtedly have some programs that you'd like to get at without having to go through the menus or without searching around the Desktop. To add a program to the top of the Start menu, just click on a shortcut, drag it to the Start button, and drop it on top. Then when you click on the Start button, the program will be instantly available (as shown in Figure 4.4).

Remove programs from the Start menu by selecting Start ➤ Settings ➤ Taskbar. Click on the Start Menu Programs and then the Remove button. Highlight the program you want to remove and then click on the Remove button.

As you can see in Figure 4.5, you can also use this page to add programs to the Start menu, though it requires more steps than the simple drag-and-drop method.

> **NOTE** This page is also where you can clear the Documents menu that branches off from the Start menu.

Adding a Shortcut to *Send To*

When you right-click on most things in Windows 95, one of the choices on the menu is Send To. By default, the Send To menu includes shortcuts to your floppy drive (or drives) and also may include (depending on your installation) shortcuts to mail and fax recipients.

FIGURE 4.4:
Add your favorite programs to the top of the Start menu for instant access.

To add a shortcut to Send To, follow these steps:

1. Click on the Start button and select Programs ➢ Windows Explorer.
2. In the Explorer, find your Windows folder in the left pane and double-click on it.
3. Under the Windows folder, find the Send To folder and double-click.
4. Use the right mouse button to drag and drop shortcuts into this folder to add them to the Send To menu.

You may have to open a second instance of the Explorer to get at other folders if the shortcuts you want are not on the Desktop. Or you can use Copy and Paste on the right mouse button menu.

> **NOTE** When you use Send To, you're actually doing the equivalent of drag and drop. The item you've highlighted will be dropped on the selection you make in Send To.

Shortcut Settings

Every shortcut has a Properties sheet that you can get at by right-clicking on the shortcut icon and selecting Properties from the pop-up menu. For shortcuts to Windows objects (as opposed to DOS programs), the more interesting tab is the one labeled Shortcut (shown in Figure 4.6).

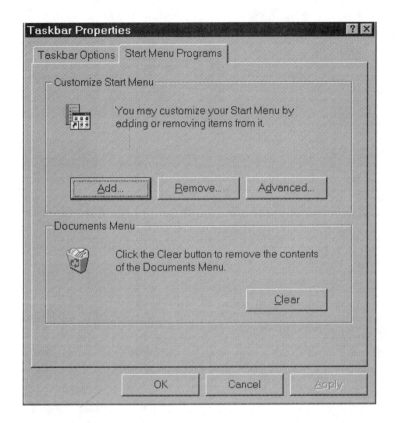

FIGURE 4.5:
You can use the Taskbar settings to add and remove programs from the Start menu.

Finding the Target

Click on the Find Target button to find out just where the shortcut is pointing. When you click on this button, a window opens into the folder containing the application or file the shortcut is for.

Changing a Shortcut's Icon

Shortcuts to programs will display the icon associated with that program. However, shortcuts to folders and documents are pretty dull. In any case, you can change the icon for a shortcut by following these steps:

1. Right-click on the icon and select Properties from the pop-up menu.
2. Select the Shortcut tab and click on the Change Icon button.
3. Highlight an icon from the default SHELL32.DLL file (see Figure 4.7) or use the browse button to look in other files (WINDOWS\MORICONS.DLL has a bunch).
4. Click on OK twice and the new icon will be displayed.

Many icons are available from icon libraries that are distributed as shareware. Icons are

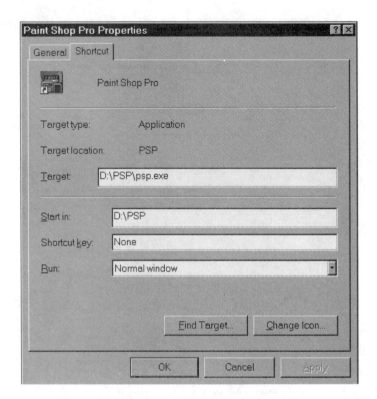

FIGURE 4.6:
The main Properties sheet for a shortcut to a Windows program

often included in executable files so if you have a shortcut to an application (a file with an .EXE extension) you can pick from those icons as well.

Using the Keyboard

If you're fond of opening certain applications with key strokes, you can still do so in Windows 95—with some limitations. At the end of this chapter, you'll find a list of the keyboard shortcuts used to move around the screen, however, you can also set up a key combination to open a shortcut to a program or folder.

1. Right-click on the shortcut and select Properties.
2. On the Shortcut page click in the Shortcut key field.
3. Type in a letter and Windows will add Ctrl+Alt. (So if you enter a **W**, the keyboard combination will be Ctrl+Alt+W.)
4. Click on OK when you're finished.

To remove a keyboard shortcut, you need to click in the Shortcut key field and press the Backspace key.

FIGURE 4.7:
The SHELL32.DLL file has a number of icons to choose from.

It's best to limit keyboard shortcuts to just a few programs or folders because these shortcuts have precedence in Windows. So if you define a keyboard combination that's also used in a program, that program loses the ability to use the key combination.

When the Linked Object Is Moved or Renamed

As I've said, the shortcut is only a pointer to the original object—a pretty smart pointer, but with limitations. If you move the original object, the shortcut can almost always find it. (It may take a few seconds the first time for the search to be made.) Even renaming the original object doesn't thwart Windows 95.

However, if you move the original object to a different drive or both move and rename the original object, the system will offer you a chance to Browse for the original object. If that doesn't appeal to you, just let the search continue. Windows 95 will come up with a suggestion.

If the proposed solution is correct, click on Yes. If it's not, select No. Click on the shortcut with the right mouse button and select Properties. In the Properties sheet, provide the correct path for the shortcut.

WARNING Shortcuts to DOS programs will not be so forgiving. So if you move your game to another drive or rename a batch file, plan on making new shortcuts.

Shortcuts to Other Places

Shortcuts quickly become a normal way of accessing files and programs on your own computer but they're a much more powerful tool than you'd suspect at first.

DOS Programs

Shortcuts to DOS programs are made in the same way as other shortcuts. Find the program file in the Explorer and do a right-mouse drag to the Desktop. However, the Properties pages for a DOS program are more complex to allow for individual configuration of older programs. Chapter 10 covers these settings in some detail.

Disk Drives

Right-click on a disk drive in the Explorer or My Computer and drag it to the Desktop to create a shortcut to the contents of a drive. When you click on the shortcut, you'll see its contents almost instantly—it's much quicker than opening the entire Explorer.

Other Computers

You can put a shortcut to another computer—or part of it—on the Desktop. It can be a computer you're connected to on a network or even a computer you connect to using Dial-Up Networking. Just use Network Neighborhood to find the computer or part of it or even a single file, right-click on it and drag it to your Desktop (or another folder) and create a shortcut there.

HyperTerminal Connections

After you've used HyperTerminal to make a connection, you can drag the connection out of the folder onto your Desktop. Double-click on it and the call will be made.

TIP | **HyperTerminal is an applet that comes with Windows 95 and is described in Chapter 16.**

In E-mail and Other Documents

Shortcuts can even be dropped into your e-mail or other documents. This still has limited use but if you're communicating with someone who's also using, say, the Microsoft Network, you can send a shortcut to a location on MSN or the Internet. The recipient has only to double-click on the shortcut and the appropriate connection will be made.

As you can see, shortcuts are a valuable tool now and have even more potential in the future. As you experiment, you'll find even more ways to use shortcuts that are specific to your needs and work habits.

Keyboard Shortcuts

Even though Windows 95 is much more mousy than earlier versions of Windows, you can still do practically everything from the keyboard. Of course, you probably can't be bothered memorizing all these keyboard combinations, but you may want to consider a few for your memory bank (the one in your head) particularly if there are actions that you do repeatedly that you find the mouse too clumsy for.

The following table includes the most useful (and in many cases, undocumented) keyboard shortcuts.

Key	Action
F1	Help.
F2	Rename the file or folder that's highlighted.
F3	Open Find.
F4	Open the drop-down list in the Toolbar. Press F4 a second time and the drop-down list will close.
F5	Refresh the view in the active window.
Tab or F6	Each time you press this key, the focus will move from the drop-down window in the Toolbar to the left pane to the right pane and back again.
F10 or Alt	Put the focus on the menu bar. To move between menus, use the left ← and right → arrow keys. The ↓ key will open the menu.
Backspace	Move up one level in the folder hierarchy.
Right arrow →	Expand the highlighted folder. If the folder is already expanded, go to the subfolder.
Left arrow ←	Collapse the highlighted folder. If it's already collapsed, move up one level in the folder hierarchy.
Alt+Esc	Switch between open applications. Hold down the Alt key and each press of Esc will take you to another application. Applications on the Taskbar, once highlighted, can be activated by then clicking on Enter once or twice.
Alt+Tab	Open a window in the middle of the screen with icons representing all

Key	Action
	open files and folders (see Figure 4.8 at the end of this table). Hold down the Alt key and press Tab to move the cursor from item to item.
Alt+Shift+Tab	Move the cursor through the open items in the opposite direction from Alt+Tab.
Ctrl+Esc	Open the Start menu.
Alt+F4	Close the current application. If no application is open, will activate the Shut Down window.
Alt+Spacebar	Open the Control Menu (same as clicking on the icon at the extreme upper-left corner of the application or folder window).
Spacebar	When the selection cursor in a dialog box is selected, will toggle the choice.
Tab	Move the selection cursor to the next choice in a folder or dialog box.
Shift+Tab	Move the selection cursor in the opposite direction from Tab.
PrintScreen	Copies the current screen to the Clipboard from which it can be pasted into Paint or another graphics application.
Alt+PrintScreen	Copy the active window to the Clipboard.

NOTE   The Clipboard mentioned above is a special place in memory and not a specific application. However, there is a Clipboard Viewer (available under Accessories) that can see whatever you copy. If it's not installed, go to Add/Remove Programs in the Control Panel. Select Windows Setup and then Accessories.

In addition to the above shortcuts, there are a number of key combinations that have a special effect when you're starting up your machine. These keys are used as soon as you see the message: *Starting Windows 95*.

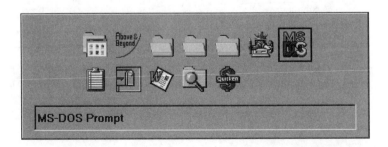

FIGURE 4.8:
Using Alt+Tab to switch between active programs and folders

Key	Action
F4	Start the previous operating system. In other words, if you have Windows 95 installed on a computer that also has a directory for DOS 6.x or earlier, this key will force the loading of DOS.
F5	Start Windows 95 in safe mode. Safe mode is a sure-fire way to get your system to boot. If you have, for example, accidentally changed something that causes your whole system to go south, use safe mode to change it back. Safe mode bypasses your AUTOEXEC.BAT and CONFIG.SYS files, if you have them.
Shift+F5	Start at the DOS 7 command line. Also bypasses AUTOEXEC.BAT and CONFIG.SYS files.
Ctrl+F5	Start at the DOS 7 command line without compressed drives. Any Doublespaced or Drivespaced drives will not be available.
F6	Start Windows 95 in safe mode but include network connections.
F8	Go to the following menu before starting Windows 95: 1. Normal 2. Logged (BOOTLOG.TXT) 3. Safe mode 4. Safe mode with network support 5. Step-by-step confirmation 6. Command prompt only 7. Safe mode command prompt only 8. Previous version of MS-DOS
Shift+F8	Go through CONFIG.SYS and AUTOEXEC.BAT one line at a time, letting you choose which commands to accept.
Shift	Bypass all the programs in the Startup folder.

Next Step

Now that you're introduced in detail to shortcuts, we'll cover some of the new strengths that Windows 95 gives to the mouse (or whatever pointing device you use).

Chapter 5

NEW MOUSE POWERS

FEATURING

- **Understanding double- and single-click**
- **Right clicks and left clicks**
- **Setting up your mouse**
- **Changing pointers**

The Windows user interface has always depended on a mouse or other pointing device and with Windows 95 that reliance is even more pronounced. You can still do most things from the keyboard (Chapter 4 has a whole list of key combinations) but everything is much easier when you're using a mouse. Fewer steps are required and there's no memorization, as there is when you use the keyboard a lot.

> **NOTE** In this chapter the term *mouse* is used but all devices that perform point-and-click actions (such as trackballs and pens) are included.

Everywhere you go in Windows 95, you can click with the mouse to produce an action—whether it's opening a file or just getting helpful information. In this chapter we'll discuss how the mouse works and how you can customize most functions for your own use.

Double- or Single-Click

It's not always easy in Windows 95 to know whether to double- or single-click the mouse button. The double-click (two rapid clicks in succession) with the left mouse button serves to open icons on the Desktop. If the icon represents a program, the program is started. If the icon represents a folder, the folder expands into a window on the Desktop so you can see and get at what's inside.

A single click with the left mouse button serves to highlight the item clicked on. So if you're choosing a file in the Explorer or other folder with the idea of moving it or acting on it in some other way—other than opening it—a single click will do the job.

Windows 95 attempts to reduce the number of clicks needed by making use of the right mouse button. Use the right mouse button to click on a file or folder and you have an array of choices on the menu that pops up. The top choice on this menu is usually Open, so you can open a program or file or folder with the right mouse button as easily as double-clicking with the left. Other functions are just as direct.

The Right Mouse Button

You can right-click on everything on the Desktop as well as the Desktop itself. As mentioned in Chapter 2, a right-click almost anywhere will provide some helpful result. All the programs that come with Windows 95 as well as programs written specifically for Windows 95 will use the right mouse button extensively. Bear in mind that programs written for Windows 3.1 will not use the right mouse button in the same way, though quite a few have some right-mouse button functionality built in.

Right-Click on a File

Right-click on a file and you're presented with a menu of multiple options, including opening the file with its associated program.

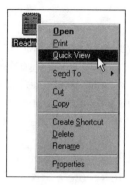

If there's a Quick Viewer associated with the file, you can get a look at the contents by choosing Quick View from the menu.

If the file is of a registered file type, you can get still another option. Hold down the Shift key while right-clicking and you get Open With—an option that lets you open the file with a different application.

A number of programs will add other entries to the right mouse button menu. For example, the archiving program WinZip puts the item Add to Zip on the menu so you can select files to be added to an archive.

Right-Click on a Folder

The menu that opens when you right-click on a folder is similar to the one for a file. If you chose Open, you'll see the contents of the folder. Explore does much the same thing, except the folder will be shown in Explorer view—two panes with the left one showing the folder and its placement on the hard drive and the right pane detailing the folder's contents.

You can also select Find to search the folder for a particular file either by name or by contents. (There's more on using Find in Chapter 7.)

Right-Click on the Start Button

Place your pointer on the Start button and right-click to bring up three choices:

- Open will open the Start Menu folder. This is the folder that contains the programs you've dropped on the Start Menu as well as another folder called Programs that contains all the shortcuts that make up the Programs menu that cascades off the Start Menu.
- Explore will open the Start Menu folder but in the Explorer view.
- Find is a shortcut to finding a file in the Start Menu folder.

The first two choices on the menu are quick ways to get at the items on the Programs menu so you can move a program up a level or two or remove one from the menu entirely. If you choose Explore, the window that opens will have two panes, the left one showing the folder and its place in the file system, the right pane showing the files inside whatever folder is chosen on the left. If you choose Open, the view is of a single window. When you double-click on a folder, another window opens showing the contents.

Right-Click on the Taskbar

When you right-click on a blank spot on the Taskbar a menu pops up with options to:

- Cascade the windows that are currently open on the Desktop.
- Tile the open windows horizontally.
- Tile the open windows vertically.
- Minimize all the open windows to the Taskbar.
- Access the Taskbar properties.

Right-Click on Icons on the Taskbar

Open programs and folders will each have an icon on the Taskbar. Right-click on the icon and, if the item isn't open on the Desktop, you'll get the option to Restore (in other words, open a window on the Desktop), Maximize (restore it full screen), or Close.

For items that have a window open on the Desktop, a left click on the icon will bring that window to the front. A right click will bring the window to the front plus open the same menu.

Move and Size are keyboard options. Select one of them and you can move the window or change its size using the arrow keys.

Right-click on other icons in the far right corner of the Taskbar and you'll get a chance to adjust the date and time or adjust the volume on your sound card. Other icons may appear in this section of the Taskbar depending on the hardware and software installed. As in other places, just try the right click and see what you get!

Right-Click on My Computer

Right-click on the My Computer icon on the Desktop and you have the option of opening My Computer in a regular window or in Explorer view. You can also connect or disconnect network drives, find files or computers, or open the Properties sheets for your system. There's considerably more about My Computer in Chapter 6.

Mouse Settings

Because the mouse (or other pointing device) is used so much in Windows 95, it's important to have it set up comfortably. To change how your mouse operates, settings are available in the Mouse icon in the Control Panel.

Right- or Left-Handed

To change your right-handed mouse to a left-handed one, double-click on the Mouse icon in the Control Panel. On the Buttons page, click on the left-handed button to swap left and right mouse buttons. On a three-button mouse, these are the two outside buttons.

Setting That Middle Mouse Button

If you have a Logitech pointing device, it probably has three buttons. The software that came with the device includes the Mouse Control Center. If you run this program after Windows 95 is installed, the middle mouse button can be set to double-click (Figure 5.1).

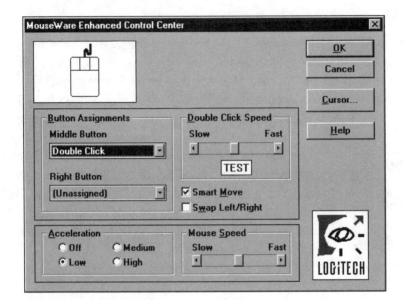

FIGURE 5.1:
Set the middle mouse button of a Logitech mouse or trackball to double-click.

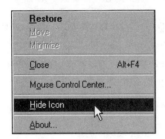

After you click on OK, the program is minimized to your Taskbar.

Right-click on the minimized icon and select Hide Icon to make it invisible.

Double-Click on Speed

You can adjust the amount of time allowed between two mouse-clicks for them to be counted as a double-click. Open the Mouse icon in the Control Panel. On the Buttons page, move the slider under Double-Click Speed toward Slow or Fast. Double-click in the Test area to try out a different setting.

TIP

If you have a three-button mouse with the middle button set to double-click, move the double-click speed here all the way to Fast. It won't change the double-click speed for your mouse's middle button but it will make all the menus in Windows 95 open much faster.

Pointer Speed

As you move the pointer around the Desktop, perhaps you find you have to move the device too much to get a small result on the screen. Or vice versa, you move the mouse just a little and the pointer moves way too far. To adjust this, double-click on the Mouse icon in the Control Panel.

1. Select the Motion tab.
2. Move the slider under Pointer Speed one notch to the left or the right.
3. Click on the Apply button and try the new setting.
4. Repeat until you have a speed you like and click on OK.

Making the Pointer More Visible

If you're working with a smaller screen—particularly the kind on a laptop, you may find the pointer "disappearing" sometimes. To make the pointer more visible, open the Mouse icon in the Control Panel and select the Motion Tab.

Click on the box next to Show Pointer Trails. Use the slider to adjust for long or short trails. You can see the results as you move the slider, without having to use the Apply button.

Mouse Pointers

Windows 95 comes with an assortment of new mouse pointers, so you can choose ones you like. You'll probably find them a big improvement on the default pointers. A few of the pointers included with Windows 95 are animated, and many more animated cursors come with the Plus! package.

Animated cursors are also on their way to becoming the kind of cottage industry that icons were with earlier versions of Windows. Animated cursors can be downloaded from many online services and are also distributed as shareware.

NOTE Your display must be set to at least 256 colors for the animated cursors to work. To check your settings, open the Display icon in the Control Panel and click on the Settings button. The color palette must be set for 256 colors, High Color, or True Color.

Figure 5.2 shows the Pointers page under Mouse Properties. These default pointers are described in the table that follows. Once you understand what each pointer represents, you're better able to select appropriate substitutes. For example, you wouldn't want an animated pointer for Text Select because the animation would make it very difficult to make a precise selection.

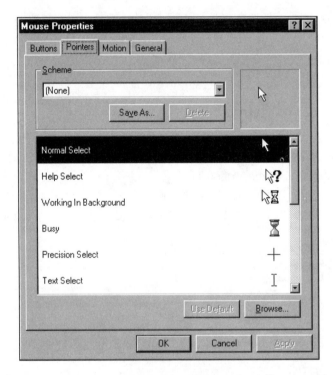

FIGURE 5.2:
The pointers that are used by default in Windows 95

Pointer	What It Does
Normal Select	The normal pointer for selecting items.
Help Select	Click on the ? button and move the pointer to the area you want information about and click again.
Working in Background	Something is going on in the background, but you can often move to another area and do something else.
Busy	Just hang in there. Windows 95 or an application is doing something and can't be disturbed.
Precision Select	Cross-hairs for very careful selection.

Pointer	What It Does
Text Select	The I-beam that's seen in word processors and used to select text.
Handwriting	When you're using a handwriting input device.
Unavailable	Sorry, you can't drag a file to this location either because the area is unacceptable or the application won't accept drag and drop.
Resizing	Cursors that appear when you're moving a window border.
Move	Select Move from the system menu or a right-click menu and you'll get this cursor, allowing you to move the window using the arrow keys.
Alternate Select	Used in the FreeCell card game. Probably other uses to come.

Changing Pointers

You can change one or more pointers and even have more than one set of pointers that you can switch among. To change one or more pointers on your system, follow these steps.

1. Double-click on the Mouse icon in the Control Panel and select the Pointers tab.
2. In the middle of the screen you'll see a display of the pointers with their function. Highlight a pointer you want to change and click on the Browse button.
3. The window shown in Figure 5.3 will open. When you click on a selection (files with the .ANI extension are animated) it will be displayed in the Preview box.
4. Click on the Open button when you have selected the one you want.

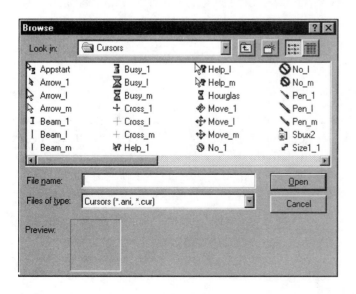

FIGURE 5.3:
The Cursors folder contains the cursor images that come with Windows 95.

If you accumulate a large number of animated cursors, you may want to gather them together in a folder inside the Cursors folder.

> **TIP**
>
> **The animated cursors that come with Plus! are located in the Program Files\Plus!\Themes folder. Copy them over rather than moving them. If you move them, your Plus! themes may not work properly.**

To save a selection of pointers as a set, click on the Save As button and enter a name for the scheme. After you save it, the set will be listed in the Scheme drop-down list and you can select it any time.

The DOS Mouse

DOS programs that use mouse movements and button presses should work fine in Windows 95. Windows 95 passes the mouse information along without the need to install special DOS mouse drivers.

However, if you have occasion to run a program in the special MS-DOS mode (described in Chapter 10) you'll have to load a mouse driver for that program. The mouse driver is a program that came with the mouse when you bought it. Or if you upgraded by installing Windows 95 over Windows 3.1, it's probably still on your machine. Consult the mouse documentation to find the name of the driver file.

Next Step

Now that you're acquainted with all the mouse functions, in the next chapter we move on to some important Desktop elements, namely the Explorer and the icon called My Computer. You'll see how, with some variations, these two elements are really much the same. Which one you use will depend on how *you* want to approach your work.

Chapter

EXPLORING

F E A T U R I N G

- **Defining Explorer and making it work**
- **File extensions: turning them on and off**
- **Connecting files to programs**
- **Using File Manager**
- **Settings in the My Computer folder**

Windows 95 is set up so you can get at most things in more than one way. This is initially a little confusing because you may think you're looking at different places...when only the view has changed. In this chapter we'll talk about the Explorer and the My Computer icon and the differences between what they offer.

What Is the Explorer?

The Explorer is the heir to the File Manager in Windows 3.1. It's the main tool for viewing the files and folders on your hard drive. Everything you see in the My Computer window is also in the Explorer.

NOTE Most of the programs you'll be using will be launched by shortcuts, either from the Start menu or from the Desktop, but you'll still need to use the Explorer to find the objects you want to create shortcuts *to*.

When you install a program on your computer, the program's folders are placed on the hard drive—usually in the form of a main folder and subfolders (folders inside the main folder). Sometimes there are even sub-subfolders. Figure 6.1 shows an open Explorer window with the hierarchy of folders shown on the left. If you look closely, you can see that one of the folders in the left column is shown as "open." The contents of that folder are displayed in the right-hand pane. You use the scroll bars on either side to move up and down through the listing.

FIGURE 6.1:
An Explorer window

In the left pane, folders may have either a plus or minus sign next to them. A plus sign means there are subfolders—click directly on the plus sign to expand the view. When expanded, the plus sign turns into a minus sign.

To open the Explorer, click on the Start button and select Programs ➤ Windows Explorer.

Understanding Explorer

Slide the scroll bar for the left pane all the way to the top. Note that the hard drive C: and the floppy drive A: are shown connected to My Computer by dotted lines. This indicates their connection to My Computer. But even further up is the top folder called Desktop.

In the Explorer's terms, the Desktop is the top of the hierarchy (see Figure 6.2) with My Computer and all its pieces connected to it.

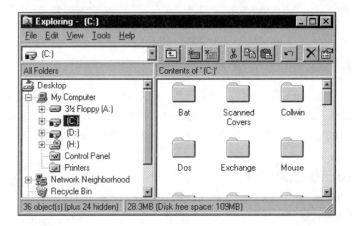

FIGURE 6.2:
How the Explorer sees your system

The dotted lines show the connections, like in a flow chart. Lines that come from the bottom of an icon and connect horizontally to other icons indicate that the destination items are contained inside the object represented by the top icon. For example, you can see that floppy drive A: and drive C: are all part of My Computer. Inside drive C: are numerous folders. The ones with plus signs next to them have subfolders (click on the plus sign to see them). Folders without plus signs have no other folders contained within them.

Looking further down the "tree" in the left pane (Figure 6.2) you can see that the Network Neighborhood is connected to the Desktop on the same level as My Computer. And why not? Other computers on the network are equivalent to your machine. The Recycle Bin is also on the same level—it spans all drives and can't be moved or deleted.

Special folders such as the Control Panel and the folder for printers are displayed on the same level as the disk drives so they're easier to find.

Folders you have placed directly on the Desktop will also show up in the left pane. Shortcuts to folders aren't in the left pane because shortcuts are only pointers to the actual folders. The original folders are found along with other folders on your hard drive. To see the shortcuts that are on your Desktop, click on the Desktop icon in the left pane.

The shortcuts will then be displayed—along with the rest of the stuff on the Desktop—in the right pane.

> **NOTE** Other items that don't show in the left pane are the Inbox for Microsoft Exchange, the icon for the Microsoft Network, and any individual files that are on the Desktop. All these are visible in Explorer's right pane when you click on the Desktop icon in the left pane.

Exploring a Folder

Right-click on any folder—including My Computer or Network Neighborhood—and select Explore. The folder will open in Explorer view, with the hierarchy of folders shown in the left pane and the content of an open folder shown in the right pane.

Making a Shortcut to Explorer

To put Explorer at the top of your Start menu, open Explorer and find the file called EXPLORER.EXE in your Windows folder. Drag and drop it on the Start button. Similarly, you can put Explorer on your Desktop. Right-click on EXPLORER.EXE and drag it to the Desktop. When you release the mouse button, select Create Shortcut(s) here.

Making a Shortcut to the Desktop

Try as you may, you can't drag the Desktop icon from the Explorer's left pane and create a shortcut that way. But you can create a shortcut to the Desktop following these steps:
1. Click on the Windows folder in the Explorer.
2. In the right pane, right-click on the Desktop folder and drag it to the Desktop.
3. Release the right mouse button and select Create Shortcut(s) here.

Or, instead of dragging it to the Desktop, drag and drop on the Start button to put the Desktop folder on the top of your Start menu.

When opened, this shortcut will contain all the folders and files and other icons on the Desktop—except the system-type folders like My Computer, the Microsoft Network, and Recycle Bin.

Opening Two Explorers

If you're moving around a number of files or folders, it's simpler if you can have two instances of the Explorer open. It's certainly easy enough to have more than one Explorer window open. All you have to do is select Explore whenever you right-click on a folder.

To arrange the Explorer windows so you can access them easily, right-click on the Taskbar and select Tile Horizontally or Tile Vertically. Figure 6.3 shows two instances of Explorer tiled vertically.

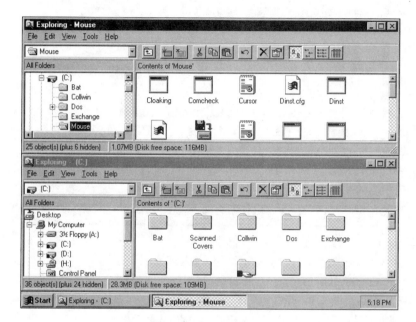

FIGURE 6.3: Tile Explorer windows so you can move back and forth between them easily.

Explorer Navigation

As mentioned before, when you see a plus sign next to an icon in the Explorer, it means that at least one subfolder is inside. Click on the plus sign to expand the view. Click on a minus sign and the subfolders will be collapsed inside the main folder. You can slide the scroll boxes to view items that are outside the pane view.

> **TIP**
>
> Scroll boxes are proportionate in Windows 95. That is, the scroll box shows how much of the window's contents is being displayed. A scroll box that fills half the bar tells you that you're looking at half of what there is to see (in that particular window).

There are several ways to get at folder contents using your mouse:

- Click on a folder in the left pane of the Explorer and the contents are displayed in the right pane.
- Right-click on a folder in the left pane and select Open. A new folder will open on the Desktop displaying the contents of the folder you clicked on.
- Double-click on a folder in the left pane and you expand that branch and display the folder contents in the right pane.

The Toolbar

The Toolbar in the Explorer is a standardization of a visual device that's been used in most Windows applications. It's a collection of icons that provide quick access to the functions on the menus. Position the mouse pointer over a button and a small window opens telling you what the button does. The Toolbar is not on by default, so you'll need to select Toolbar from the View menu for it to be visible.

From left to right, the functions on the Toolbar are

- Move to another folder by selecting it from this drop-down list.
- Move up one level in the folder hierarchy.
- Map a network drive. In other words, assign a letter to a drive on another computer on the network so your computer can access it.
- Disconnect a network drive (un-map it).
- Cut the highlighted item(s).
- Copy the highlighted item(s).
- Paste what you've just cut or copied.
- Undo the last operation.
- Delete the highlighted item(s).
- View the Properties sheet for the highlighted item.
- Change the view to Large Icons.
- Change the view to Small Icons.
- Change the view to a list.
- Change the view to a list with details about file size, date, and so forth.

Other Tools and Buttons

The Explorer, like the other folder windows, has a number of additional tools and buttons—many of them new in Windows 95.

Minimize, Maximize, and Restore

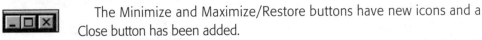

The Minimize and Maximize/Restore buttons have new icons and a Close button has been added.

Click on the rightmost button and the window will close. The button on the left will minimize the window to the Taskbar. The middle button maximizes the window. If the window is already at its maximum size, the middle button will restore the window to its normal size.

Sizing Handles

The odd little graphic effect in the bottom right corner of some windows is called a sizing handle.

Click and drag a sizing handle to change the size of a window. A Windows 95 window without a sizing handle can't be resized. Application windows can be resized as they always have been—by dragging a corner or border.

Sort Buttons

A folder that's being displayed in the form of a detailed list will have several sort buttons at the top of the display.

Click on a button to get the following results:

Name Contents will be sorted in alphabetical order. A second click will sort the files in *reverse* alphabetical order.

Size Files will be sorted in order of their ascending size. A second click will reverse the size order.

Type Files will be sorted alphabetically by type with folders first, then files. A second click will reverse the order.

Modified Files will be sorted by the date they were last changed—most recent to oldest. A second click will reverse the order.

All of the above sort methods are also available on the View menu under Arrange Icons.

Setting the Display of a Folder's Contents

The contents of folders can be viewed as large icons, small icons, a list, or a detailed list. Pull down the View menu in any folder window to try out different looks.

If you use large or small icons, you can select View ➤ Arrange Icons and toggle Auto Arrange on or off. Remove the check mark from in front of Auto Arrange and you can drag the icons around inside the folder. With Auto Arrange selected, the icons snap to an invisible grid and can't be moved about arbitrarily.

If you turn off Auto Arrange and have moved your folder icons every which way until you've made a mess, you can select Line Up Icons from the View menu and the file icons all snap to an invisible grid.

File Extensions

If you've ever used any version of DOS or Windows, you're very familiar with the file-naming conventions used. A file name can have a maximum of eight characters plus a three-character extension. This has historically been one of the more irritating facts about using a PC. Not because naming a file is especially hard—but because six months later you're probably going to have a hard time remembering what CZMLHTL.DOC is all about.

With Windows 95, long file names are finally permitted, so you can give that file a name like LETTER TO HOTEL IN COZUMEL. But because the underlying file structure is unchanged, the actual name of that file will be LETTER TO HOTEL IN COZUMEL.DOC.

By default, Windows 95 hides most file extensions. If Windows 95 knows what program *made* the file, the extension doesn't need to be seen. All you have to do is click on the file and Windows 95 will open the associated application.

Seeing Extensions

If you want the file extensions displayed, follow these steps:

1. Select Options from the View menu.
2. On the View page, remove the check from in front of Hide MS-DOS File Extensions for file types that are registered.
3. Click on OK.

Note that the reference is to all *registered* file types. If Windows 95 doesn't know what program is associated with a particular file extension, the extension will continue to be displayed.

Seeing All Files

Windows 95 also hides from normal view a whole assortment of files, including system files and various kinds of device drivers. These are hidden for two reasons. First, because most users don't need to see these files and they just clutter up the Desktop. Secondly, if you were to accidentally change or delete one of these files, it could cause a particular program—or even your whole system—not to work.

However, there's certainly no harm in displaying them, so if you really want to see all the files on your system, you can do so easily. Just select Option from the View menu and on the View page of the Properties sheet (Figure 6.4), select Show All Files.

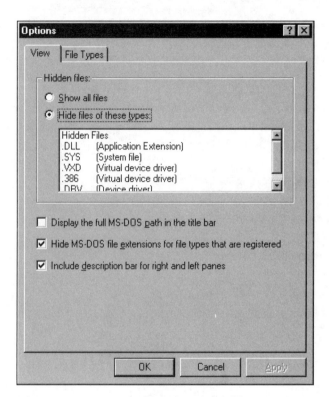

FIGURE 6.4:
Hidden files can be un-hidden using the View menu.

Unfortunately, there's no way to pick and choose among the files that are designated as hidden. Either they're all displayed or none are.

Associating Files with Programs

Windows 95 does a pretty good job of determining which files go with which programs. Once Windows 95 knows that a certain type of file is associated with a particular program, you can click on *any* file with that extension and cause the program to open.

> **NOTE** Associating a file type with a program is the same as registering it. So when Windows 95 talks about registered file types, the reference is also to associated files.

Making a New Association

Most of the time, merely installing a program is enough to teach Windows 95 which files go with that program, but not always. If a file is of a registered type, when you right-click on it the first option on the menu is Open. If it's not registered, the first option will be Open With. Select Open With and you can select from the list of applications as shown in Figure 6.5.

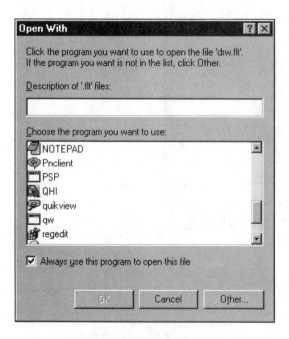

FIGURE 6.5:
Choosing an application for an unregistered file type

If you want to have all your files of a particular type always open with a particular application, you need to tell Windows 95 about it.

To register a file type, follow these steps:

1. Open Explorer and from the View menu, select Options.
2. Select File Types and click on New Type.
3. In the Description of Type box, enter how you want this type of file to be shown in windows that display in Details view. This is for your information, so you can describe it in any way you choose.

4. In the Associated Extension box, enter the three letters that make up this file type's extension (see Figure 6.6). These three letters *are* important because all files with the same extension will display a particular icon and be acted on in the same way as far as the operating system is concerned.

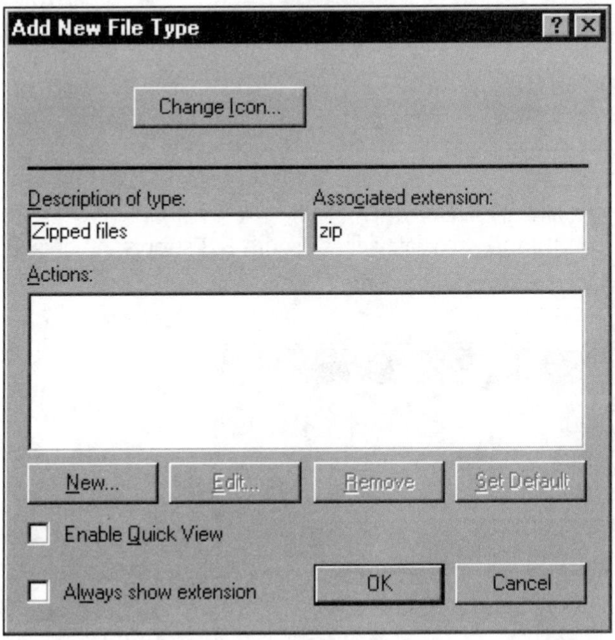

FIGURE 6.6:
Fill in a description of the file type and the file extension.

5. Click on the New button. In the New Action box, type in the action you want performed when you double-click on files of this type and the application used to perform the action (see Figure 6.7).

NOTE Almost all the time, you'll want the program to open the file. That is, the program will start and then load a file with the specified extension.

6. Use the Browse button to find the exact location of the application you want used. Click on OK.

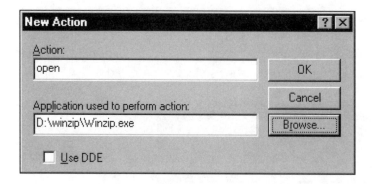

FIGURE 6.7:
Designate the action you want taken and the program that will do it.

7. Back in the Add New File Type box, you can click on the Change Icon button to select a different icon for the associated files. Figure 6.8 shows the finished window. Click on Close when you're done.

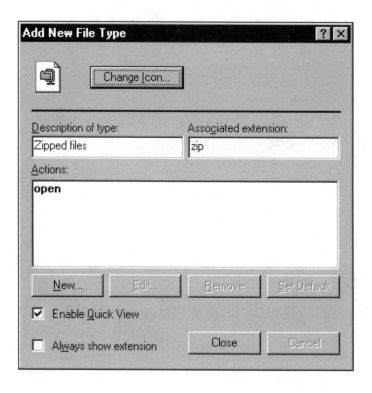

FIGURE 6.8:
With this arrangement, double-clicking any file with the .ZIP extension will open the associated program WINZIP.EXE.

One File Type, Multiple Programs

Most file types are associated with a single program—but there are exceptions. For example, when confronted with bitmapped files (extension .BMP) you may want to open some in Microsoft Paint, others in Collage Plus, still others in PaintShop Pro or another program.

To have multiple associations, follow these steps, substituting the file types and programs you want to use:

1. Open Explorer and from the View menu, select Options.
2. Click on the File Types tab. In the Registered File Types window, find the file type you want to add another association for and highlight it.
3. Click on the Edit button. (Figure 6.9 shows the default actions for text documents [.TXT].) If you double-click on a .TXT file, it will open (the action in bold type). The print action is available from the right-click menu.

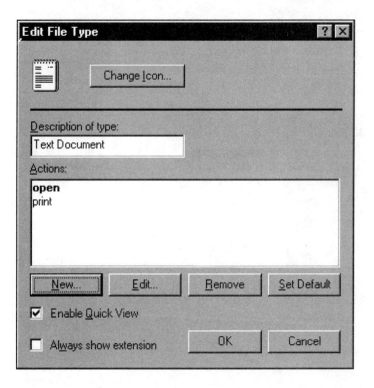

FIGURE 6.9:
Default actions for documents with the .TXT extension

4. Click on the New button to add an action. In the New Action window, enter the action you want performed as well as the application to perform the action. In Figure 6.10 we're adding the option to open the file in Word for Windows.

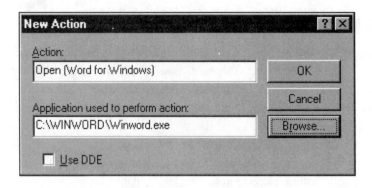

FIGURE 6.10:
Adding open in Word for Windows as an association for text files

5. Click on OK. Back in the Edit File Type window, all the actions will be listed. The item in bold will be the default (double-click) action. To change the default, highlight the one you want and click on the Set Default button. Click on OK again when you've finished.

Figure 6.11 shows the results of the above steps. Now a right click on a text file gives the additional option of opening the file in Word for Windows.

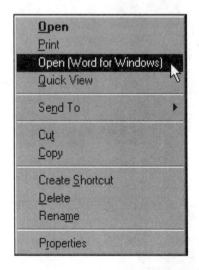

FIGURE 6.11:
A right mouse-click on a .TXT file now produces a menu with an additional option—open in Word for Windows.

You can clutter up your right-click menu with as many associations as you want.

Changing Associations

To change an association between a file type and a program, follow these steps:

1. Open the Explorer and select Options from the View menu.

2. Under File Types, highlight the type you want to change and click on the Edit button.
3. Highlight the Action you want to change.
4. Click on Edit to make a change and make the change in the Editing action box.
5. When you're finished, select OK several times until you're back on the Desktop.

Deleting Associations

To delete an association, open the Explorer and select Options from the View menu. Under File Types, highlight the file type you want to unregister and click on Remove.

Using File Manager

If you're a convert from a previous version of Windows, you're probably missing File Manager about now. Fortunately, it's still included with Windows 95.

To open File Manager, open Explorer and then open the Windows folder. Inside, you'll see a file called WINFILE (or WINFILE.EXE if you have the display extensions turned on). Double-click on WINFILE and the File Manager will open.

You can create shortcuts to the File Manager so they can be available in areas where you're likely to need them. The advantages of File Manager are

- It's faster than the Explorer.
- You can rename a group of files (as long as the file names are in the old-style eight characters/three characters form).

The disadvantages stem from File Manager's origins in older versions of Windows:

- Long file names aren't recognized, only the shortened versions are.
- Right-clicking doesn't work.

Nevertheless, there are times when using File Manager can be more efficient; so a shortcut on the Desktop or the Start menu may be in order.

My Computer

When you first set up Windows 95, there'll be several icons on the left side of your screen. The number will vary, depending on the options you chose when installing. One of them—in fact, the first one—is called My Computer. Double-click on it and you'll see a window like the one shown in Figure 6.12. It may not be exactly the same because computers vary.

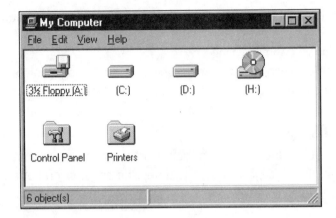

FIGURE 6.12:
The My Computer folder

The items displayed in the window are symbols for the physical contents of your computer, including the floppy drives, hard drives, and CD-ROM drives. There'll also be a folder labeled Printers (even if you have only one or none) and one for the Control Panel.

NOTE Because so many settings are accessed through the Control Panel, it makes sense for them to be available in a variety of locations: off the Start menu, in My Computer, and in the Explorer. Plus you can make shortcuts to the Control Panel and put them wherever you like.

Click once on a drive and the disk's capacity and free space appear in the status bar at the bottom of the window. Double-click on one of the icons and a window will open displaying the contents. For example, double-click on the hard drive labeled C: and you'll see all the folders contained on the C: drive.

My Computer's Properties

Right-click on the My Computer icon and select Properties. There's a great deal of information to be found in these Properties sheets. Of particular interest is the Device Manager page (see Figure 6.13). Double-click on any of the hardware items in the list to see exactly what's installed on your system.

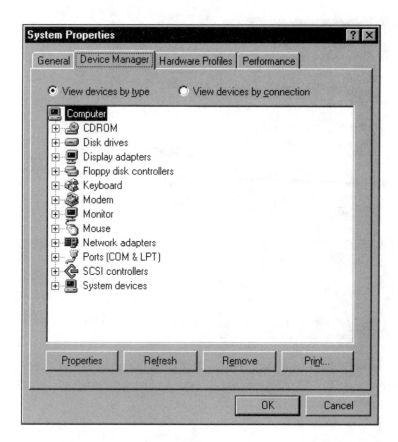

FIGURE 6.13:
The Device
Manager lists all
your hardware.

Highlight a specific piece of hardware and click on the Properties button to see some of what Windows 95 knows about it. There are a number of other settings—particularly under the Performance tab—that you may want to take a look at. Most of these settings *never* need to be changed, but you should know where they are.

TIP   To create a shortcut to the Device manager, right-click on the Desktop and select New ➤ Shortcut. In the Command line box, type this exactly: c:\windows\control.exe sysdm.cpl,system,1.

Disk Properties

Right-click on one of the disk drives and select Properties. You'll get a Properties sheet (see Figure 6.14) that reports the used space and free space in detail. You can also supply a name (what the dialog box calls a Label) for the hard drive.

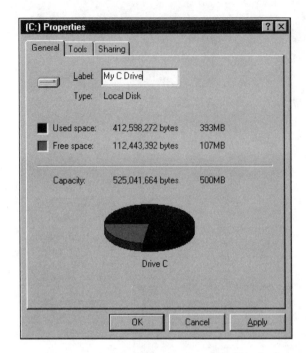

FIGURE 6.14:
The Properties sheet for a hard drive

The Tools tab will let you check the disk for errors, back it up, or defragment it. There's more on these tools in Chapter 17. If you're on a network, the Sharing tab lets you share this drive with others on the network.

One Window or Many

Click on the View menu and select Options in a window (like My Computer) and you can choose from two ways to open folders:

- Separate window. With this choice, every double-click on a folder will open a new window, leaving open all previous windows. This will fill up your screen pretty quickly, but it will give you a clear indication of where you are and how you got there.
- Single window. This means that as you double-click through multiple layers of folders, the contents of the current folder fill the window.

You can experiment to see which one you prefer.

TIP

> **Select the single window option and you'll be able to make some view settings permanent. Using single window browse, if you select (let's say) Large Icons for the parent window, all the child windows will also display Large Icons. For another parent window, another view setting can be selected and all the subfolders will retain that setting.**

Reducing Multiple Window Clutter

It's possible to keep the clutter to a minimum using the multiple window option. Open folder windows until you get to the one you want. Then hold down the Shift key and click on the Close box of the parent folder of the folder you want left open. This will close all windows leading down to the current folder.

Changing to Single Window on the Spot

If you like the multiple window option most of the time, you can switch to a single window on occasion. Instead of a simple double-click on a folder to open a new window, hold down the Ctrl key as you double-click. This will open the contents of the clicked folder in the current folder.

Changing a Folder to Explorer View

Hold down the Shift key as you double-click on a folder and the folder will open in the Explorer view. Make sure the focus is on the folder you want to open this way, otherwise Windows 95 will open all the folders between where you clicked and the folder where the focus actually was.

In a folder where none of the objects are highlighted, the focus is on the object with a dotted line around the name. If an item is highlighted, that's the focus object. Every open folder has an item that is the focus.

Next Step

In the next chapter we'll continue some of the themes of this one, except that we'll go into more detail about the nuts and bolts of moving, selecting, and manipulating files on your system.

Chapter 7

FILES AND FOLDERS

FEATURING

- **Making selections**
- **Making new files and folders**
- **Moving, copying, and deleting files and folders**
- **Undoing a mistake**
- **Using long file names**
- **Formatting and copying floppy disks**
- **Locating anything with the Find command**

In this chapter we'll continue some of the discussion from Chapter 6 with an emphasis on the basics of making and manipulating files and folders, and getting them organized in ways you find comfortable.

Selecting Files and Folders

A single file or folder is selected by clicking on it once. As soon as you click, you'll see that the object is highlighted. You can do this with the left mouse button and then move or rename or copy the object as described later in this chapter. Or you can click on the object with the right mouse button and a menu will open with possible actions.

Selecting Everything

To select a bunch of files or folders, open the window where the objects in question are and then click on the Edit menu and click on Select All. Everything in the window will be highlighted. Right-click on one of the highlighted icons (see Figure 7.1) and choose the action you want to take from the pop-up menu.

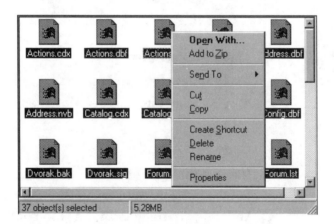

FIGURE 7.1:
All the files are selected and the right mouse menu lets you choose what you want to do with them.

Selecting Some but Not All

There are lots of ways to select some of the objects in a window. The easiest way often depends on how you have the files and folders displayed.

If you have large icons displayed, you might want to simply lasso the items in question. Right-click on an area near the first item and, holding the mouse button down, draw a line around the icons you want to select. When you're finished drawing the box, the icons will be highlighted and the pop-up menu will appear, giving you a choice of actions. Figure 7.2 shows some icons selected in just this way.

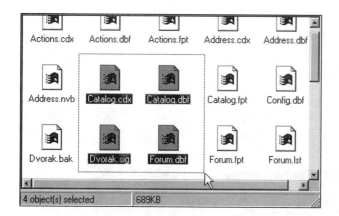

FIGURE 7.2:
Some icons captured by lassoing

You can also draw the box using the left mouse button but when you go to grab the icon group you must click on one of the highlighted icons with the right mouse button. Otherwise, the highlighting will disappear and you'll need to start over.

If you have the icons displayed as a list or in the details view, it's probably easier to select them using Ctrl+click. Hold down the Ctrl key while clicking on the items you want.

If you want all the files in a series, click on the first one, then hold down the Shift key while clicking on the last one. All the objects in between the two clicks will be selected.

Making a New Folder

Folders are the Windows 95 equivalent of DOS and Windows 3.1 directories. There are differences in that Windows 95 folders can contain shortcuts, can be shortcuts to *real* folders in other locations, and can be placed right on the Desktop.

On the Desktop

To create a new folder on the Desktop, right-click on the Desktop in some unoccupied space and select New ➢ Folder from the menu. A folder like the one in Figure 7.3 will appear with the cursor already placed for you to type in a name.

FIGURE 7.3:
A newly made
folder on the
Desktop

This folder is actually located on your hard drive in the Desktop folder inside the Windows folder. Figure 7.4 shows this new folder as it appears in Explorer.

FIGURE 7.4:
The New Folder on
the Desktop can
also be seen in the
Explorer.

TIP

If you can't see the Desktop folder, it's because **Hide Files of These Types** is checked under **View ➢ Options. Check Show All Files** instead and the **Desktop** folder appears.

Inside Another Folder

To make a folder inside another folder, for example in Explorer, follow these steps:

1. Open Explorer. Use the scroll bars to locate the folder where you want to place the new folder.

2. Expand the existing folder by double-clicking on it.

3. Move your pointer to a blank spot in the right pane and click once with the right mouse button.

4. Select New ➢ Folder from the menu.

5. Type in the name for the new folder.

You can do this with a folder on the Desktop. Just open the folder where you want to place the new folder and right-click once in a blank spot inside the open window.

TIP	Make a folder in the wrong place? Just right-click on the errant folder and select Delete. You'll be asked to confirm that you want to send the folder to the Recycle Bin.

Folder Properties

Since everything else has Properties sheets, it should come as no surprise that folders do too. Right-click on a folder and select Properties from the menu. You'll see a window like the one shown in Figure 7.5.

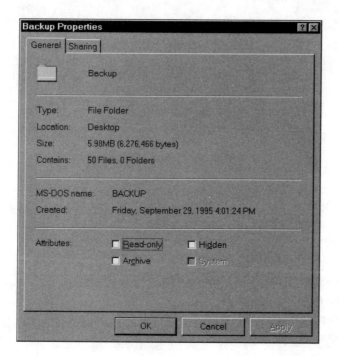

FIGURE 7.5:
Folder Properties

General Page

The General page provides information about the folder including its size and the number of files and other folders to be found inside. As with Properties sheets for individual files, there are also check boxes for setting attributes:

Read only Set this attribute and the folder cannot be written to. This is not a security measure except in that it makes it harder to accidentally change something. A determined person can easily figure out how to change this attribute.

Archive A check in this box means that all the files in the folder have been backed up by a program that sets the archive bit. If the box is filled, it means that some of the files are backed up but others are not.

Hidden Folders and files that are hidden will disappear from the Windows 95 interface. They'll still work as usual, but just won't be visible to the Explorer or other programs.

System System files are required by Windows 95. You don't want to delete them. In any case, a whole folder cannot be designated as System, so this box is always grayed out when you're looking at a folder.

> **TIP**
>
> To change a file or folder from hidden to visible, go to View ➤ Options on a window's toolbar and select Show All Files. Find the file you want to change and open its Properties page so you can change the Hidden attribute.

Sharing Page

You can share your folder with others on the network by selecting the Sharing page. You can give other users read-only or read-write access. You can require a password from other users. You can also allow sharing at the drive level or the individual file level. If you set drive C: as shared on the network, you can't *un*-share anything on drive C:. Everything will be accessible. Similarly, if you share a folder, all files in that folder are shared.

> **TIP**
>
> If there's no Sharing tab on the Properties sheet, you'll need to go to the Network icon in the Control Panel and activate File and Printer Sharing on the Configuration page. This will make the Sharing tab visible.

Making a New File

As long as you're using older software, not specifically made for Windows 95, you'll probably make new files as you always have: by opening the application and selecting New from the File menu. However, a number of applications do place themselves on a New File menu and you can make new files from there.

On the Desktop

To create a new file on the Desktop, right-click on the Desktop in some unoccupied space and select New from the menu. Select the type of file you want to make. A file like the one in Figure 7.6 will appear with the cursor already placed for you to type in a name.

FIGURE 7.6:
A newly made file on the Desktop

This file is located on your hard drive in the Desktop folder inside the Windows folder. Figure 7.7 shows this new file as it appears in Explorer.

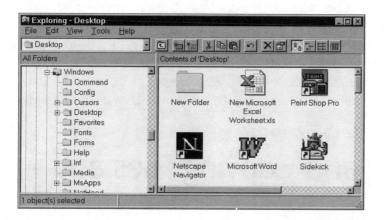

FIGURE 7.7:
The New File on the Desktop can also be seen in the Explorer.

TIP Types is checked under View ➢ Options. Check Show All Files instead and the Desktop folder appears.

Inside Another Folder

To make a file inside another folder, for example in Explorer, open the folder that'll be the outside folder. Right-click on a blank spot and select New from the pop-up menu. Then select the type of file from the list and type in the name for the new file.

TIP Make a file in the wrong place? Just right-click on the errant file and select Delete. You'll be asked to confirm that you want to send the file to the Recycle Bin.

File Properties

As a rule, most Properties sheets for files are a single page like the one shown in Figure 7.8. It will include some information about the file's location, size, and creation date. There will also be boxes for setting and removing attributes as described previously under Folder Properties.

A few programs include other pages on the Properties sheets for files. For example, Word for Windows files include a page of statistics about the file and another page of summary information about the file. As more programs are written specifically for Windows 95, this trend toward including ever more data on the Properties sheets is bound to continue.

Moving and Copying Files and Folders

There are at least three different methods for moving and copying files or folders. You can adopt one method and use it all the time or you can pick and choose from the various methods, depending on the circumstances.

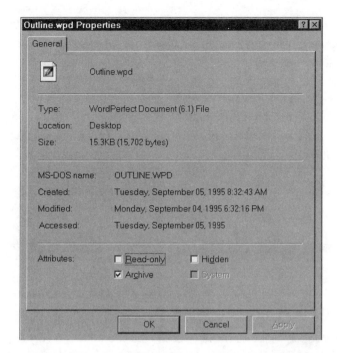

FIGURE 7.8:
A Properties sheet
for a specific file

Move or Copy Using Right Drag and Drop

This is my personal favorite because it requires a minimum of thought:

1. Locate the file or folder using the Explorer or My Computer.
2. Click on the file or folder using the right mouse button.
3. Hold the button down and drag the object to its new location.
4. Release the mouse button and choose Move or Copy from the pop-up menu.

For the shortest distance between two points, you may want to open a second instance of the Explorer so you can drag and drop directly. Or you can move or copy the object to the Desktop, and then open the destination folder or drive and drag the object a second time.

Move or Copy Using Left Drag and Drop

This method requires a bit more mental attention because when you use the left mouse button to drag and drop, the result is a move only if the source and destination are on the same hard drive. If they are on different drives, the result will be a copy.

Winpix

If you're dragging a *program* file (one with the extension .EXE, .COM or .BAT) Windows 95 will create a shortcut to the original file at the destination. You can tell that a shortcut is going to be made because a shortcut arrow can be seen in the transparent icon that you're dragging.

If you see a black plus sign in the transparent icon as you drag, that means that a copy will be made when you release the left mouse button.

In both cases you can force a move to happen by pressing and holding the Shift key before you release the left mouse button.

TIP

If you decide while dragging to cancel the move or copy, just hit the Escape key before you release the mouse button. This stops the drag but leaves the files or folders highlighted.

Move or Copy Using Cut/Copy and Paste

Using the right mouse button menu to move or copy files and folders is very efficient because you don't have to have both source and destination available at the same time.

To move or copy a file, follow these steps:

1. Locate the file or folder you want to move or copy, using My Computer or the Explorer.
2. Right-click on the object and select Cut (to move) or Copy from the pop-up menu.
3. Find the destination folder and open it.
4. Right-click on a blank spot inside the folder and select Paste from the pop-up menu.

NOTE

There are a few objects, such as disk icons, that you can't move or copy. If you try to, you'll get a message informing you of this fact and asking if you want a shortcut instead.

Deleting Files and Folders

The easiest way to delete a file or folder is to click on it once with the right mouse button and select Delete from the pop-up menu. Or you can click on the object with the left mouse button and then press the Del key on your keyboard.

Another method is to drag and drop the object on the Recycle Bin icon. A plus of this method is that you won't be asked to confirm that you want to delete the file.

In any of the above methods, the Recycle Bin protects the user from over-hasty deletions because the data is not instantly deleted but can be retrieved from the Recycle Bin if you later decide you want it back. There's much more on the Recycle Bin in Chapter 9.

TIP

To delete a file or folder without sending it to the Recycle Bin, press the Shift key while you select Delete from the pop-up menu or while pressing the Del key.

Renaming Files and Folders

There are two easy ways to change the name of a file or folder.
1. You can click on the name twice (with about a second between each click) and the name will be highlighted so you can type in a new one.
2. Or you can right-click once on the file and select Rename from the pop-up menu.

NOTE

Unfortunately, there's no provision for renaming a group of files. For that you'll need to use File Manager (discussed in Chapter 6).

The Undo Command

When you move, copy, or rename something, the command to undo that action gets added to a stack maintained by Windows 95. The stack is built up as you move, copy, and rename. The most recent action is on top.

To undo an action you can click on the Undo button on the window's toolbar or you can right-click on the Desktop or in a free area of a folder, and the Undo command will be on the pop-up menu.

The unwieldy thing about Undo is that it's a big and global stack. You can merrily undo dozens of commands and you may not be able to see where the Undo is taking place and just what moves and copies and renames are being undone. (Particularly if you've been working in a variety of folders.) So it's best to use Undo quickly and to do it in the folder where you performed the original action. That way you can see the results of Undo.

TIP

If you don't remember what you did last, and therefore don't know what Undo will undo, rest your mouse pointer on the button and the pop-up help will tell you whether it was a move, copy, or rename.

Long File Names

One of the most attractive features in Windows 95 is the ability to give files and folders long file names. In fact a name can be as long as 250 characters. However, you don't want to get carried away because the full path, including folder and subfolder names, can't exceed 258 characters.

File names can now include spaces as well as characters you couldn't use before like the comma, semicolon, equals sign (=) and square brackets ([]). However, the following characters are still not allowed in either file or folder names:

\ / * < > : ? " |

File and folder names can also have both upper- and lowercase letters and the system will preserve them. However, this is for display purposes. When you type in the name, you don't have to remember whether you capitalized some part of it or not. Windows 95 will find it as long as the spelling is correct.

NOTE

Passwords in Windows 95 are case-sensitive—as they are everywhere.

Long File Names in DOS

The DOS commands that come with Windows 95 know how to handle long file names. Figure 7.9 shows some files and shortcuts as they appear in an open window in Windows 95.

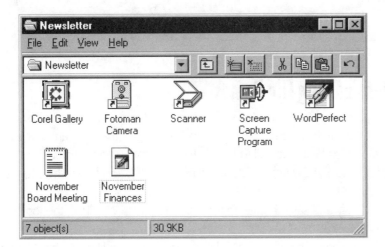

FIGURE 7.9:
The Newsletter folder on the Desktop

Figure 7.10 shows those same items in a DOS window.

FIGURE 7.10:
The same objects displayed in a DOS window

As you can see, the long file names are preserved on the right while shortened versions appear on the left. As a rule, DOS will make the short file name by taking the first six letters of the long file name and appending a tilde (~) and a number. So if you have a series of files called Chapter 1, Chapter 2, and Chapter 3, they'll show up in a DOS window as Chapte~1, Chapte~2, and so forth.

WARNING　　Numbers added to make short file names are used in the order that the files are created. So if you create Chapter 3 first, it will be named Chapte~1, not Chapte~3 as you might expect.

Limitations of Long File Names

Unless you're running all Windows 95 programs (and few of us are), the long file names will be truncated when you view them from inside the program. For example, if you've made a file in WordPad called Luisa's Party Invitation and then want to open it in Word for Windows 2.0 (which predates Windows 95), you'll see the file name has changed to luisas~1.

After you modify and save the file, though, and return to WordPad, the long name will still be intact.

Similarly if you copy some files to a diskette and take those files to a computer running DOS or some previous version of Windows, you can edit the files on the floppy disk and, when you return to the Windows 95 machine, the long file names will be intact. However, if you copy those files to the other machine's hard drive and edit them, later copying them back to the floppy, when you return to your Windows 95 machine, the long names will be replaced by short names.

Dealing with Floppy Disks

Floppy disks remain part of the computing arsenal even for people on networks. Sooner or later, you have to put something on a floppy or take it off (by formatting). Windows 95 includes tools to do all the floppy tasks, though some may not work exactly as you expect.

Formatting a Floppy

To format a floppy disk, put the disk in the drive and follow these steps:

1. Open Explorer.
2. Use the scroll bars to move up to the point where you can see your floppy drive in the left window.

3. Right-click on the floppy drive and select Format.
4. The window shown in Figure 7.11 will open. Make sure the choices selected are the ones you want. If not, change them.
5. Click on the Start button. When the formatting is complete (you'll see a progress bar at the bottom of the window), click on the Close button.

TIP Make sure you right-click on the floppy drive. If the contents of the floppy are displayed in the right panel of the Explorer, you won't be allowed to format it because Windows 95 will see the floppy as "in use." This is true even if the floppy has no files on it.

Copying a Floppy

To make an exact copy of a floppy disk, put the floppy in the drive and follow these steps:

1. Open Explorer.
2. Use the scroll bars to move up to the point where you can see your floppy drive in the left window.
3. Right-click on the floppy drive and select Copy Disk.
4. If you have more than one floppy drive, you'll have to specify the Copy From drive and click on Start. With only one floppy drive, just click on Start.

The system will read the entire disk then prompt you to insert the disk you want to copy to.

Copying Files to a Floppy

There are two approaches to copying folders or files to a floppy disk, depending on whether the material to be copied is smaller or larger than the capacity of a single floppy.

Copying to a Single Floppy

When the material you want to copy will fit on a single floppy, the process is easy. Put the floppy disk in the drive and use one of these approaches:

• Highlight the file or folder and then right-click and select Send To ➤ and then the specific floppy drive.
• Drag and drop the items to the floppy drive icon in the Explorer or My Computer.
• If you have a shortcut to a floppy drive on your desktop or in a folder, drag and drop the items there.

You may even find other ways over time!

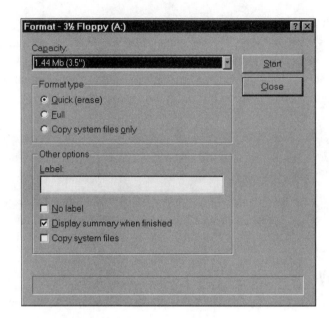

FIGURE 7.11:
The window that opens to format a floppy disk

Copying to Multiple Floppies

If you have to copy a large file or folder or even a whole drive onto multiple floppies, you'll use an MS-DOS window and the program XCOPY32.

Click on the Start button and select Programs ➤ MS-DOS Prompt.

The basic syntax of XCOPY32 is:

```
Xcopy32 fromwhere towhere
```

This means if you were copying a big folder on your C: drive called Documents to floppies on the A: drive, you'd type in:

```
Xcopy32 C:\Documents A:
```

If the Documents folder included subfolders that you wanted to copy intact, you'd use an extra parameter:

```
Xcopy32 C:\Documents A: /E
```

Want to copy the directory structure and any hidden or system files? Add one more parameter:

```
Xcopy32 C:\Documents A: /E /H
```

NOTE It's important to type in the commands as shown—including spaces—though the case used is irrelevant.

The Xcopy32 program has lots of parameters that you can use to customize the copying process. To see them, open the MS-DOS window and type in:

```
Xcopy32 /?|MORE
```

The MORE command is so you can view the two pages of parameters one at a time.

Using Find

Windows 95 comes with a very sophisticated file-finding tool that makes it possible to find almost anything on your hard disk, even if you know very little about it.

When You Know the Name

To find a file or folder when you know the name (or part of it), follow these steps:

1. Click on the Start button, slide the pointer to Find, and then click on Files or Folders.
2. Type in the file name, either whole or in part. Unlike previous find tools, you don't need to know how the file begins or ends. For example, a search for files with "part" in their names, yielded the results shown in Figure 7.12.
3. The Look In box tells the program where to search. If you haven't a clue, use the drop-down list or the Browse button to select My Computer and the program will look everywhere on your system.
4. Click on Find Now to start the search.

NOTE The results of file and folder searches can be saved by selecting Save Results from the Option menu. The search results will be saved in the form of an icon on your Desktop. Double-click on the icon to open the Find window with the search criteria and results displayed.

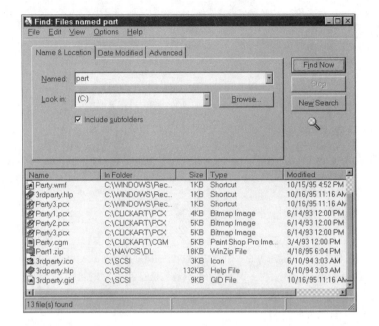

FIGURE 7.12:
Searching with only part of the name

When You Know Something Else

And then there are the times when you don't know *any* part of the file name. If you have an idea of when the file was last worked on, you can use the Date Modified tab. You can specify a search between specific days or just look for files created or modified in some previous months or days.

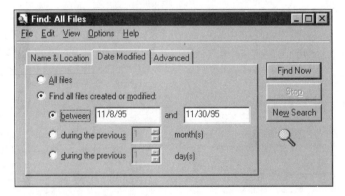

Maybe all you know is that the document you want is a letter written in WordPerfect and that it was addressed to a branch office in Poughkeepsie. Click on the Advanced tab, select the file type from the drop-down window, and enter Poughkeepsie in the Containing text box.

Searches can be based on even skimpier information. You can have the program search All files and folders (look in the Of Type drop-down list) for files containing a certain word or

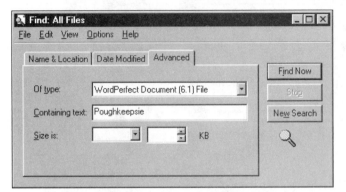

phrase. Of course, the more information you can tell the program, the faster the search will be.

> **NOTE**
>
> Once you find the file you want, you can drag it to the Desktop or into another folder. You can double-click on program files to open the program. If a file is associated with a program (as discussed in Chapter 6) double-click on the file and the program will open with the file loaded.

Finding a Computer on the Network

You can use Find to locate a particular computer on your network. Again, you don't have to know the entire name of the computer. Just click on the Start button, slide the pointer to Find, and select Computer. Type in what you know of the name and click on the Find Now button. Figure 7.13 shows the result of a search for computers with "ci" in their names.

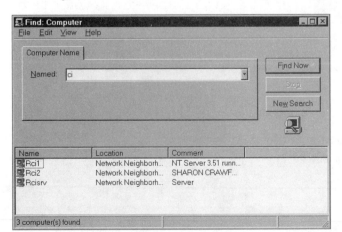

FIGURE 7.13:
A search for computers with "ci" in their names

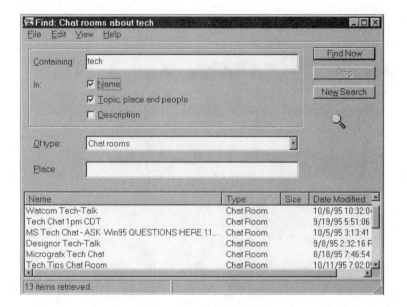

FIGURE 7.14:
Lots of chat rooms on Microsoft Network with tech as part of their names

Finding Things on the Microsoft Network

Another function in Find is the ability to search the Microsoft Network. Click on Find and then on the Microsoft Network. Type in the topic or name of the place you want to find. Select the area you want searched from the Of Type drop-down list. Click on the Find Now button. The Microsoft Network will launch (if it's not already open) and will be searched using the criteria you specified. Figure 7.14 shows the results of a search looking for chat rooms with "tech" in their names.

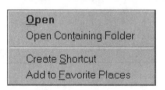

Double-click on any of the found items and you'll be sent there. Or right-click and, in addition to the Open option, you get the choice to open the folder containing the object in question, create a shortcut to the place, or add it to the MSN Favorite Places folder.

Next Step

Now that we've learned how to navigate the Desktop and handle files, we'll move on in the next chapter to launching programs and setting up your programs to be launched in the easiest way for you.

Chapter 8

RUNNING PROGRAMS

- **Using the Start menu**
- **Using the right mouse button**
- **Arranging menus**
- **Putting programs in the Startup group**
- **Finding and using Program Manager**

In this chapter we'll cover the essentials of launching programs. There are lots of ways to get programs started and where you'll start them from depends a lot on how often you use certain ones. The more frequently used programs can be placed in the most easily accessible spots and the infrequently used can be easily accessible but still out of the way.

Starting a Program

As you might suspect by now, there are a lot of different ways to start a program. You may prefer having shortcuts to your favorite programs on your Desktop or on the Start button. Here's a refresher on how to do that.

Shortcut to a Program

To make a shortcut to a program on your Desktop, follow these steps:

1. Open Explorer (Start ➤ Programs ➤ Windows Explorer).
2. Using the scroll bars, find the folder for your program. Double-click on the folder.
3. In the right pane of the Explorer, click on the File Type button at the top of the list until you see a file or a group of files labeled Application.
4. If there's a single file labeled Application, right-click on the file and drag it to your Desktop. When you release the mouse button, select Create Shortcut(s) here from the pop-up menu.

TIP | If there's more than one file labeled Application, you may have to guess which one is the actual main program file—either by the name or the icon. If worse comes to worse, double-click on a file you think might be "it." If the program opens, you've hit the jackpot. If it doesn't, just close whatever did open and try again.

A shortcut to a program can be put wherever you find handy—on the Desktop or inside a folder, either on the Desktop or somewhere else.

Putting a Program on the Start Menu

If you want a program to appear on the Start menu (as shown in Figure 8.1) the necessary steps are very similar to the ones above.

1. Open Explorer (Start ➤ Programs ➤ Windows Explorer).
2. Using the scroll bars, find the folder for your program. Double-click on the folder.
3. In the right pane of the Explorer, click on the File Type button at the top of the list until you see a file or a group of files labeled Application.
4. Look for a file labeled Application, right-click on the file and drag it to the Start button. When the pointer is above the Start button, release the mouse.

FIGURE 8.1:
The Start menu with some programs and a folder added

> **TIP**
>
> Like the idea of having a shortcut to the Desktop on your Start menu? Open the Explorer and find the Desktop subfolder inside your Windows folder. Right-click on the Desktop folder, drag it to the Start button, and drop it.

Forcing the Order on the Start Menu

Programs on the Start menu are listed in alphabetical order, but suppose this isn't what you want. To change the order, follow these steps:

1. Right-click on the Start button and select Explore.
2. In the window that opens, you'll see a Programs folder (what you see when you select Start ➢ Programs) and shortcuts for the programs you've placed on the Start button (see Figure 8.2).

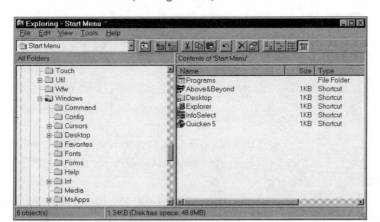

FIGURE 8.2:
Programs on the Start menu are listed in alphabetical order.

3. Right-click on the program you want to move to the top of the list.
4. Rename it, making sure that the first character is an underscore (_).
5. Click on the Start button and you'll see that the name that begins with an underscore has been moved to the top (Figure 8.3).

FIGURE 8.3:
The underscore character moves the program to the top of the list.

To force a program to be second on the list, no matter what its alphabetical ranking, just rename the shortcut, making a tilde (~) the first character.

> **TIP**
> Rename several files using the underscore as the first character and they'll be listed together at the top of the menu, in alphabetical order. Rename several with the tilde as the first character and they'll also be listed together in alphabetical order but *after* the group with the underscore.

Using the Right Mouse Button

The right mouse button, not surprisingly, is useful for launching programs in addition to all its other talents. Right-click on a program in the Explorer or on the Desktop and select Open from the menu.

If the top item is Open With... and you haven't a clue as to what program might be able to handle the file, make a shortcut to the file viewers by following these steps:

1. Click on the Start button and select Find.
2. Search for QUIKVIEW.EXE (note the spelling!). Or you can open Explorer and

look in the following folders Windows ➤ System ➤ Viewers. You'll find QUIKVIEW.EXE in the last folder.

3.   Right-click on QUIKVIEW.EXE and drag it to the Desktop, selecting Create Shortcut(s) here when you release the mouse button.

4.   Next open the Explorer and open the folder Windows ➤ SendTo. Drag the shortcut to QUIKVIEW.EXE to the SendTo folder and drop it inside.

Now when you right-click on an object, one of the options under SendTo will be Quikview. So when you see a file that you don't recognize, you can always send it to Quikview for a fast look.

Launching from Start ➤ Programs

Click once on the Start menu, slide the pointer up to Programs and then select the program you want. This is an easy way to start up any program on your system. However, you may dislike the multilevel menus—first there's a folder for each application and then another menu for all the stuff inside (see Figure 8.4). This is the default setup for Windows 95 but you can change almost all aspects of it.

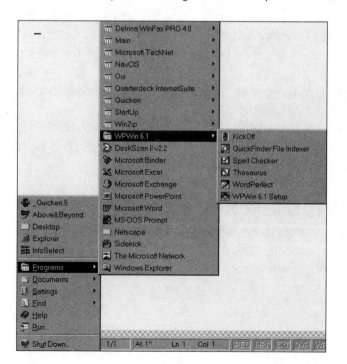

FIGURE 8.4:
Maybe you'd rather not have your programs set up this way.

Many of the menus in Windows 95 contain just a series of shortcuts easily accessible through Explorer. Find the window that represents the menu and you can add to it or subtract from it. To change the Programs menu, follow these steps:

1. Right-click on the Start button and select Explore.
2. Double-click on Programs and you'll see a listing of folders and shortcuts that correspond to the Start ➤ Programs menu.
3. Double-click on a folder to see the program inside. To move a program up a level, right-click on the shortcut and select Cut from the pop-up menu.

4. Click on the up-one-level icon on the toolbar.
5. Right-click in the right pane and select Paste from the menu.

Remember that these are all shortcuts, so you can rename them or delete them without a thought. You can also drag new shortcuts to any level of the menu.

Adding a Program to the Start ➤ Programs Menu

You can add a program to the Start ➤ Programs menu quite easily. Just follow these steps:

1. Find the program (or a shortcut to the program) you want, either by searching the Explorer or by using Start ➤ Find.
2. Once you locate the program or shortcut, right-click on it and drag it to the Desktop, creating a new shortcut when you get there.
3. Right-click on the Start button and select Explore. Double-click on the Programs icon.
4. You can drag and drop your newly made shortcut to this window. That will put it on the first level of the Programs menu.

If you want, you can create a new folder in Programs (right-click on a blank spot inside the folder and select New ➤ Folder). Then you can put other shortcuts in the folder— these will then be on the second level of the Programs menu.

Removing a Program from the Start ➤ Programs Menu

Removing stuff from the Programs menu is equally easy:

1. Right-click on the Start button and select Explore.
2. Double-click on the Programs icon.
3. Right-click on anything you want to get rid of and select Delete from the pop-up menu.

WARNING

All the items in the Programs folder and any subfolders *should* be shortcuts, though the icons are too small in many cases to verify this at a glance. If you have any doubts, right-click on the object and select Properties. If there's not a Shortcut page with the Properties sheet, don't delete the file until you're sure it's not the *only* copy.

Starting Programs When You Start Windows

Everyone has a program or two that they know they'll be using every single day. So you might as well have the program start when you start up your computer.

To add a program to the StartUp group, just right-click on the Start button and select Explore. Double-click on the Programs icon in the right pane. Then double-click on StartUp, a folder under Programs. In this folder are all the programs that will launch when you turn on the computer.

Next, open a second instance of Explorer and find the programs you want in StartUp. Right-click on your choice and drag it to StartUp. Release the mouse button and select Create Shortcut(s) here from the menu. Or you can right-click on any shortcut on your Desktop and drag it to StartUp, also selecting Create Shortcut(s) when the menu appears.

Using Program Manager

If you really miss Program Manager from Windows 3.1, there's good news for you. It's included with Windows 95. Look in your Windows folder for a file called PROGMAN.EXE. Right-click on it and drag it to the Desktop and make a shortcut.

TIP

When you know the name of the file, it's almost always fastest to use Find from the Start menu. Once Find locates the file, you can right-click on the file and make a shortcut or a copy, or even move it from its folder.

Sometimes—even if you don't miss Program Manager—you'll still need to use it. Some older programs that work perfectly well in Windows 95, have a devil of a time *installing* in Windows 95. If you run into one of these uncooperative programs, try installing it from Program Manager:

1. Use Find to locate PROGMAN.EXE in Windows 95.

2. Right-click on it and drag it to your Desktop and make a shortcut there.

3. Double-click on the shortcut to PROGMAN.EXE.

4. Select Run from Program Manager's File menu.

5. If you've been prudent enough to check the program's floppy disk for the name of the install program (almost always INSTALL.EXE or SETUP.EXE), type in the path in the command line box. Otherwise, click on Browse and check the floppy drive for the name of the install file.

6. Click on OK twice and the program should install.

The program will still be available to Windows 95, though if you want to put it in the Start ➤ Programs menu, you may have to do it by dragging a shortcut to the Programs folder (described in the section "Adding Programs to the Start ➤ Programs Menu" earlier in this chapter).

Next Step

In the next chapter we'll move on to one of the best tools in Windows 95, the Recycle Bin. We'll cover how to use it to its best advantage, as well as some of the Recycle Bin's limitations and how to overcome them.

Chapter 9

THE RECYCLE BIN

FEATURING

- **How the Recycle Bin works**
- **Deleting files safely**
- **Recovering deleted files**
- **Setup and configuration**

In the bad old days of computing, it was far too easy to accidentally delete a file from your system—and all you could do was wave bye-bye. Because there was no going back. You could buy a package of tools like the Norton Utilities that included a utility to retrieve deleted files (providing you acted quickly enough). And DOS itself, starting with version 5, included a program to undelete files. The weakness of both approaches was that if you didn't undelete right away, your file could easily be overwritten by another file and then there was *no way* to recover.

The Recycle Bin will retain all your deleted files for as long as you want and you can adjust the amount of security from "just a little" to "all I can get" to match your own personal comfort level.

What It Is

Recycle Bin

The Recycle Bin is a reserved space on your hard drive. When you delete a file or drag it to the Recycle Bin icon, the file is actually moved to that reserved space. If you have more than one hard drive, each drive has its own reserved space. There's an icon that represents the Recycle Bin on each drive—though the contents displayed when you double-click on any icon will be the same as the Recycle Bin on any other drive. If you want a deleted file back, you can double-click on the Recycle Bin icon to open it and retrieve any file.

The Recycle Bin functions as a first-in, first-out system. That is, when the bin is full, the oldest files are deleted to make room for the newest ones.

As configurable as the rest of Windows 95 is, this is one place where Microsoft draws the line. The Recycle Bin cannot be

- Deleted
- Renamed
- Removed from the Desktop

though there are a number of settings you can change to make the Recycle Bin suitable for your use.

NOTE See "Settings" later in this chapter for information on how to determine the amount of disk space used by the Recycle Bin as well as other settings.

Sending Files to the Recycle Bin

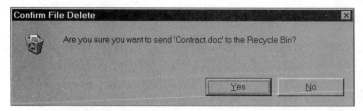

By default, Windows 95 is set up to deposit all deleted files in the Recycle Bin. When you right-click on a file and select delete or highlight a file and press the Del key, you'll be asked to confirm if you want to send the file to the Recycle Bin. After you click on Yes, that's where the file is moved to. Deleted shortcuts are also sent to the Recycle Bin.

> **TIP**
>
> If you delete an empty folder, it's not sent to the Recycle Bin but you can recover it by immediately selecting Undo Delete from the Recycle Bin's Edit menu. If the folder was on the Desktop or in an open window, just right-click on a blank spot where it was and select Undo Delete from the pop-up menu.

Sending a Floppy Disk's Files to the Recycle Bin

Normally, files that you delete from a floppy drive are *not* sent to the Recycle Bin. They're just deleted. However, if that strikes you as just a little too impetuous, there's an easy way to make sure that the files on your floppy do go to the Recycle Bin.

1. Open Explorer. Use the scroll bar for the left pane to move up so you can see the entry for your floppy drive.
2. Click with the left mouse button on the Floppy Drive icon. In the right pane, select the file(s) you want to delete but still want in the Recycle Bin.
3. Right-click on the file(s) and select Cut. Right-click on the Desktop and select Paste.
4. Highlight the file on the Desktop. (If there's more than one, hold down the Shift key while you click on each one in turn.) Right-click on a highlighted file and select Delete. You'll be prompted to confirm that you want to send the file(s) to the Recycle Bin.

There's no more direct way to do this function because the Recycle Bin stubbornly refuses to see any files that are sent directly from a floppy.

Bypassing the Recycle Bin

If you've got a file that you know for sure you want to delete and that you therefore don't want taking up space in the Recycle Bin, just hold down the Shift key when you select Delete. But be sure that's what you want to do because there's no way in Windows 95 to recover a deleted file that's bypassed the Recycle Bin.

NOTE   If you have the Norton Utilities for Windows 95, you can use their Unerase program to recover deleted files that are not in the Recycle Bin. Again, you must do this very quickly before another file overwrites the one you want to recover.

Files That Won't Go Willingly

Some older programs (not written specifically for Windows 95) allow you to delete files from within the program. Files deleted this way will not be sent to the Recycle Bin. Similarly, files you delete at the DOS prompt will also disappear into never-never land rather than the Recycle Bin.

Therefore, you should make all your deletions through the Explorer or My Computer, or on the Desktop. If Windows 95 knows about the deletion, the file will automatically go to the Recycle Bin.

NOTE   Using the DOS prompt is covered in Chapter 10.

Recovering a Deleted File

Retrieving a file from the Recycle Bin is remarkably easy. Just double-click on the Recycle Bin icon. The Recycle Bin window can be set up in any of the usual choices on the View menu. The most useful are probably Large Icons (as shown in Figure 9.1) and Details.

The Details view (Figure 9.2) is the best view if you're looking for a file that was recently deleted. Just click on the Date Deleted bar to arrange the files in date order. A second click will reverse the order. Similarly, if you know the file name, a click on the Name bar will list the files in alphabetical order.

To retrieve a single file, click on it with either the left or right button and drag it to a folder or the Desktop. If you just want to send it back to its original location, right-click on the file name and select Restore from the pop-up menu.

More Than One File

To recover more than one file at a time, hold down the Ctrl key while selecting the file names. Then right-click on one of the highlighted names and select Restore. Or use cut and

FIGURE 9.1:
In the Large Icons view you can quickly identify files that were made by a particular program.

paste to send the whole bunch to a different location. Using either the right or left button, you can click and drag the files to your Desktop or another open folder.

To retrieve a number of files all in a series, click on the first one and then hold down the Shift key while selecting the last one in the series.

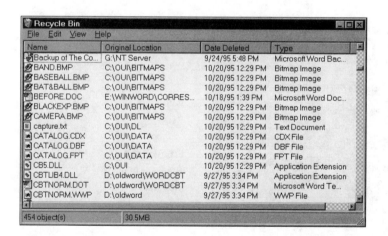

FIGURE 9.2:
The Details view is useful if you're searching by date or name.

Let's say you deleted a whole folder and the only thing all the parts of the folder have in common is that all were deleted at the same time. Here's how to recover them.

1. Open the Recycle Bin with a double-click on the icon.
2. Select Details from the View menu.
3. Click on the Date Deleted button. Use the scroll bar to move through the list until you find the group of files you want to retrieve.

4. Click on the first one's name. Then, while holding down the Shift key, click on the name of the last one you want. All the files between the first and last click will be highlighted.

5. Right-click on one of the highlighted files and select Recover from the pop-up menu.

All the files will be returned to their original home and even though the original folder is not listed in the Recycle Bin, the files will be in the original folder.

Settings

You can adjust the amount of space the Recycle Bin claims and change other settings that affect how the Recycle Bin works. Mostly you have to decide just how much safety you want and are comfortable with.

How Much Space?

Right-click on the Recycle Bin icon and select Properties. The Recycle Bin's Properties sheets will open as shown in Figure 9.3.

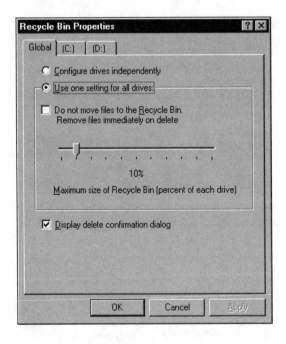

FIGURE 9.3:
The Recycle Bin's Properties sheets

As you can see, you can set the amount of space reserved for the Recycle Bin for each hard disk drive individually, or make a global setting. By default, 10 percent of each drive is set aside for the Recycle Bin. On a large drive, that's a lot of megabytes, so you may want to reduce the size a bit.

Click on Configure Drives Independently and then click on each drive tab in turn. Click on the sliding arrow and move it up or down until the Space Reserved is to your liking.

> **NOTE** There's also a field below the slider, showing the percentage of the drive that is reserved. If your drives are different sizes, you might want to make things easier for yourself by just reserving the same percentage on each drive.

Remember that the Recycle Bin is first-in, first-out, so if you make the reserved space very small, deleted files may pass into oblivion faster than you might wish.

Getting Rid of Confirmations

On the first page of the Recycle Bin Properties sheet, there's a box to clear if you don't want to be questioned every time you delete a file.

If there's no check in this box, you won't see any messages when you select Delete. If you like the comfort of being consulted about every deletion, clear this box.

☑ Display delete confirmation dialog

Doing Away with the Recycle Bin

Well, you can't exactly do away with the Recycle Bin completely. As mentioned before, you can't delete it or remove it from the Desktop. However, you can check this box on the Recycle Bin Properties sheet. If you have selected Configure Drives Independently you can pick which drives you want this to apply to. This is a *very bad* idea unless you have another program for undeleting files. Files that are deleted and not sent to the Recycle Bin are gone forever.

☐ Do not move files to the Recycle Bin. Remove files immediately on delete

Even if you do have a program that will rescue files deleted in error, it's still not a good idea to bypass the Recycle Bin completely because most of the undelete programs are dependent on you getting to the deleted file before it is overwritten by something else. And that can easily happen in Windows 95 where there's almost always something going on behind the scenes.

> **TIP**
>
> If you begrudge large portions of your hard drive, make the reserved space on the hard drive very small—maybe 5 or 10MB. Check the box on the Properties sheet to disable the confirmation requests. Then the Recycle Bin will be quite unobtrusive but you'll still have some margin of safety.

Emptying the Recycle Bin

To get rid of everything in the Recycle Bin, right-click on the Recycle Bin icon and select Empty Recycle Bin. There's also an option to Empty Recycle Bin under the File menu.

To remove just *some* of the items in the Recycle Bin, highlight the file names, right-click on one of them and select Delete from the pop-up menu. You'll be asked to confirm the deletion (assuming you have the confirmation option turned on) and when you say Yes, the files will be deleted permanently.

Next Step

Up until now we've talked about Windows 95 as a graphical environment—and an excellent one it is. In the next chapter we'll see how Windows 95 runs DOS programs better and faster than plain DOS ever did, and many, many times better than any previous version of Windows.

Chapter 10

USING DOS

FEATURING

- **DOS: better than ever**
- **Fine tuning DOS settings**
- **Making even unruly DOS programs work perfectly**
- **Configuring the default DOS prompt**
- **Available DOS commands**

Windows 95 comes with a set of DOS commands that, when referred to, are called DOS 7. They aren't referred to very often because you don't need to have much to do with them. If you have DOS programs, most of them can be run in a window on the Desktop or full screen. Only the most aggressive DOS programs (games for the most part) require any fiddling with settings. In this chapter we'll talk about the simple way to run DOS programs and how you can cajole even the most poorly behaved DOS program to run without complaint.

There's also information in the latter part of the chapter about the available DOS commands.

DOS the Easy Way

DOS programs aren't automatically placed on your Programs menu the way Windows programs are when you first install them. But you can create a shortcut to a DOS program and put the shortcut either on your Desktop or in one of the folders that make up the Programs menu (as discussed in Chapter 8).

Open the Explorer and find the folder with your program in it. Right-click on the program name and drag it to the Desktop to make a shortcut. Put it on your Start menu or in a folder. In other words, you can handle DOS programs like Windows programs. Almost every DOS program will open with a simple double-click on the icon. But what if it won't? Or it opens in a window and you'd like it to run full screen? Fortunately, every DOS program has a very extensive collection of Properties sheets that you can use to tweak your DOS performance.

DOS Properties Sheets

When you run a DOS program, whether from the Desktop or off the Start menu, you can set a wide variety of properties for the program. As elsewhere in Windows 95, you get to those properties by right-clicking on the icon for the program or its shortcut in any of three different places.

- Highlight the program's executable file in the Explorer or My Computer, and right-click on it.
- Right-click on a shortcut to the program.
- Open a DOS window and click once on the little icon in the upper-left corner.

In all cases, you'll select Properties from the menu that opens. This will open up a Properties sheet for the DOS program like the one in Figure 10.1.

There are six pages on the Properties sheet—five if you got here by right-clicking in the upper-left corner of a running program or DOS Window.

- General shows information about the file and file attributes. You won't see this one if you examine the properties of a running program or DOS window.
- Program sets command line options and sets the program's icon.
- Font sets the font to be used when the program is run in a window.
- Memory sets how much and what kind of memory is made available to the DOS program.
- Screen changes whether the program runs full screen or in a window, and the characteristics of the window.

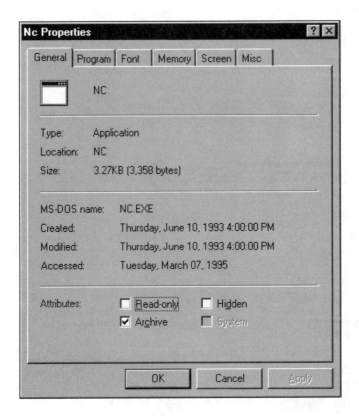

FIGURE 10.1:
The first page of a DOS program's many Properties sheets

• Misc, like miscellaneous files everywhere, sets stuff that doesn't fit in any other category.

The default settings are usually adequate for most programs but if you need to fuss with one or more of these pages, the following sections contain some guidance.

General Properties

The General tab shows information about the program, as well as allowing you to set the attributes of the underlying file. As you can see in Figure 10.1, this tab shows you the type of program or file, its location and size, the DOS file name associated with it, and when the file was created, modified, and last accessed.

If you're looking at a shortcut, the information about the file size, location, and type will refer to the shortcut and not to the original object (the file itself). If you are looking at an open DOS window or program, you won't see this page.

On this tab you can change the MS-DOS attributes of the program, including whether the archive bit is set, whether the file can be modified or not (read-only bit), and whether the file is a hidden or system file. Generally you won't want to change these bits except in very special circumstances. And then only if you're sure you know why you're making the change.

Program Properties

The Program tab of the Properties window (see Figure 10.2) lets you change the running parameters of the program as well as the name and icon associated with it.

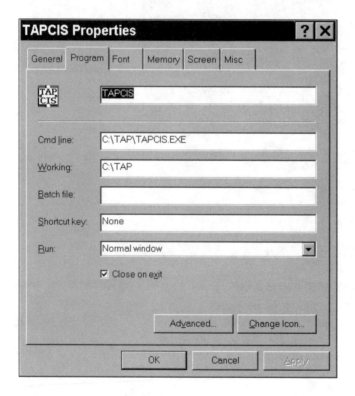

FIGURE 10.2:
The Program tab lets you control the command options of a DOS program.

Some Basic Settings

Here's what those settings mean:

Cmd line This box shows the actual command line executed. Here you can add any command line parameters that you need. (If you want to be able to add parameters each time you run the program, add a question mark as the only command line option and Windows 95 will prompt you for parameters.)

Working If your program has a favorite working directory, set that here. This isn't common any more but some older programs need to be told this information. If there's already an entry in this box,

Windows 95 and the program have figured out that it's necessary. Don't change this setting unless you're sure you know why.

Batch file If you want to run a batch file either before or as part of the program, place the name (and full path, if necessary) for that batch file in this box.

Shortcut key This box lets you add a shortcut key. (Some DOS programs may not work well with this option, but there's no harm in trying.)

Run You can decide whether the program will run in a normal window, maximized, or minimized. Some DOS programs may pay no attention to this setting.

Close on exit When this box is checked, the DOS window will close when you close the program.

Advanced Settings

Use the Advanced button only if you have an extremely ill-behaved or avaricious application—such as a game or other very specialized, hardware-dependent program. Click on Advanced to open the Advanced Program Settings dialog box shown in Figure 10.3.

Here you can keep the program from knowing it's even running in Windows. If really drastic measures are required, you can set the program to run in MS-DOS mode. This closes all your applications, restarts your computer in DOS mode, and may reboot your computer.

> **NOTE**
>
> It's not necessary for you to guess whether your game needs DOS mode to run. Go ahead and run the game. By default, the system will suggest DOS mode when the program requires it. So except in unusual situations, the system will let you know when a particular program needs DOS mode to run.

In MS-DOS mode you can only run a single program, and when you exit from it, the system starts Windows 95. Again, this may well mean a reboot, so don't be startled. If you need to set up a specialized configuration for the program, you can type in new CONFIG.SYS and AUTOEXEC.BAT files. And you'll need to load your older 16-bit (pre-Windows 95) drivers in order to have access to your mouse, CD-ROM, and sound card in MS-DOS mode.

The Last Resort

Running programs in MS-DOS mode should be a last resort. Almost everything should run fine in a full-screen DOS session or a DOS window. It is unlikely you will want or need to run anything in MS-DOS mode. Even DOOM and Flight Simulator run fine without it.

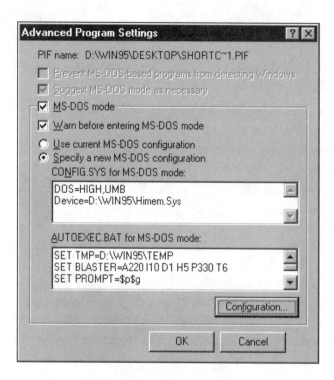

FIGURE 10.3:
This program will run in DOS mode, because it's one that has to have its own CONFIG.SYS and AUTOEXEC.BAT to make sure it's happy.

A primary reason for not running anything in DOS mode is that you lose the multitasking advantages of Windows 95. Plus, since a reboot may be required, the whole process takes a substantial amount of time.

Change the Icon

Click on the Change Icon button on the Program page to change the way the program displays in icon form. You can accept one of the icons offered or use the Browse button to look elsewhere.

Font Properties

The Font tab of the Properties sheet (see Figure 10.4) lets you set which fonts will be available when the program is running in a window on the Desktop. You can select from either bit-mapped or TrueType fonts or have both available.

In general, bit-map fonts look better on high resolution displays and are easier to read. If you want to be able to scale the window when it's open on your Desktop, set the Font size to Auto, and the fonts will change as you resize the open window.

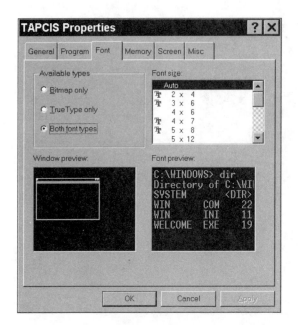

FIGURE 10.4:
The Font tab of the Properties sheet lets you control which fonts are available and used for the DOS program when it's running in a window.

Resizing the DOS Window

To change the size of a DOS window, go to the program's Properties sheet and try setting the font size to Auto and then clicking on and dragging the edge of the DOS window. Sometimes setting the Font to a fixed size and then dragging the edge of the window will work also. Different programs have different abilities to shrink and expand.

Memory Properties

The Memory tab of the Properties sheet (see Figure 10.5) lets you control how much and what kind of memory DOS programs have available when they run.

On this tab you can make sure your program has a specific amount of conventional, expanded, and extended memory. You can also let Windows 95 automatically determine how much to make available. Generally, you'll want to leave the settings here on Auto, but if you know you have a program that requires a specific amount of expanded memory to run well, you can set that here.

And Memory Problems

If you have a program that has a habit of crashing occasionally, and you want to be sure it doesn't cause problems for the rest of the system, check the Protected box in the Conventional Memory section. This may slow down the program a little but will provide an additional layer of protection.

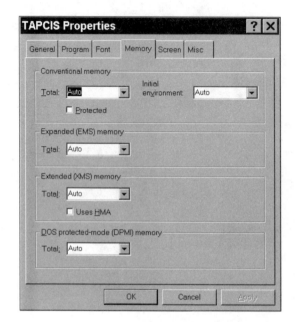

FIGURE 10.5:
The Memory tab lets you fine-tune the memory available for your DOS programs.

Some programs can actually have a problem with too much memory. Older versions of Paradox, for example, have difficulty coping with unlimited extended memory. If you leave the Expanded and Extended sections set to Auto, programs like this may not run reliably. Try setting expanded and extended memory to some reasonable maximum number, such as 8192, which should be enough for most programs.

Screen Properties

The Screen tab of the Properties sheet (shown in Figure 10.6) lets you set your program's display. If you're running a graphical program, set it for full screen. Most text-based programs run better in a window. Unlike Windows 3.1, Windows 95 handles windowed DOS programs extremely well, and there is no real gain to running them full screen unless you need the extra space for the program to look good.

Except for the full-screen versus window option, the options on this page are best left alone unless you know why you're changing them. If you're sure you need to make a change, right-click on an item and select What's This? If you understand what's in the box, you're hereby authorized to make the change.

Switching from a Window to Full Screen (and Back Again)

To switch a DOS program window to full screen, just press Alt+↵. Press Alt+↵ a second time to return to the window.

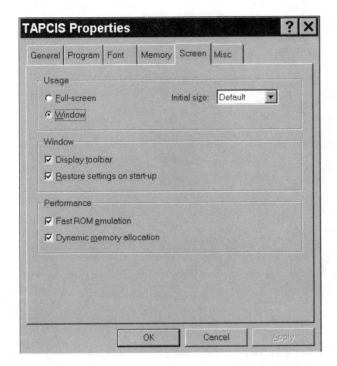

FIGURE 10.6:
The Screen tab lets you decide how your DOS programs are displayed.

To switch from a DOS Program running full screen to the Windows 95 Desktop, press Alt+Tab.

Miscellaneous Properties

The Misc tab of the Properties sheet (shown in Figure 10.7) lets you tweak several characteristics that don't fit in any of the other categories.

The properties you can set here include the following areas:

Allow screen saver When this box is checked, the Windows screen saver is allowed to come on when this program is in the foreground. If this box isn't checked, an active DOS program will keep your screen saver from kicking in.

Quick Edit Allows you to use your mouse to select text for cut-and-copy operations. If this box is cleared, you must use Mark on the Edit menu of the program to mark text.

Exclusive mode Lets the mouse work exclusively with this program. This means that when this program is open, the mouse won't be available outside this program's window.

Always suspend When this box is checked, no system resources are allocated to this program while it's in the background (open but not the active window). If this is a communications or other type of program that you want churning away in the background while you do something else, don't check this box.

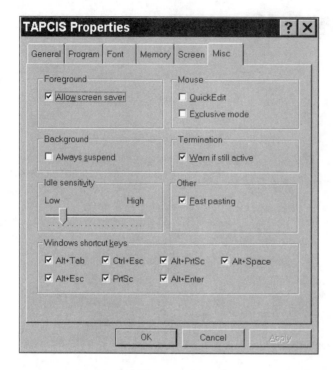

FIGURE 10.7:
The Misc tab lets you set other characteristics of your DOS program's behavior.

Warn if still active Some DOS programs are very fussy about being closed properly (like WordPerfect for DOS). When this box is checked, you'll get a warning message if you try to close the window without closing the program first.

Idle sensitivity When this slider is set to high, the DOS program will release resources and processing time more quickly to other, foreground tasks. For communications programs, however, you will probably want to set this to the low side.

Fast pasting This allows a faster method of pasting, but if you have troubles with pasting correctly in this application, clear the box.

Windows shortcut keys Generally you will want to leave these alone unless your DOS program absolutely needs to use one of these keystrokes. Clear the appropriate box or boxes if there are special keystrokes normally used by Windows 95 that you want passed on to your DOS program instead.

Making Stubborn DOS Programs Run

If your favorite DOS application is having trouble running in Windows 95, there are a variety of ways to get it going. They are presented here in approximately the order you should try them—from the relatively mild to the seriously serious. You should try these only if you have problems running a program after you have installed it.

> **NOTE**   The default settings in Windows 95 are excellent for the vast majority of DOS-based programs and should only be messed with if you're having problems.

- Run the program full screen. You can do this by pressing Alt+↵ when the program is active, or from the program's Properties sheet. Select Full-screen from the Screen page. This should be all that most graphical programs need, and with text-only programs this step can usually be skipped.
- Give the program only the kind of memory it absolutely needs. From the Memory page of the Properties sheet, select None for any memory types that you know the program doesn't need. Most DOS programs will not use Extended (XMS) memory or DPMI memory, so those are good choices to try turning off first.
- Give the program the exact amount of memory it needs. If there's a minimum amount of memory that you know the program requires, set the conventional memory setting of the Memory page to some figure slightly above that. This will ensure that the program will only attempt to run when there is sufficient memory available.
- Protect the memory that the program uses. On the Memory sheet, check the Protected box in the conventional memory section.
- Turn off dynamic memory allocation on the Screen page. If the program uses both text mode and graphics mode (an example would be Symantec's TimeLine), this will prevent Windows 95 from trying to change the amount of memory allocated when there's a mode change.
- Turn off fast ROM emulation on the Screen page. This may make the program run a bit more slowly, especially in text mode, but if the program is having problems with writing text to the screen, this may help.

- Turn off the Windows 95 screen saver by clearing the Allow Screen Saver check box on the Misc page.
- Turn the idle sensitivity down to the minimum by moving the slider on the Misc page all the way to the left.
- If your program refuses to run from within Windows, try lying to it. Click on the Advanced button on the Program page, and check the Prevent MS-DOS-based Programs from Detecting Windows box. Only do this as a last resort before trying DOS mode.
- OK, everything else failed, so it's time to get serious. Run the program in MS-DOS mode. This is the last resort for reasons we have already gone into. If nothing else works, this will. From the Advanced Program Settings dialog box of the Program page of the Properties sheet, check the MS-DOS mode box. If the program needs special CONFIG.SYS and AUTOEXEC.BAT files, type them into the appropriate boxes, or use the current versions by checking the Use Current MS-DOS Configuration box.

> **TIP** This list of troubleshooting tips should help you get that recalcitrant DOS program to behave. But a word of warning: Never change more than one thing at a time!

If you try something and it doesn't work, return to the default settings and try the next one on the list. If you try to change too many things at once, you're likely to make the situation worse, and even if it does work, you won't be sure which setting was the important one.

MS-DOS Prompt

As you've probably noticed by now, there's an MS-DOS Prompt listing on your Start ➤ Programs menu. Select it and you get a DOS window on your Desktop. You can use this window to run most DOS commands.

If you're the sort of person who uses a DOS window a lot, you can put a shortcut to the DOS prompt on your Desktop or in the Startup folder so it'll be ready and waiting on the Taskbar each time you start the computer. To make a shortcut to the DOS prompt window, follow these steps:

1. Right-click on the Start button and select Open.
2. Double-click on the Programs folder.

3. Scroll down until you see the MS-DOS icon (see Figure 10.8).
4. Right-click on the icon and either select Create Shortcut to make a shortcut on the spot or drag and drop to another location and select Create Shortcut(s) when you get there.

FIGURE 10.8:
Inside the Programs folder using the Large Icons view

DOS Commands

The DOS commands that come with Windows 95 are fairly few in number compared to DOS 6.22 or earlier. All the external DOS commands are in the Command folder inside your Windows folder.

This table lists the commands and a brief description of what each one does.

Command Name	What It Does
attrib.exe	Displays or changes file attributes.
chkdsk.exe	Reports on disk status and any errors found. Has been superseded by scandisk.exe.
choice.com	Allows for user input in a batch file.
debug.exe	Hexadecimal editor and viewer.
diskcopy.com	Makes a full copy of a diskette. Same function also available in Explorer.

Command Name	What It Does
doskey.com	Beloved of all DOS-geeks, edits command lines, makes macros.
edit.com	New version of older file editor.
extract.exe	Extracts files from a cabinet (.CAB) file.
fc.exe	File compare.
fdisk.exe	Makes and removes hard drive partitions.
find.exe	Locates text in a file.
format.com	Formats disks.
label.exe	Adds, removes, or changes a disk label.
mem.exe	Displays total memory, amount in use, and amount available.
mode.com	Configures system devices.
more.com	Displays output one screen at a time.
move.exe	Moves one or more files.
scandisk.exe	Checks a disk for errors and makes corrections.
share.exe	Sets file locking. No longer needed in a DOS window, but can be used in MS-DOS mode.
sort.exe	Sorts input.
start.exe	Runs a program.
subst.exe	Associates a drive letter with a particular path.
sys.com	Copies system files to a disk, making the disk bootable.
xcopy.exe	Copies whole directories including subdirectories.
xcopy32.exe	A juiced-up version of xcopy with more functions plus the ability to copy long file names.

There's not a whole lot of help available in Windows 95 for DOS commands but you can get basic information if you go to a DOS prompt, type in the name of the command followed by / ?, and then press ⏎.

Next Step

Now that we've covered many of the software issues of Windows 95, it's time to cast an eye toward hardware. This is where Windows 95 has made some remarkable improvements. In the next chapter we'll talk about adding and removing hardware, and—if Windows 95 is reluctant—getting it to recognize all the pieces of your system now and in the future.

Chapter

11

HARDWARE MADE EASY

FEATURING

- **Adding new hardware**
- **Making a modem work**
- **Adding or removing a printer**
- **Troubleshooting the troublesome**

Changing hardware on a PC has always been a challenge to say the least, because most PCs are made up of perhaps a hard drive from one manufacturer, a video card from another, a sound card built somewhere in Asia, and a modem manufactured by someone you never heard of. Before Windows 95, getting all these disparate parts to work together was a real chore. And once everything was functioning, changing your system by installing a new hard drive or a different modem was more grief than most could bear.

This has begun to change with the wide adoption of what's called the *Plug-and-Play* standard. Any hardware built to this standard will be recognized and installed by Windows 95 without fuss or muss. But even older hardware—like that modem handed down to you by your annoyingly techie brother-in-law—can be installed in just a few steps. In this chapter you'll see how easy it is to get Windows 95 to recognize your new hardware as well as how to troubleshoot any hardware that gets flaky.

Add New Hardware

With hardware built to the Plug-and-Play specification, you can shut down the computer, install the new hardware and, when you turn the computer on again, Windows 95 will detect the new hardware and do whatever's necessary to make the device work.

This is, of course, the ideal situation. You do nothing. Windows 95 does everything. Always try this approach first.

WARNING Be cautious of phrases such as "works with Plug and Play" or "works with Windows 95." Neither phrase is very meaningful because practically everything works with both Plug and Play and Windows 95. What you're looking for when you buy new hardware is a device that's built to the Plug-and-Play standard. Also watch out for anything that's a too-good-to-be-true bargain. It may well be from a company dumping the last of their non-Plug-and-Play stock. You don't want to buy old technology.

Add New
Hardware

Other devices (most notably modems) have to be pointed out to Windows 95, which is where the Add New Hardware Wizard comes in.

Double-click on this icon in the Control Panel and the first page of the Wizard opens (see Figure 11.1).

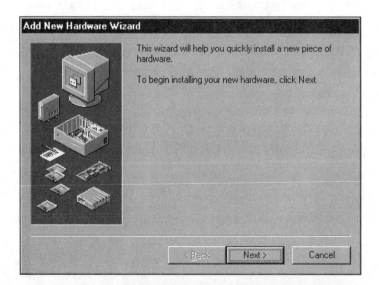

FIGURE 11.1:
The first page of the hardware installing Wizard

On the second page of the Wizard, you'll be asked if you want Windows 95 to detect the hardware or if you want to supply the information yourself. Let Windows 95 do the detecting. That usually works very well. Carefully read every page of the Wizard as you go so you know what's going on.

You'll see the page shown in Figure 11.2 with a bar across the bottom showing how near you are to finishing. The bar will sometimes look as if it's stalled and nothing's happening, but be patient. Unless the computer is completely silent for at least five minutes, there's still activity going on.

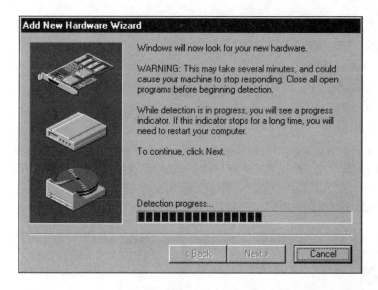

FIGURE 11.2:
The hardware detection process in action

After the search, the Wizard will tell you what it found and ask you to confirm its findings. If it's all correct, click on Finish and the installation process will be completed.

When You Have to Help

But what if, at the end of the search, Windows 95 comes up empty (as shown in Figure 11.3)?

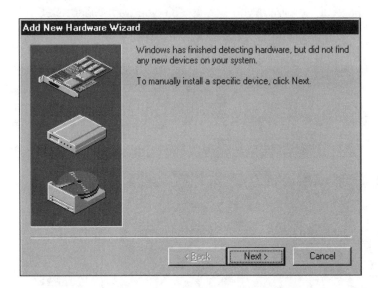

FIGURE 11.3:
Windows 95 has made an attempt but can't see your new hardware.

Don't worry, this just means that you have to provide some help. Click on the Next button and you'll be presented with a list of hardware types (Figure 11.4). Let's say you're adding a sound card to your system. Scroll down until you see Sound, Video, and Game Controllers and click on it once. Click on the Next button again.

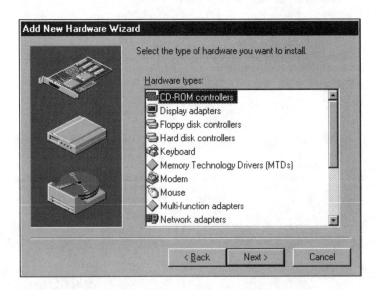

FIGURE 11.4:
Now you get to tell Windows 95 what hardware has been added to your system.

The Wizard now shows a box with two panes. The left one is a list of manufacturers. Find the name of the company that made your new piece of hardware and highlight it by clicking once on the name. That will open a list of models on the right (as shown in Figure 11.5).

NOTE The name or number of your model may be on the hardware itself; it certainly will be in the documentation. Don't have the documentation? Then guess. Seriously—if you guess wrong, no harm done. You'll just have to run the Add New Hardware Wizard and try again.

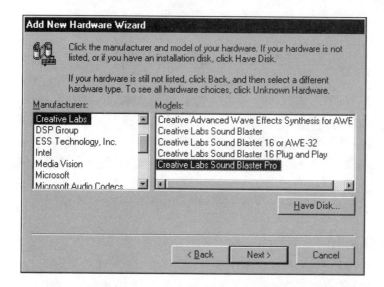

FIGURE 11.5:
Picking the manufacturer and model

TIP The Have Disk button is used only when you know that the hardware in question requires some files (called *drivers*) that Windows 95 doesn't provide. These files would be on a disk that came with the hardware. This doesn't happen very often. Most of the time the Windows 95 drivers will work best.

Highlight the model and click on the Next button. What happens next depends on the hardware being installed. Just be sure to read all the instructions you receive. For example, installing a sound card may produce something like the screen shown in Figure 11.6. It's wise to print out such settings on the off chance that these settings are in conflict with some other piece of hardware.

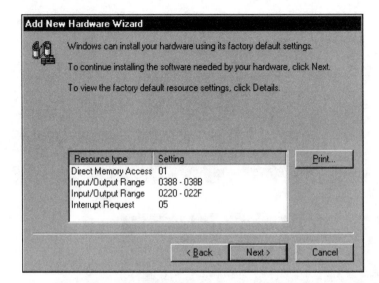

FIGURE 11.6:
Some installations will produce a window like this one. Print out and save this information. If everything works fine, you can throw the printout away.

 **TIP**   Modems and printers can be installed from Add New Hardware but installation is easier using other methods as described later in this chapter.

Continue following the Wizard's instructions until the installation is complete.

Still Not Working?

If you've tried the above steps and your system still can't see the hardware in question, there's plenty more you can do before calling in an expert. Of course, you can go for the expert now and forget the rest of this if you're too uncomfortable messing around with your computer. But you're unlikely to do any harm trying these steps and you might actually fix the problem yourself!

Check for Conflicts

Open the System Properties dialog box (Properties of My Computer or System from the Control Panel), and click on the Device Manager tab. Click on the + beside the type of device you are having trouble with, then choose the particular device. Click on Properties, then the Resources page, and see if there are any conflicts shown. If there are, then you'll probably want to run one of the Troubleshooting Wizards from the Windows 95 Help system.

External Devices

If the thing that isn't working is attached to your computer, as opposed to something inside the box, here are a few things to check per lists below:

Power Check that the power is on to the device. Even if it is, try turning the power off and back on. This single step will clear an amazing percentage of all hardware problems.

Cable connections Make sure that the cable that connects it is solidly attached at both ends, with all the screws that lock the connectors screwed in.

Cable integrity Check the cable and make sure that your cat hasn't decided that it looked like a tasty supplement to her kibble.

Internal Devices

If the problem is with something inside the computer box, it gets trickier. First, shut down Windows 95 completely and turn the power off. Then carefully remove the screws that hold your computer's box together and put them somewhere safe and remove the cover. Here are a few things to check:

Cables Check that all the cables are firmly attached and that there is no obvious physical evidence of problems (a worn spot or burn mark).

Cards Make sure that all the cards are firmly placed in their slots. It's easy to install a card in such a way that it's sort of loose. This will cause the device to work intermittently or not at all.

Dirt Over time, the amount of dust and dirt that builds up inside your computer's box is astounding. This can actually degrade performance or cause a device to stop working since the dirt can provide a conductive path. Remove dirt either by using a small amount of compressed air or one of those tiny computer vacuums. Or you can just do what everybody else does, huff and puff and blow the dirt loose.

When you have checked everything you can inside the computer box, before you put the cover back on, power the computer back up and see if you have corrected the problem.

Video Problems

Most video problems can be traced to a driver problem and are out of your scope of control. But here are a few things to look at:

Distortion If your picture is highly distorted, especially along one edge, you may be suffering from interference with other equipment or monitors in the area. Check where your cable is running, and try moving it to see if that helps. If not, you may need to figure out which piece of equipment is causing the interference and move either it or the computer.

Setting defaults Your video card needs to have its options set from DOS and won't let you just run the utilities in a DOS window from inside Windows 95? Well, in the first place, shame on the manufacturer! But to get around this problem, shut down Windows 95, selecting Re-start the Computer in MS-DOS mode. Once you've run the utility that the video card requires, you can exit and reboot into Windows 95 again.

With video problems it's almost always fruitful to get in touch with the manufacturer of the card and ask about "new drivers." Don't be shy, this is one inquiry they're *very* used to getting.

Modems

In the past, modems (along with printers, discussed in the next section) have been the worst possible pains-in-the-neck to get installed. There's been some steady improvement over the years and Windows 95 is a big step forward. Modems are still quirky animals, but Windows 95 gives you a lot of help in solving whatever problems might occur.

Modems

All the steps for getting a modem up and running are included with the (what else?) Modem Wizard. To get started, double-click on the Modems icon in the Control Panel.

In the window that opens, you'll see which modem (or modems) are set up on the computer.

Adding a Modem

If you have no modem on the computer and want to install one, follow these steps:

1. Shut down Windows 95 (click on the Start button and select Shut Down). Then turn the computer off. Connect the modem to the computer.
   - If it's an external modem, you need to plug it into a serial port on the back of the computer box. You'll also need to plug the modem's electrical cord into an outlet, then make sure to turn the modem *on* before proceeding.
   - For an internal modem, you'll need to open the computer box. The instructions that came with the modem should help.
2. Turn your computer back on and let Windows 95 start. Double-click on the Modems icon in the Control Panel.
3. In the Modems Properties window, click on the Add button.
4. Windows 95 will volunteer to find the modem for you and install it. Take advantage of this offer and click on Next.
5. The system will search the communications ports and report its findings. Figure 11.7 shows what was found on my computer.

6.   If the finding is correct, click on the Next button. If Windows 95 came up with wrong information, click on the Change button and select the right manufacturer and type from the list provided and *then* click on Next.

The process will continue and you'll be notified of a successful installation.

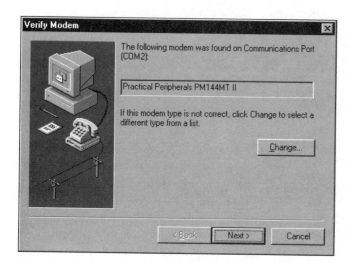

FIGURE 11.7:
Windows 95 reports on the kind of modem it found.

Removing a Modem

If you change modems (or install the wrong one), it's easy to correct the situation.

1.   Open the Modems icon in the Control Panel.
2.   On the General page, highlight the modem name.
3.   Click on the Remove button, and it's gone!

TIP   Some modem problems in Windows 95 arise when pre-Windows 95 communications software intervenes and changes a modem setting without your knowledge. If you repeatedly get a *modem will not initialize* message, try removing the modem from Windows 95 and then installing it again. Sometimes, just shutting down the computer and starting it up again will do the trick. You may even need to switch software or upgrade your existing software to a Windows 95 version.

Modem Settings

To find the hardware-type settings for your modem, double-click on the Modems icon in the Control Panel. Highlight your modem (if it isn't already) and select Properties. What opens is the Properties sheet for this particular modem (see Figure 11.8).

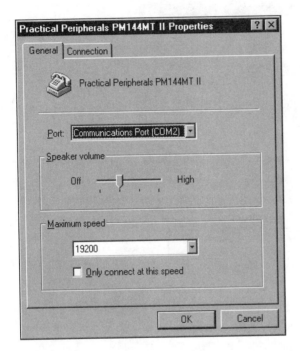

FIGURE 11.8:
This is the place to check up on the settings for your modem.

On the General page are
- The full name of the modem
- The port it's connected to
- A slider for setting the volume of the modem speaker
- A drop-down box for setting the maximum speed

NOTE These settings (except for volume, which is strictly a matter of preference) rarely need to be fooled with. That's because they come from what Windows 95 knows about your specific modem. Only change the settings when you've had some difficulty with your modem being recognized or you're sure a particular setting is wrong.

The Connection Page

On the Connection page are more of the hardware settings. Again, unless you have a good reason for changing the Connection preferences, leave them alone. The Call Preferences can be changed if you find the default ones unsuitable.

Advanced Settings

If you click on the Advanced button, you'll see the window in Figure 11.9. These settings are rarely anything to be concerned about. They're just here for those odd and infrequent times when it might be necessary to force error correction or use software for error control. The one thing on this page that might be used more often is the log file. If you're troubleshooting a bad connection, check Record a Log File before you try to connect, and Windows 95 will produce a text file of exactly what happened. The file will be called MODEMLOG.TXT and will be placed in the Windows folder. Some communications software will not produce a MODEMLOG.TXT.

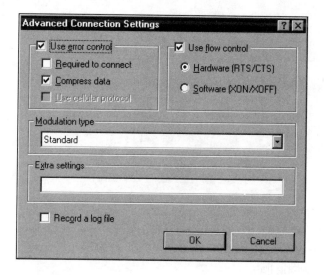

FIGURE 11.9:
The Advanced settings can sometimes help with a difficult connection.

Dialing Properties

In addition to centralizing the modem's hardware and software settings, you also want to enter information about how you're dialing and where you're dialing from. Windows 95 allows for the configuring of multiple dialing locations, so if you travel with your computer, you can make calls from your branch office (or the ski resort in Gstaad where you take your vacations) without making complex changes.

Double-click on the Modems icon in the Control Panel, then click on Dialing Properties on the General page and fill out the information for your location. Click on the New button to supply additional locations. When you change physical locations, you need only tell Windows 95 where you are (see Figure 11.10) and all your necessary dialing information will be loaded.

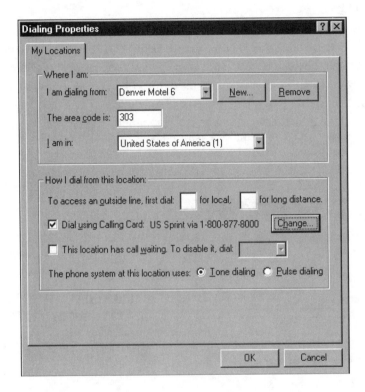

FIGURE 11.10:
When you travel with your computer, you don't have to redo your communications settings when you change locations.

Modem Solutions

As a general rule, when your modem is uncooperative, it's for obvious reasons:
- It's not plugged into a phone line.
- The modem's turned off or it's not plugged into an active electrical socket (external modems).
- One or more programs have confused the settings.

This last item happens more often in Windows 95 because of the new TAPI (short for Telephony Applications Programming Interface) standard. Like most technology designed to make things better in the future, it has a way of making life somewhat worse here in the present.

TIP   For more on TAPI and what it means, see Chapter 15.

Suffice it to say here that communications programs written for Windows 3.1 and not updated for Windows 95 can change your modem's settings. Not all older programs—just some. If this happens, you'll try to use another communications program and get an error message that says something like *initialization failure* or *modem not recognized.*

The problem can usually be fixed by removing your modem (as described earlier in this chapter) and then reinstalling it. This isn't really difficult but it is a pain and a delay. More permanent solutions are

- Upgrade to the Windows 95 version of the software.
- Change to a communications program that doesn't cause other programs to fail.

Another problem in Windows 95 is that most programs can't share a communications port. You become aware of this when you have fax software loaded and ready to receive a fax and then try to connect to America Online or CompuServe or your Internet provider. In this case you'll get a message like *the modem can't be found* or *the modem is not responding.* The immediate solution is to close the fax software before starting another communications program. The long-term fixes are

- Upgrade all your communications programs to ones that are TAPI-aware.
- Use programs that combine fax and communications in one package.

Printers

Printing is generally a lot easier in Windows 95 than in any previous system. As in Windows 3.1, printers are set up to use a common set of drivers so you don't have to configure each program independently for printing. Adding or removing a printer is as easy as point and click, and sharing printers over a network is painless.

Printers are accessible through the Printers folder inside My Computer, off the Start menu under Settings, or the Printers folder in the Control Panel. And of course, you can drag a shortcut to the Printers folder (or any of the printers in it) to your desktop. Open the Printers folder to see what printers are installed for your system.

Adding a Printer

Setting up a printer is part of the installation routine. But if your printer isn't installed or you want to add another printer or a network printer, it's very easy to do.

For a printer that's connected directly to your computer, double-click on the Printers folder and follow these steps (clicking on the Next button after each entry):

1. Select Add Printer.
2. When the Add Printer Wizard starts, click on Next, and check the Local printer entry. (This step will be skipped if you're not on a network.)
3. Highlight the name of the printer's manufacturer and the model name.
4. Select the port you want to use. Unless you know of some special circumstances, choose LPT1.
5. Type in the name you want the printer to be known by and indicate whether this is to be the default printer for all your Windows programs. If this is the printer you plan to use practically all the time, select Yes. Otherwise say no—you'll still be able to select the printer when you want to use it.
6. Print a test page to verify all is well. Then click on Finish.

Adding a Network Printer

A network printer (indicated by this icon) is plugged into someone else's computer—a computer you have access to via a network.

HP LaserJet 4

To install a network printer so you can use it, double-click on the Printers folder and follow these steps (clicking on Next after each entry):

1. Double-click on Add Printer. When the Add Printer Wizard starts, click on Next, and then select Network printer.
2. You'll need to tell the system the address of the printer, so click on the Browse button to look for available printers. Highlight the printer (as shown in Figure 11.11) and click on OK.
3. If you expect to print from DOS programs, click on Yes so the system can add the necessary information to the printer setup.
4. Enter the name you want to call the printer and check whether you want this printer to be the default printer. Only check Yes if you expect to be using the network printer for the majority of your printing.
5. Print a test page to make sure everything's running properly and click on Finish.

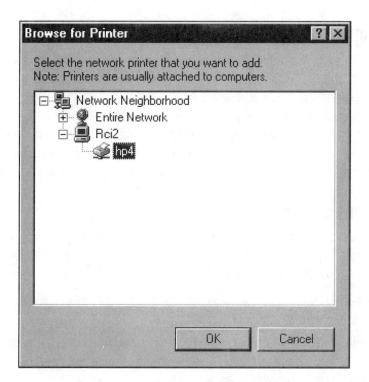

FIGURE 11.11:
Here's where you select a printer on the network.

TIP

To be able to use a printer set up this way, both the printer and the computer it's connected to must be switched on.

Removing a Printer

Sometimes you may need to uninstall a printer, which is quite easily done. Just right-click on the printer's icon in the Printers folder and select Delete. You'll be asked to confirm the deletion. You may also be asked if you want to delete files that are associated with this printer that won't be necessary if the printer is gone. If you're getting rid of the printer permanently, select Yes. If you're planning on reinstalling the same printer soon, select No.

Printer Settings

To get at the settings for a printer, you need to right-click on the printer's icon and select Properties. On the Properties sheet that opens, you can set details as to fonts, paper, how the printer treats graphics, and so on.

Most of these settings are made by the printer driver that Windows 95 installed to run the printer. Change ones that you need to change but avoid changing settings if you're not clear what the setting does. You can inadvertently disable your printer. If this happens, you can usually cure it by removing the printer (see the previous section) and then installing it again.

Printer Solutions

Besides the usual paper jam problems that we all hate, you can easily run into subtle conflicts between your application program and the printer drivers, as well as downright bugs in either. Here are some things to try, in roughly the order to try them.

Printer Online This happens all the time, especially if the printer's not right next to you where you can see it. Make sure the Online light is on.

Power Turn the power off and back on. This does two things. It forces you to check that the power is actually on, and, more to the point, it causes the printer to do a complete reset getting back to the known starting point that Windows 95 expects to find it in.

Cable Check the cable connections on both ends.

Switch Boxes, "Buffalo Boxes," Spoolers There are all sorts of ways to share a printer that are left over from the bad old DOS days. With networking built into Windows 95 these probably won't last long but if you have one of these boxes, temporarily connect the printer directly to your computer, with nothing in between except the actual cable (and that one a nice short one). Now try printing. If you can print now, you know the problem isn't the printer itself. It's the device between your computer and the printer.

Network Print Servers Same approach as for switch boxes. Try connecting directly to the printer without the intervening network connection.

Test File Print a simple test file from Notepad—a few words are enough to know if the printer is being recognized by Windows 95. If the test file prints, but you have a problem with more complicated printing from your application, chances are you have a problem with the application or possibly the printer driver. Check with the company that makes the application for a newer version or check with the manufacturer of your printer to see if there's a newer driver.

If none of these help, try the print troubleshooter that comes with Windows 95. Select Help from the Start menu. On the Contents page, double-click on Troubleshooting and select If You Have Trouble Printing. The guide is interactive in that you select the problem you're having, and then you're stepped through the process of finding a solution.

Solving Hardware Conflicts

No matter how much Windows 95 does to let you simply plug in your new hardware, and play with it immediately, sooner or later you're going to have problems with either a new piece of hardware or an existing one. Sometimes the source of the problem is a subtle conflict between two (or more) pieces of hardware but much more often the root cause is something fairly simple and straightforward.

Open the System Properties dialog box (Properties of My Computer or System from the Control Panel) and click on the Device Manager tab. Click on the type of device you are having trouble with and see if there are any conflicts shown. If there are, then you'll probably want to run one of the Troubleshooting Wizards from the Windows 95 Help system.

Windows 95 provides an outstanding tool for resolving conflicts and getting stuff working called the Hardware Conflict Troubleshooter shown in Figure 11.12. This little gem, reached off the Help menu, will resolve the vast majority of any hardware problems you might have. Just follow the directions, and click on the buttons as required. We're not going to trace through every step of using this tool because there are just too many directions it could branch in, depending on what it finds, and how you respond to its questions.

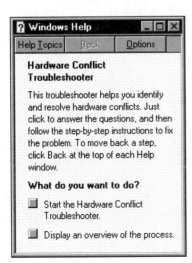

FIGURE 11.12:
The Hardware Conflict Troubleshooter is an excellent tool for resolving hardware problems.

If your problem is a sort of general "it doesn't work" where "it" is some device, there are a few things to look for or think about. If none of these seem to fit the bill, start the Windows 95 Help system and see if there's a Wizard for it in the Troubleshooting section, as shown in Figure 11.13.

FIGURE 11.13:
The Windows Help system has excellent Troubleshooting Wizards to help you locate and resolve problems.

Next Step

In this chapter we've covered some of the most common hardware questions and answers. Next we'll move on to the features and programs that come with Windows 95, starting with some treats for your eyes and ears.

Chapter 12

SIGHTS AND SOUNDS

- **Setting up multimedia**
- **Playing and programming CDs**
- **Playing video**
- **Recording and playing sound**
- **Turning the volume up (and down)**

The multimedia capabilities built into many computers and now implemented by Windows 95 may strike you as more of a toy than anything useful. People who use computers intensely, as writers, accountants, and computer consultants do, are not looking for more ways to get distracted but for ways to remove distractions. Who needs moving pictures or music to get a book written?

Turns out that's the wrong question. The fact is that publishing is different in the age of the computer, and so are accounting and data crunching. Books can be published online with animation, pictures, or music. Spreadsheets can include pictures of products or factories to make data more concrete. Databases can include pictures of clients and employees to make information more personal.

This chapter examines the CD Player, Media Player, and Sound Recorder built into Windows 95. The first can be used for your private enjoyment or to accompany a presentation with a soundtrack. The second and third can be used to display and enhance multimedia presentations.

You'll find all the Multimedia applications by clicking on the Start button and proceeding through Programs ➤ Accessories ➤ Multimedia.

Can't Find Multimedia?

You won't have a Multimedia menu in your Accessories menu if the Multimedia applications weren't installed at the time Windows 95 was installed. If this is the case, it's easily remedied:

1. Go to the Control Panel and click on Add/Remove Programs.
2. Click on the Windows Setup tab at the top of the Add/Remove Programs Properties dialog box.
3. Scroll through the list of options in the dialog box until you locate Multimedia.
4. Double-click on Multimedia to see a list of multimedia programs available.
5. Click on the check boxes next to as many programs as you want to install. (For the purposes of this chapter, make sure CD Player, Media Player, Sound Recorder, and Volume Control are selected.)
6. OK your way out and insert your Windows 95 disk(s) as requested to complete the installation.

> **NOTE** You can associate sounds with different events—for example a program opens and a particular sound plays. Chapter 13 covers how to do this.

The CD Player

The CD Player lets you play audio CDs using your CD-ROM drive, sound card, and speakers. If you want to listen through external speakers, a sound card is required. But even without a sound card, you can listen through headphones plugged into the CD-ROM drive itself.

To open the CD Player, follow these steps:

1. Click on the Start button on the Taskbar.

2. Select Programs.

3. Select Accessories in the Program menu.

4. Select Multimedia in the Accessories menu to open the Multimedia menu.

Depending on the programs you selected when you installed Windows 95, you'll probably have several applications on this menu.

Starting It Up

To start the CD Player, follow these steps:

1. Locate CD Player among the programs in the Multimedia menu.

2. Click on the CD Player option. That will start the program. You will see the window shown in Figure 12.1.

All you have to do is supply a music CD. The player will play it through your sound card and speakers (plugged into the audio jacks on the back of the CD-ROM controller) or through the headphone jack in the front of your CD-ROM drive.

FIGURE 12.1:
To change the look of the CD Player, check out the View menu.

TIP

By default, the CD Player will start playing the minute you put a music CD in the drive. To overrule the automatic play for a particular CD, hold down the Shift key while you insert the CD. To turn this automatic play feature off completely (or back on), right-click on the My Computer icon and select Properties. On the Device Manager page, double-click on CD-ROM, highlight your CD-ROM drive's name, and click on Properties. On the Settings page, click on Auto Insert Notification. With a check in the box, music CDs will play automatically. Without the check, you need to open the CD Player applet yourself.

How It Works

Just as a demonstration, I popped a Gipsy Kings CD in the drive and clicked on the large triangle next to the digital read-out (the play button). The CD Player (with Disk/Track info enabled from the View menu) can be seen in Figure 12.2.

FIGURE 12.2:
Here's what the CD Player at work looks like.

Notice that several of the buttons that were gray and unavailable in Figure 12.1 when there was no CD in the drive are now black and available in Figure 12.2.

Play At the top, the large triangle is gray because the CD is playing. (There's no reason to click on the Play button when the CD is playing; but if you do, no harm is done.)

Pause Next to the play button is a button with two vertical bars. This is the Pause button. Click on it to hold your playback while you run to answer the door or the phone.

Stop The last button at the right end of the top tier is the Stop button. Click on it when you're tired of listening to the music or when the boss walks into your office. It will stop playback dead.

Previous Cut The first button at the left end of the second tier of buttons looks like a double arrowhead pointing left toward a vertical line. Click once to move to the beginning of the current piece, click twice to move to the previous cut on the CD.

Skip Back The second button on the second tier looks like a double arrowhead pointing left. This is the Skip Back button. Each time you click on it, you will move back one second in the music.

Skip Forward The third button on the second tier is the Skip Forward button. It looks like a double arrowhead pointing to the right. Each time you click on it, you will move one second forward in the music.

Next Track The fourth button on the second tier is the Next Track button. It looks like a double arrowhead pointing right toward a vertical bar. It will take you instantly to the next song.

Eject The final button at the right end of the second tier of buttons looks like an arrow pointing upward. It is the Eject button. It will cause your CD-ROM drive to stick its tongue out at you—which is what it looks like when your CD is ejected from most drives.

Setting Time and Play Options

Is that all there is? Certainly not. If you're an information freak, click on the digital read-out. Before you click, the readout will tell you the current track number and the elapsed time for that track. The first time you click, you'll see the track number and the time remaining on the track. The second click will display the time remaining for the whole CD (shown in Figure 12.3).

FIGURE 12.3:
Getting instant information about the play time remaining on the whole CD

If you want to set these without clicking on the digital display, pull down the View menu and select from:
- Track time elapsed
- Track time remaining
- Disc time remaining

The Options menu lets you opt for continuous play, random play, or intro play. Select the Preferences option. It allows you to set the font size for the digital readout as well as the length of intro play (10 seconds is the default).

> **TIP**
> **Want a shortcut to CD Player or Media Player on your Desktop? Open the Windows folder and look for the file CDPLAYER.EXE or MPLAYER.EXE, then right-click and drag the file to the Desktop. Release the right mouse button and select Create Shortcut(s) here.**

Editing the Play List

And if that's not enough, there's an entire layer of the CD Player we haven't even touched yet. Here's how to access it.

1. Pull down the Disc menu.
2. Select Edit Play List. You will see the dialog box shown in Figure 12.4.

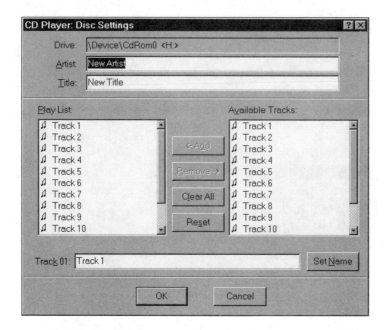

FIGURE 12.4:
The Disc Settings dialog box lets you program a play list.

Using this dialog box, you can do something that owners of CD players often never get the hang of—programming your player to play specific songs in a specific order.

By Track Number

As an example, let's set up the CD Player to play Tracks 5, 12, and 3 on this particular disk. Here's how:

1. Click on the Clear All button to clear all the entries on the Play List.
2. Double-click on Track 5 in the Available Tracks list box. It will appear in the Play List.
3. Double-click on Track 12, and then double-click on Track 3 in the Available Tracks list box.

By Track Name

If you'd rather deal with track names than track numbers, you can insert names for each of the tracks (or just the ones you care about) as follows:

1. Click on a track—for this example, we'll click on Track 3 in the Available Tracks list.
2. Click on the text box next to the Set Name button.
3. Refer to your CD packaging to get the name of the third song on the CD.
4. Type the name in the text box. (You can type it next to Track 3, or delete the track and type the name instead.)
5. Click on the Set Name button. In the Available Tracks list and in the Play List, Track 3 will be replaced with the name you just typed.

6. Just for the sake of completeness, click on the text box marked Artist and type the performer(s) name.

7. Highlight the text box marked Title and type the CD's title.

8. Click on the OK button.

Once you've supplied your CD Player with this information, the program will remember it, recognize the CD, and follow your programmed instructions every time you play it.

TIP If you have a CD-ROM player capable of playing multiple disks, Multidisc Play will be an option on the Options menu. Select it, and when you click on the downward-pointing arrow at the right end of the Artist box, you will see each of the CDs available to you. Select the CD you want to play.

The Media Player

These days the word *media* conjures up more talk show blather about how everything's the fault of the media. Not this media. The media in this section are fun—never trouble.

Let's begin, as always, by first opening the program:

1. Click on the Start button on the Taskbar.

2. Select Programs.

3. Select Accessories from the Programs menu.

4. Select Multimedia from the Accessories menu.

5. Select Media Player from the Multimedia menu.

You should see something similar to the window shown in Figure 12.5.

FIGURE 12.5:
The Media Player looks like this.

The Media Player will play Video for Windows animated files (.AVI), sound files (.WAV), MIDI files (.MID and .RMI), or your audio CD. Yes, that's right. You can use Media Player to play your music CDs just like CD Player except that Media Player offers fewer customization options.

Playing Files

Windows 95 comes with a variety of multimedia files—especially on the CD-ROM version. To play a file, follow these steps:

1. Pull down the Media Player Device menu and select the type of file you want to play.
2. Locate the file you want to play, double-click or highlight it, and select Open.
3. Click on the right-pointing arrow (the Play button).

You can select sections of animation or movies just like you select recorded music tracks (see the CD Player section earlier in this chapter). Although the buttons are in different places than the ones on the CD Player, you should be able to identify them by their icons.

Copying and Pasting Files

 You can copy and paste sound, animation, or movie files using the Select buttons, which look like tiny arrows pointing down (begin selection) and up (end selection) above a horizontal bar.

Selecting a Section

To select a section of either an audio or video file:

1. Listen (or watch) until you reach the point where the section begins.
2. Click on the begin selection button.
3. Continue listening or watching until you reach the end of the section.
4. Click on the end selection button.
5. Pull down the Edit menu and select Copy Object. (The piece you have selected will be placed on the Clipboard for pasting into any document that supports sound or video files.)

Getting Looped

If you want a piece of music, film, or animation to repeat continuously, pull down the Edit menu and select Options. Click on the option marked Auto Repeat. Your media file will play over and over until:

1. the end of time,
2. you turn off the media player,
3. or you lose your mind and destroy your computer with a fire ax.

The Sound Recorder

If you have an audio input device on your computer (either a microphone or a CD-ROM player), you can use the Sound Recorder to make a .WAV file you can associate with a Windows event or send in a message.

Making .WAV Files

Here's how to make a .WAV file with the Sound Recorder:

1. Open Sound Recorder in the Multimedia menu under Accessories.
2. Select New from the File menu.
3. To begin recording, click on the button with the dark red dot.
4. Start the CD or start speaking into the microphone.
5. Click on the button with the black square to stop recording.
6. Select Save from the File menu to save the sound clip.

Figure 12.6 shows the Sound Recorder recording from a CD being played in the Media Player.

FIGURE 12.6:
Make your own .WAV files from a CD-ROM with the Sound Recorder.

The Sound Recorder also lets you play other types of sound clips in the Media Player and record them as .WAV files. The .WAV files you make can be played back with the Sound Recorder or the Media Player.

TIP

To easily associate a .WAV file with an event in Windows 95, move the file to the Media folder (inside the Windows folder). See Chapter 13 for the specifics on how to use sound files in this way.

Special Effects and Editing

Use the Effects menu to change some of the sound's qualities—to add an echo or decrease the speed. The sound can also be edited, using the menu controls.

Volume Control

The Volume Control panel not only lets you adjust the sound level but also individually tune different types of files. The easiest way to reach the Volume Control panel is to right-click on the small speaker icon at the end of the Taskbar and select Volume Controls. You can also open it from the Multimedia menu under Accessories (Figure 12.7).

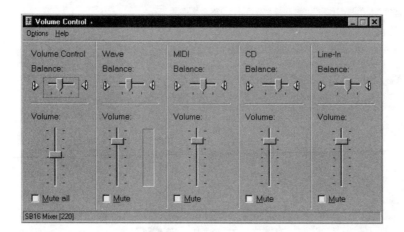

FIGURE 12.7:
The Volume Control panel lets you make adjustments in your sound files.

Tone Controls

For tone controls (bass and treble), select Advanced Controls from the Options menu. This will put an Advanced button at the bottom of the Volume Control window. Click on this button to open the page shown in Figure 12.8.

Use the slider controls to increase or decrease the treble and bass tones. These settings will affect all the sound files you play.

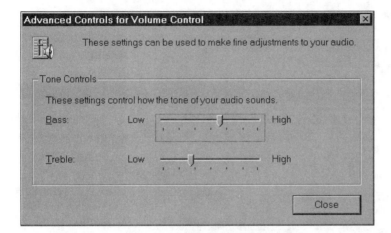

FIGURE 12.8:
Use the slider controls to adjust tone.

NOTE If Advanced Controls is dimmed on your screen, it just means that your hardware doesn't support these functions.

Setting Volume Control Display

Figure 12.7 shows the default settings for volume control, but you can decide which devices you want to show on the Volume Control panel. Open Volume Control and select Properties from the Options menu. This will open the window shown in Figure 12.9.

Select Playback and check the devices you want shown on Volume Control. Likewise you can display recording levels. The choices will probably differ based on your specific computer hardware.

More Multimedia Settings

Multimedia

There's also a Multimedia icon in the Control Panel that contains mostly advanced settings but some basic ones too.

Double-click on this icon and poke around, right-clicking on anything you don't understand to get a box of explanation. There are a lot of

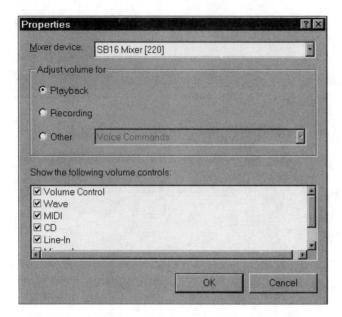

FIGURE 12.9:
Deciding which controls you want shown in the Volume Control window

terms here that will be unfamiliar to anyone who's a novice at computer-based sound and video. Experiment but also take care not to remove a device unintentionally. If you do, you may have run the Add New Hardware icon in the Control Panel to get the device back.

Next Step

This chapter hasn't exhausted all the features for eyes and ears. In the next chapter, we'll go on to some neat functions in the Control Panel that also affect how your computer looks and sounds and you'll learn how to customize settings that make your computer truly your own. And if the computer is not 100 percent your own, you'll also see how to share with other users by creating User Profiles.

Chapter 13

IN THE CONTROL PANEL

FEATURING

- **Adding and removing programs and hardware**
- **Configuring your mouse, keyboard, and printer**
- **Using all the Control Panel icons (in alphabetical order)**

If you've fiddled around with the Control Panel at all, you can see that it acts as a sort of Mission Central for Windows 95. Some of the settings behind the icons can be reached from other directions, but others can be reached only by way of the Control Panel. Most of the items in the Control Panel help you customize your Windows 95 even further. And if you share your computer with other people, the section on passwords will show you how each of you can have a unique Desktop.

You'll find a heading in this chapter for all the usual icons in the Control Panel (listed alphabetically). If the settings behind an icon are detailed elsewhere, you'll be pointed to the correct location.

Accessibility Options

The Accessibility Options are installed automatically when Windows 95 is installed. If you want them and they're not on your system, use Add/Remove Programs to add them.

Accessibility Options

Double-click on this icon and you'll find options for adding sound to the usual visual cues, adding visual cues to the sound ones, and making the keyboard and mouse easier to use for those of us with dexterity problems.

Not all the settings are obvious, so when you come across one that's unclear, right-click on the text and then click on the What's This? button for more information.

After you've made your settings, don't leave until you click on the General tab and check the Automatic Reset section. Put a check next to Turn Off Accessibility Features after Idle if you want the options to be turned off if the computer isn't used for the period specified in the minutes box. Clear the check box if you want to make the selection of options permanent.

Add New Hardware

The functions behind this icon are covered in detail in Chapter 11, "Hardware Made Easy."

Add/Remove Programs

Windows 95 provides a good deal of aid and comfort when it comes to adding or removing programs from your system, especially adding and removing parts of Windows 95 itself. Click on this icon in the Control Panel.

The Add/Remove function has three parts, one on each tab:

- Installing or uninstalling software applications
- Installing or removing portions of Windows 95
- Making a current Startup Disk to boot from if there's trouble

Install/Uninstall

A software producer who wants the right to put a Windows 95 logo on a product is supposed to make sure the program can uninstall itself. The idea is to correct a problem in Windows 3.1 which made it very difficult to completely remove a program and all of its associated files.

Programs written for 3.1 (and that's the software we're mostly using) don't have this uninstall capability. And some programs actually written for Windows 95 can be uninstalled and still leave bits of themselves cluttering your hard disk. This will probably improve over time. How the major programs written for Windows 95 handle Add/Remove varies widely. Some will just uninstall themselves without a fuss; others give you the option of removing all or just parts of the program. You'll have to click on the program and select Remove to see. *Nothing* will be uninstalled without your OK.

For now, this is an easy-to-use tool for installing new programs. Just put the program's first floppy disk in the drive (or if the program came on a compact disk, insert the CD in the proper drive) and click on the Install/Uninstall tab. Click on the Install button.

The program searches for an install routine first in drive A:, then drive B:, and finally in the CD drive. Figure 13.1 shows the result of one search. Click on Finish to continue. After this, the install routine of the program being installed takes over.

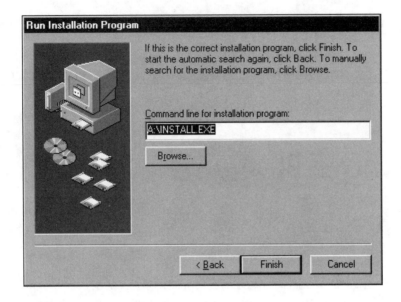

FIGURE 13.1:
The Installation program finds the INSTALL or SETUP file and proceeds to install the program.

Windows Setup

Click on the Windows Setup tab to add or remove a component of Windows 95. The various parts are organized by groups (see Figure 13.2). You can highlight any group and click on Details to see the individual components.

FIGURE 13.2:
Here's where you can install or uninstall various parts of Windows 95.

As you click on each item in a group, a description of the item's function displays at the bottom of the page. The rules are simple.

- If an item is checked, it's installed. Remove the check mark and it'll be removed.
- If an item is not checked, it's not currently installed on your system. Put a check mark next to it, and it'll be installed.
- If the check box is gray, a part of the component is selected for installation. Click on the Details button to specify which parts you want.

Click on OK once or twice until the window closes. If your Windows installation came on floppies, you'll be asked for one or more disks. If you installed from a CD, you'll have to return the Windows 95 compact disk to the CD drive.

Startup Disk

If your computer came with Windows 95 already installed, you probably don't have a startup disk. You may have made a startup disk if you installed Windows 95 yourself. Of course, you may have since lost the disk or made major changes to your system, in which case it's wise to make a new one. Simply click on this tab and select Create Disk. You'll be prompted for a floppy and the new Startup disk will be made.

A current startup disk can be helpful (if not invaluable) to a technician if one day your system fails to boot on its own, so it's best to make a new startup disk either monthly or whenever you make a major change in software or any change at all in hardware.

Date and Time

To reset the day and time shown on your computer, double-click on this icon.

This function comes in handy when traveling and using Windows 95 on a laptop. You can use it to change the time zone or reset your computer clock. By default, Windows 95 will reset your clock for daylight saving time in the time zone you've selected. It even knows that Arizona and eastern Indiana don't use daylight time, but you have to be sure the time zone is set properly. Use the drop-down box if you can't seem to get the right time zone by clicking on the map.

Other time and date information:

- Position the mouse pointer over the time display at the end of the Taskbar to see the current month, day, and year.
- For a shortcut to the Date/Time windows, right-click on the time display on the Taskbar and select Adjust Date/Time.

- To remove the time from the Taskbar, click on the Start button and select Settings ➤ Taskbar. Clear the check mark from before Show Clock.

Display

Behind the Display icon in the Control Panel are all the settings that affect your screen display including colors, screen savers, type faces in windows and dialog boxes, and resolutions. See "Desktop Settings" in Chapter 3 for details on these settings.

Fonts

TrueType fonts are managed in Windows 95 in a clear and understandable way. To see the list of fonts on your computer, click on this icon in the Control Panel.

Selecting and Viewing Fonts

The Fonts folder is a little different from the usual run of folders in that the menus show some new items. In the View menu shown in Figure 13.3, you'll find, in addition to the choices for viewing icons and lists, an option called List Fonts by Similarity.

TIP

If your font list is very long and unwieldy, select View ➤ Hide Variations. That will conceal font variations such as italic and bold and make the list easier to look through.

Select a font in the drop-down box at the top and the other fonts will line up in terms of their degree of similarity (see Figure 13.4). Before you make a commitment, you can right-click on any of the font names and select Open (or just double-click). A window will open with a complete view of the font in question.

TrueType fonts that you may have located elsewhere can be moved into this folder. Figure 13.5 shows a newly acquired font being dragged into the folder.

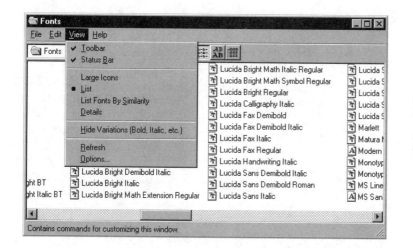

FIGURE 13.3:
The View menu is a little different in the Fonts folder.

Fonts don't have to be physically located in the Windows/Fonts folder to be recognized by Windows 95. You can make a shortcut to a font in another folder and put the shortcut in the Fonts folder. The shortcut is all you need for the font to be installed.

Fonts that are identified with an icon like this are not TrueType fonts. They're not scaleable, which means that at large point sizes they tend to look quite crummy (see Figure 13.6). Many of these fonts can be used only in certain, limited point sizes.

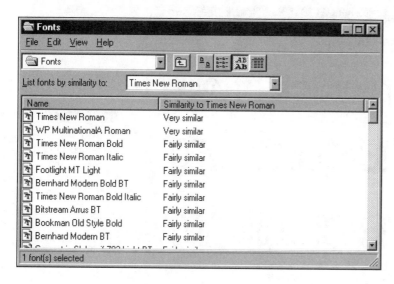

FIGURE 13.4:
Fonts can be viewed in terms of their resemblance to one another.

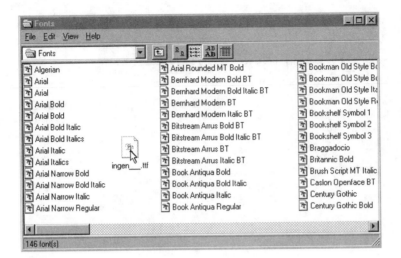

FIGURE 13.5:
Move fonts into
the Fonts folder
just as you'd
move any object—
drag and drop
or cut and paste.

Installing New Fonts

Installing new fonts is a pretty easy project. Just open the Fonts icon in the Control Panel and select Install New Font from the File menu. In the Add Fonts window (Figure 13.7) you can tell the system the drive and directory where the font(s) reside. If there's one or more TrueType fonts at the location you specify, they'll show up in the List of Fonts window.

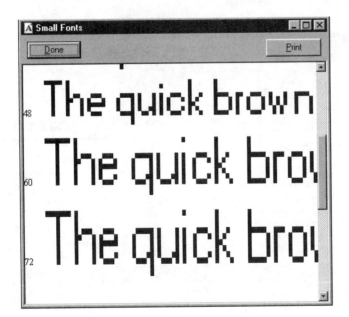

FIGURE 13.6:
The non-TrueType
fonts are not much
to look at in the
larger sizes.

Highlight the font or fonts you want installed and click on the OK button. Packages like Microsoft's TrueType Fonts for Windows (designed for Windows 3.1) may need to be installed like other programs. Use Add/Remove Programs, described earlier in this chapter.

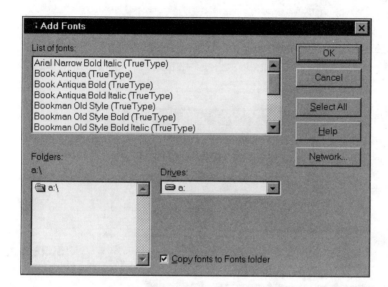

FIGURE 13.7:
Here's where you add fonts to the Fonts folder.

NOTE   Other types of fonts, such as those installed by the Adobe Type Manager, will reside elsewhere on your hard drive, depending on the location you selected. You can't put them in the Fonts folder or view them by double-clicking. However, numerous applications can display fonts and most font installing programs have their own viewers.

Joystick

If you have a joystick attached to your computer when Windows 95 is installed, this icon will appear in the Control Panel.

Double-click on it to open a Properties sheet for calibrating your existing joystick or adding a second (or third or fourth) joystick to the setup.

NOTE

To add a joystick at a later time, turn off your computer and plug the joystick in. Restart your computer. If the joystick icon doesn't appear in the Control Panel, then Windows 95 was unable to detect it. Use Add New Hardware to install it.

There's a troubleshooting button in case your joystick stops working in a particular game. As you can see in Figure 13.8, there's a joystick type for all occasions.

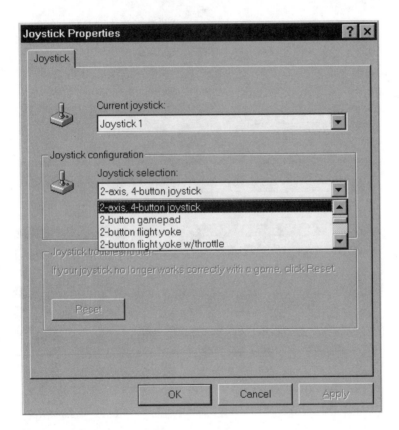

FIGURE 13.8:
Seventeen varieties of game devices are listed, or you can choose Custom and configure your own.

Keyboard

The installation routine of Windows 95 finds the keyboard plugged into your computer and recognizes it, so you normally don't have to fuss with these settings. But if you need

Keyboard

to change keyboards, adjust the keyboard's speed, or install a keyboard designed for another language, click on this icon in the Control Panel.

The three tabs on the Keyboard Properties sheet cover these different types of settings—explained in the following sections.

Changing Your Keyboard

If you're changing keyboards or Windows 95 recognizes one type of keyboard when in fact you have a different kind, go directly to the General tab. The Keyboard Type window shows what Windows 95 thinks is your keyboard. If that's wrong, click on the Change button and follow these steps:

1. On the Select Device page, click on Show All Devices.
2. Select the correct keyboard from the list shown. If you have some special installation software, click on Have Disk.
3. Click on OK and Windows 95 will install the correct keyboard either from your disk or from its own set.

You *may* have to shut down and restart your computer for the keyboard to be completely recognized.

Keyboard Speed

Click on the Speed tab to adjust keyboard rates. Here are the available settings:

Repeat delay Determines how long a key has to be held down before it starts repeating. The difference between the Long and Short setting is only about a second.

Repeat rate Determines how fast a key repeats. Fast means if you hold down a key you almost instantly get vvvvvvvvvvery long streams of letters. (Click on the practice area to test this setting.)

Cursor blink rate Makes the cursor blink faster or slower. The blinking cursor on the left demonstrates the setting.

Keyboard Languages

If you need multiple language support for your keyboard, click on the Language tab. Click on the Add button to select languages from Afrikaans to Swedish—including 15 varieties of Spanish. If you have more than one language selected, the settings on the Language tab let you choose a keyboard combination to switch between languages (see Figure 13.9).

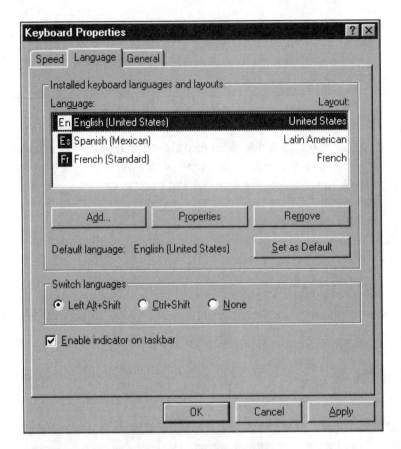

FIGURE 13.9:
Set up your keyboard for more than one language.

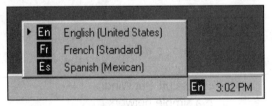

Highlight the language you want to be the default (the one that's enabled when your start you computer) and click on the Set as Default button.

Check Enable Indicator on Taskbar and an icon will appear on your Taskbar. Right-click on it and you can instantly switch between languages.

Mail and Fax

Mail and fax services have most of a chapter devoted to them.
Check Chapter 15 for mail, fax, and other communications information.

Modems

The settings behind this icon are covered in the "Modems" section of Chapter 11.

Mouse

Everything you ever wanted to know (and more) about mouse settings—including the use of settings connected to this icon can be found in Chapter 5, devoted entirely to mouses and their uses.

Multimedia

Read Chapter 12 for information on multimedia applications that come with Windows 95 and how to set them up. The settings behind this icon are covered there as well.

Network

Normally, anything to do with networks would be way beyond the scope of a book like this, and setting up multiple computers with one machine acting as a server is still pretty advanced stuff. But Windows 95 has networking tools that allow *anyone* to make a simple network connecting a couple of computers (both running Windows 95) so you can share programs and a printer.

How to setup the absolutely basic network and even some not-so-basic options are all covered in Chapter 14.

ODBC

ODBC (Open Database Connection) is a Microsoft standard for providing a uniform access method to local databases like Access or dBASE for Windows, network server databases such as Paradox for Windows, and relational databases like Oracle, Sybase, or InterBase. Since many vendors provide ODBC drivers, both for their own databases and often for others, keeping track of which ODBC driver is being used for which database can be a pain.

In Windows 95, you control which data sources are accessed with which driver using the ODBC application on the Control Panel.

When you double-click on the ODBC icon, it brings up the Data Sources dialog box shown in Figure 13.10. From here you can add, delete, and configure the drivers for the supported databases on your system. Which databases you have drivers for will depend on which applications you have.

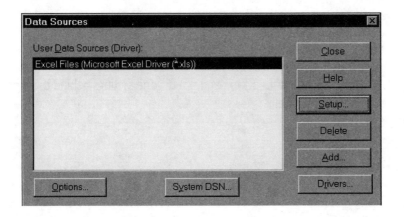

FIGURE 13.10: The Data Sources dialog box lets you add, delete, or configure your various ODBC drivers.

Passwords

When you sign on to Windows 95 the first time, you're asked to provide a name and password. If you're the only one using a computer and you don't want to deal with a password every time you turn the machine on, leave the password blank. Then double-click on the Network icon in the Control Panel, and under Primary Network Logon (on the Configuration page) make sure Windows Logon is selected. You won't be troubled with a request for a password again.

On the other hand, if you later want to start using a password or change the one you have, double-click on this icon in the Control Panel.

Click on the Change Windows Password button and enter the information requested. (If you had no previous password, leave the Old Password field empty.)

One Computer, Many Users

Everyone who sets up Windows 95 does the Desktop in a unique way. This is great—until you have to share your computer with another person (or even persons). Fortunately, Windows 95 allows you to set up a profile for each user. You'll each have to log on with your name and particular password, but once you do, the Desktop that appears will be the one you set up—programs, shortcuts, colors, and so forth, all just as you arranged.

Setting Up a User Profile

To allow user profiles, you'll need to follow these steps:

1. Double-click on the Passwords icon in the Control Panel.
2. Select the User Profiles tab. Click on the button for the second choice: Users can customize their preferences.
3. Select the kinds of settings you want individual users to be able to change and save:
   - Desktop icons and Network Neighborhood
   - Start menu and Program groups

   You can allow either, both, or none of these. Any changes you allow the other users to make will affect their profiles only.
4. Click on OK when you're finished.

After enabling user profiles, every time you restart Windows 95, you (and everyone else who uses the computer) will need to sign on with a name and password. The first time a new user signs on, the Desktop will look like it did at the time user profiles were enabled. But all changes, subject to the restrictions you set in step 3 above, will be saved for that user.

Removing a User Profile

To get rid of a user profile, sign on under a different name and password. Use the Find function to search for the user's name. For example, if the user signed on as Alfie, you should find ALFIE.PWL in the Windows folder and a folder named Alfie in the Profiles folder. Delete both the file and the folder to get rid of the profile and all things associated with it. (Don't be put off by the alarming message about deleting USER.DAT; it's just a copy and the original is still in the Windows directory.)

To eliminate all user profiles, log on and go back to the Passwords Properties sheet and change the User Profile setting.

You can also bypass all user profiles at startup by clicking on Cancel in the dialog box that asks for name and password; so don't be misled into thinking these are *security* devices, they're strictly for convenience.

Security Issues

Windows 95 was not designed to be a high-security system, even though there are some security provisions. User profiles and passwords provide some security though they can be bypassed. All someone has to do is boot in Safe Mode by pressing F8 at bootup and selecting Safe Mode from the menu.

You can prevent this by opening the file MSDOS.SYS in a text editor such as Notepad. Under Options, add the line

```
BootKeys=0
```

then save the file. Shut down and restart your computer.

On a network, you can improve the security for your computer through using some or all of these:

- Share resources selectively.
- Don't enable remote administration (in Password properties).
- Always use a password.
- Prevent others from having physical access to your computer.

This last is probably the most important because that's how most security breaches occur. It's all very much like the old saying that "locks are for honest people." The security measures in Windows 95 will not discourage a knowledgeable person determined to make mischief, but they can help protect against inadvertent misuse.

TIP

If you're in a situation where you absolutely, positively need maximum security, you should investigate running Microsoft Windows NT—a system that can be made very secure.

Printers

This icon in the Control Panel is a shortcut to your Printers folder (also seen in My Computer and the Explorer).

Details on how to install, remove, or change the settings of printers are all in Chapter 11, "Hardware Made Easy."

Regional Settings

The Regional Settings icon in the Control Panel is where you set the variations in how numbers, time, and dates are formatted in different parts of the world. For example, if

you're using a program that supports international symbols, changing the Regional Settings can affect how the program displays currency, time, and numbers. To change these settings, double-click on the icon shown here.

First select the geographic area you want to use, then confirm or change the individual settings. Your system will have to be rebooted for the settings to take effect system-wide.

Sounds

What with Windows 95's emphasis on multimedia, it's no surprise that using sound with your computer is easier than ever. Double-click on the Sounds icon in the Control Panel to set and change sound schemes.

NOTE To play the sounds that come with Windows 95, you'll need a sound card and speakers (or wear headphones all the time).

A Sheet Full of Sounds

The Sounds Properties sheet is shown in Figure 13.11. The Events window lists everything on your system that can be associated with a sound. Most are Windows events. For example, opening a program can cause a sound, as can maximizing or minimizing a window, and many other actions.

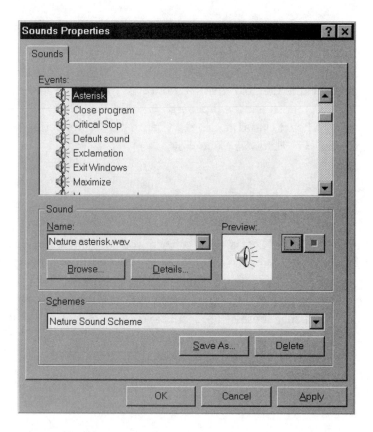

FIGURE 13.11:
Use the Sounds
Properties sheet to
associate a sound
with an event.

Many of the new programs coming out now also include sound capabilities. Their sounds may not end up in the list shown on this sheet because they're configured in the program.

If there's a Speaker icon next to the event, a sound is associated with it. Highlight the event—the name of the sound file will appear in the Name window—and click on the button next to the Preview window to hear its sound.

Sound schemes are included with Windows 95 (many more if you have the Plus! for Windows 95 package installed) and you can choose one of them from the drop-down list.

NOTE

If sound schemes don't appear in the Schemes drop-down list, you'll need to install them. Go to the Add/Remove Programs icon in the Control Panel. Under the Windows Setup, click on Multimedia and select the sound schemes you want. Select OK, and then follow the instructions.

Customizing a Sound Scheme

All the sound schemes that come with Windows are nice enough but none of them is perfect. There are either too many sounds, not enough, the wrong sounds attached to various events, or whatever. Fortunately, there's a way to make as many customized sound schemes as you like. Here's how:

1. Double-click on the Sounds icon in the Control Panel.
2. If there's a sound scheme that's close to the one you want, select it from the Schemes drop-down list. Otherwise, select Windows default.
3. Starting at the top of the Events list, select an item that you want a sound associated with.
4. Select a file from the Name drop-down list. To make sure it's the one you want, click on the Preview button to hear it.
5. Select (none) in the Name list for events that you want to keep silent.
6. Repeat steps 3–5 until you've completed the list.
7. Select Save As to save this particular assortment of sounds under a specific name. (The new scheme will appear in the Schemes drop-down list.)

TIP Windows 95 stores all its sound files in the Windows\Media folder. You'll probably want to move any additional sound files you acquire to that folder because using a single location makes setting up and changing sound schemes much easier.

System

The Properties sheet that opens when you double-click on the System icon in the Control Panel can also be accessed by right-clicking on My Computer and choosing Properties.

You won't use most of the settings if your computer is working properly. It's only when things go awry that you need to be changing anything here.

General

The General page only tells you the version of Windows 95, the registered owner, and a little bit about the type of computer. The main computer information starts on the next page.

Device Manager

The Device Manager page is where you can see what your system thinks is going on. Usually this is a reflection of reality, but when something is wrong with your computer, this is often the place you'll see it first.

The plus sign to the left of an item indicates there's more to see under that entry. To get the details of the setup for each item, highlight it, and click on Properties.

> **TIP**
>
> A list of hardware interrupts, DMA addresses, and memory addresses can be found by highlighting Computer and selecting Properties.

Hardware Profiles

Hardware profiles are something you may need if you're using a portable computer with a docking station. In a limited number of circumstances, you may need to configure alternate setups when the hardware on your system changes.

If you think this might be your situation, consult the Windows 95 help files for instructions.

Performance

The Performance tab is used almost exclusively for troubleshooting. For example, Windows 95 is pretty good at figuring out what will work best on your system, but it's not always perfect. Because of the mixture of older (16-bit) applications in a newer (32-bit) system, there may come a time when you want to check that your system is running optimally (see Figure 13.12).

Troubleshooting

Behind the File System button on the Performance page is a Troubleshooting page with options for changing some fundamental operations (see Figure 13.13). For example, let's say you have a piece of hardware that refuses to run properly under Windows 95. Sometimes, you can isolate the problem by disabling one or more of the options in Troubleshooting. In any case, the Performance entries are for solving problems. If you don't have problems, leave them alone.

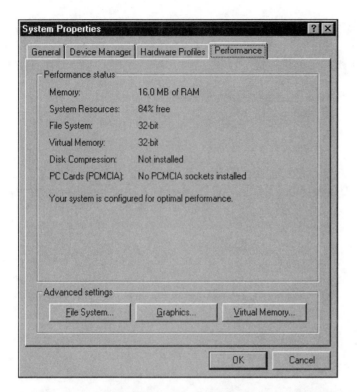

FIGURE 13.12:
The Performance tab tells you how your system is running.

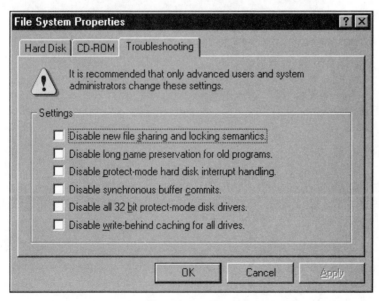

FIGURE 13.13:
Here are some troubleshooting options.

NOTE   There's much more on hardware troubleshooting in Chapter 11.

Next Step

In the next chapter we move on to some of the Windows 95 connections to the outside world. In particular, we'll address the mysterious Exchange icon and the Microsoft Network.

Chapter 14

MAKING YOUR OWN NETWORK

- **Selecting the network type**
- **Choosing hardware**
- **Building a network**
- **An even easier network**

One of the best things aboutWindows 95 is that it comes with networking already in the box. The first part of this chapter talks about the basic types of networks you might consider, how they work, and the choices available for hardware. If you want to make a network and you'd like to understand what you're doing, this is necessary information.

On the other hand, if you want to make a network and you don't care if you understand what you're doing or not, skip ahead to the section called "Networking for *Anyone*" at the end of the chapter. You'll find instructions on how to make a very simple but fully functional network (called a peer-to-peer network)—which is all that's ever needed for a home or small business setup.

NOTE

A few words of advice: If you've never used a network, you'll come across some terms you haven't seen before, but don't worry. All the terms are explained and defined to the extent that's necessary. The point of this chapter is not to turn you into a networking guru (*that's many books' worth*), but to make it possible for you to build a network to do what you need to do.

Picking Among Networks

There are essentially two types of networks—client/server and peer-to-peer. The latter is the type discussed in this chapter.

- **Client/Server:** This type of network, the most typical being one that uses Novell NetWare, has one or more computers that are servers. A server can't be used for anything other than taking care of the network's needs and it runs a special operating system. While there are very definite advantages to this kind of network, they really don't become compelling until your network gets to be a lot bigger than the two to five computers we're talking about here. The costs in hardware, software, and general complexity are additional reasons that client/server networks are uninviting for someone trying to connect just a few computers.
- **Peer-to-Peer:** This second network type is the topic of this chapter. In a peer-to-peer network, each computer has just as much importance as any other computer in the network. If you only need to connect a couple of computers together to share some files and a printer, this is the way to go. It's easy to set up, requires almost no network administration to maintain, and the cost is minimal. You don't need to buy any additional hardware except for the actual networking boards themselves and the cable. You don't need any special software, either, since the networking is built right into Windows 95.

Hardware Basics

To set up your network, all you really need is one network card per computer, enough pieces of network cable to connect them all, and the actual connectors, terminators, and so on for the cable.

Before you jump in and start buying network cards and cabling, you have to decide what kind of cabling to get, and how you are going to arrange your network. There are at least four different options for cabling, but as you'll learn in the following sections, only two of them make any sense in a small network situation.

Thin Ethernet

Up until the last couple of years, the most common way to connect personal computers in a network was to run a thin piece of coaxial cable from computer to computer. The cable looks a lot like cable-TV wire (although it isn't the same stuff), with a single, often solid, copper wire down the center with a braided shield, like that shown in Figure 14.1. This is easily the simplest (and cheapest) way to connect two or three computers in reasonably close proximity to one another.

> **NOTE**
>
> The cable for this connection method can be called: Thinnet, 10Base-2, Thin Ethernet, or co-ax (short for coaxial)—you may hear any of these variations. All Thin Ethernet is Ethernet but not all Ethernet is Thin Ethernet.

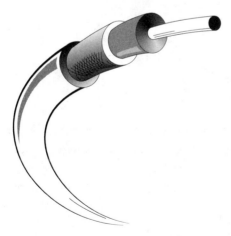

FIGURE 14.1:
Thin Ethernet uses a coaxial RG-58 cable with a single central conductor and a braided shield.

The total cost to connect two computers, including all cabling, cards, terminators, and connectors can easily be under $200; and if you are really scrimping, you could manage it for under $100, not that I'd recommend going for the absolute cheapest. (Remember, it's the cheap person who ends up paying the most!)

The Thin Ethernet Advantage

Thin Ethernet has some definite advantages besides its simplicity. Because the cabling is shielded, it's fairly resistant to electrical noise, and the maximum, practical total distance your network can span is higher than with its primary competitor: unshielded twisted pair. Of course, distance isn't likely to be a major concern with a small network of the type we're talking about here.

Hooking It Up

The most common method of hooking up a Thin Ethernet network is to hook each computer to the next one with a piece of cable between them as shown in Figure 14.2.

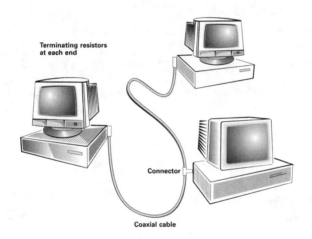

FIGURE 14.2:
The simplest way to connect computers on Thin Ethernet is to use a daisy chain.

Hooking one computer to the next is called daisy chaining. It has the advantage of being simple and easy to understand, and it does not require any extra hardware. Once you get everything set up (assuming good quality cable and connectors), you pretty much don't need to worry about it or think about it again. At least until you decide to start moving furniture around.

One Shortcoming

Daisy chaining has one major disadvantage. If you have one bad piece of cable or a single bad connector in the network, the entire network is down. Finding the bad connector or bad piece of cabling can be one of the most frustrating tasks you will ever face if you don't have specialized (read expensive) tools. But if you buy good quality cable, connectors, and terminators, this problem should not arise.

Or Twisted Pair

In recent years, wiring based on twisted pair (or more properly, unshielded twisted pair cable) has started to replace Thin Ethernet cable as the network cabling of choice. It's easy to install, requiring essentially the same skills as installing phone cable, and since it's smaller and flatter, it's easier to hide it and more wires will fit through a given space.

The cable, called variously 10Base-T, twisted pair, unshielded twisted pair, and UTP, looks a lot like standard phone cable and uses four pair of wires twisted together as shown in Figure 14.3. It has no shielding other than the inherent shielding effect of the twisted wires themselves, and while it looks a lot like standard phone cable, the two types are not interchangeable.

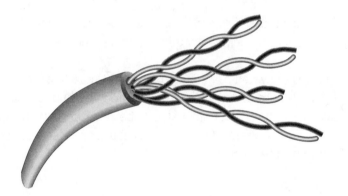

FIGURE 14.3:
Twisted pair, or 10Base-T, wiring resembles a standard phone cable.

The Star Connection

Unlike Thin Ethernet, twisted-pair cables are not connected in a daisy chain but are connected in a star configuration as shown in Figure 14.4. The cabling to each individual workstation radiates out from a central hub. This has the distinct advantage of keeping a single bad cable or connector from bringing the whole network down—making it much easier to find the source of the trouble.

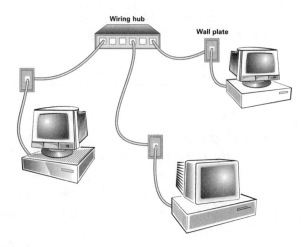

FIGURE 14.4:
A star configuration means that a single bad connector or piece of cable won't bring down the entire network.

Some Disadvantages

The disadvantage of twisted-pair, however, is that you need to buy at least one hub for the center of your star, and hubs aren't cheap—ranging from $300 to thousands of dollars for the best hubs. Of course this cost is spread across the number of computers attached to the hub, but if you're hooking up only two or three machines, the cost per machine is still steep.

The other disadvantages of twisted-pair are not particularly important for most small networks. The effective maximum cable length of a cable from the hub to an individual workstation is substantially less than the maximum length between workstations with Thin Ethernet, and the cabling itself is less resistant to physical abuse and electrical noise, but neither of these is likely to be a big deal.

The Network Card

You can't have a network without some way for your computers to connect to the cable. This takes a network card of some sort, or one of those network gizmos that attach to the parallel port of your laptop.

NOTE For the purposes of this chapter, I'll treat laptop versions no differently from a card that plugs into your PC. The network itself doesn't much care, after all, so why should we?

First Choose Your Cable

Before you buy a network card you must decide what kind of cable you want to use. Network cards come with one or more connectors on them and you need to make sure that your card supports the connection you'll need. If you aren't sure, you can always get a combo card that supports multiple types of cabling, but they cost a bit more than single interface types.

> **TIP**
>
> Combo cards let you easily change your mind about cabling without having to buy all new network cards. Because permanent cable installation is such a major undertaking, however, you're unlikely to be changing it very often. You're probably better off just buying the card you need for the cabling you're buying *now*.

And Then Pick a Card

Should you get a 16-bit card, or a 32-bit card? Should it be a standard ISA bus card, or a VLB or PCI card? The answers to these questions depend on how you intend to use your network, but here are some general rules:

16-Bit ISA Bus Card: This is more than adequate. On a small network you are unlikely to need anything more than this card can handle, and they're generally pretty cheap.

PCI Network Card: If your machine has a PCI bus with an available expansion slot, you might want to consider getting one of these. They're just becoming available and they're fast and relatively cheap. Plus Windows 95 will support them as full Plug-and-Play devices.

EISA Bus Card: If you have an EISA bus computer, there are excellent and very fast network cards available. If you expect to use your network a lot or have more than a couple of machines on it, you will probably want to consider this option. Like all EISA cards, however, an EISA network card is going to cost you substantially more than a simple ISA card from the same manufacturer.

VLB Card: Don't spend the extra money for a VLB card. The VL bus, while perfectly adequate for video, its original purpose, is just not up to the electrical demands of a network card.

> **TIP**
>
> It's absolutely necessary that you have the documentation for your computer to know what kinds of devices your machine will or will not work with. Otherwise, you'll have to call in one of those expensive consultants—and that would defeat the whole purpose of this chapter.

Connectors and Terminators

To the later regret of both users and administrators, two types of hardware that frequently get ignored (both in planning and implementation) are connectors and terminators. This is because the most common point of failure on a network isn't the cable or the network cards but the hardware that connects the cables to the cards and marks the start and end of the network.

> **NOTE**
>
> **Connectors are T-shaped with the middle leg connecting to the network card. Another leg is connected to the network cable coming *to* the computer. On a machine that's in the middle of the network chain, the third leg is for cable going on to the next computer. On the first and last machine in the chain, the third leg takes a terminator.**

For a typical small network, these little pieces will run as much as a quarter of the cable's cost, and they are the first place that people tend to get cheap. After all, a $2.95 generic T-connector at the local Computers 'R Us looks just as good as an $8.75 AMP brand one from the Black Box catalog.

Wrong! This is one place it doesn't pay to get frugal. Get the best ones you can. It will save you time, aggravation, and grief. In the long run, it will save you money.

IRQs, Addresses, Memory, and Such

Old-fashioned network cards required you to manually configure their IRQs, addresses, and other depressingly obscure stuff. Every time you acquired a new piece of hardware, you ran the risk of it interfering with your network card, and having to go through the whole process again. If you got it wrong, you were out of business—usually your computer wouldn't even boot, much less work properly, if it did manage to struggle into life. You had no choice but to open the box, pull the card out, take another guess about what jumper to change to what position, and try the whole process again.

Well, those days are gone, thank heavens. The modern network card, even a simple 16-bit ISA card, uses an EEPROM (Electrically Erasable Read Only Memory) or Flash ROM to control its settings, and they can be configured by a simple software program included with the card. (There are still some of the old cards around, so make sure you don't get one.)

If you do end up with a conflict, just use Windows 95's Hardware Conflict

Troubleshooter Wizard to figure out where the problem is and resolve it. For more on this amazing Wizard and further help in resolving hardware conflicts, see Chapter 11.

Adding Cards and Protocols

Before you can actually use Windows 95 as a network, you need to install the network card into your computer, and bind one or more network protocols to use the card.

> **NOTE**   A *protocol* is just a fancy word for the method that your software, Windows 95 in this case, uses to talk to your hardware—and through cabling, to other computers.

The Add New Hardware Wizard

When you physically install the card, Windows 95 will notice the change the next time it boots up and will run the Add New Hardware Wizard to configure it. This process should happen automatically, but you can always run it manually if for some reason it doesn't happen by itself. Just click on the Add New Hardware icon in the Control Panel.

The Add New Hardware Wizard shown in Figure 14.5 will walk you through the process of adding your new network card to your system. In addition, it will automatically install the minimal level of network support—adding the Microsoft client layer, so you can use files on someone else's Windows 95 computer and both the NetBEUI protocol and the IPX/SPX-compatible protocol. (For more instruction on using the Add New Hardware Wizard, see Chapter 13.)

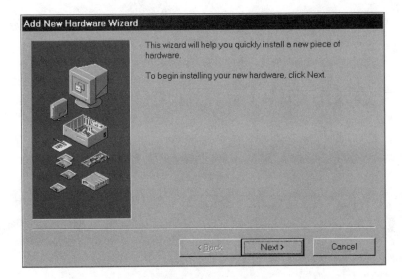

FIGURE 14.5:
The Add New Hardware Wizard will help you add and configure your new network card.

> **NOTE** You can use either protocol. NetBEUI was used by most Microsoft networking products until recently. IPX/SPX is the protocol used on Novell NetWare networks and is now being used in Microsoft's newer networking products as the default. On a Windows 95 network, you're marginally better off using IPX/SPX.

The Network Wizard

The Add New Hardware Wizard usually produces the Network Properties sheets for you (shown in Figure 14.6), but if it doesn't, you can run it yourself. Just open the Control Panel and double-click on the Network icon.

The Network icon opens up the Network dialog box where you can add all sorts of neat stuff. Some or all of it may have been added already when you installed the new network card into your computer. If it isn't there, or if you didn't get all you need or want, this is where you can add in the rest.

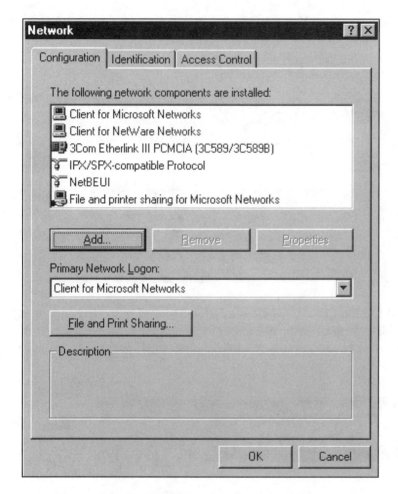

FIGURE 14.6:
The Network Properties sheet lets you add, remove, or configure your networking hardware and software.

The Network dialog box lets you add client protocols, hardware adapters, networking "stacks" or protocols, and networking services to your Windows 95 configuration.

NOTE In the following sections, we'll just cover how to add the most basic of protocols and the minimum services for your small network.

Select Network Client

You select a network client so you can use services on another machine (like their locally attached printer or their hard disk). The default configuration includes clients for both Microsoft Networks and Novell NetWare Networks. If you're using Windows 95 as a peer-to-peer network, you can pass on the Client for NetWare choice because you will only be using the built-in Microsoft networking.

> **NOTE** To remove the NetWare client, just highlight it, and then click on the Remove button. You can always add it later if you need to.

> **TIP** Unless you have an unlimited amount of memory and a Pentium-120 (or better) processor, save both memory and resources by installing only the network protocols you really need. While the memory hit is well hidden by Windows 95, there's still, sadly, no free lunch.

If you don't see the Client for Microsoft Networks listed in the Network dialog box under the heading: "The following network components are installed," click on the Add button, and then double-click on the Client icon in the Select Network Component Type box as shown in Figure 14.7.

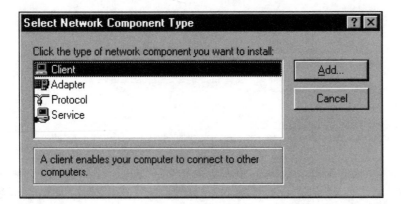

FIGURE 14.7:
The Select Network Component Type box lets you add clients, adapters, protocols, and services to your network configuration.

Clicking on the Client icon opens the Select Network Client box shown in Figure 14.8. Highlight Microsoft, select Client for Microsoft Networks, and then click on OK.

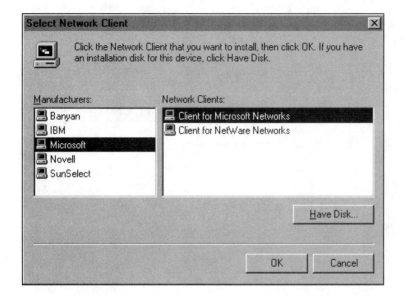

FIGURE 14.8:
Adding the Microsoft client for Microsoft's own network is easy.

Service Choices

The default installation doesn't install services, which is OK if you don't want anyone else to use the resources of your computer. If you're setting up your local network to have one main machine—the one with the fax modem, the big hard drive, the printer, and such—that everyone else would share, then you install the File and Printer Sharing (described in the next paragraph) on that machine alone. But if you're going to have computers sharing with each other, you'll need to add File and Printer Sharing to all the computers that will share their resources with others.

Select the Service choice from the Select Network Component Type box shown in Figure 14.7. Again, highlight Microsoft in the resulting Select Network Service dialog box shown in Figure 14.9, select File and Printer Sharing for Microsoft Networks, and click on OK. This will add the necessary network services to allow you to let others on the network use your documents and folders as well as any printers or fax modems attached to your computer.

NOTE   File and Printer Sharing is necessary only on machines that will share their resources with others.

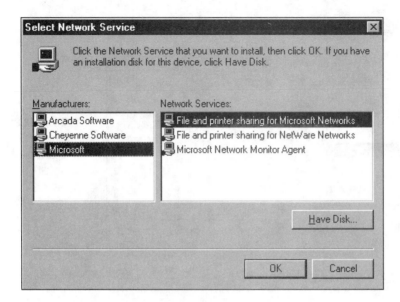

FIGURE 14.9:
Adding file and printer sharing allows others to use the resources on your computer.

These actions should be enough to get our network configured and ready to go. You will need to reboot each machine when you get done. The reboot will add the necessary hardware and software components, because these changes are more than Windows 95 can do on the fly.

TIP

If you have a notebook computer with PC Card support, once you have done the initial installation of the network components, you can insert or remove the network PC Card and Windows 95 will detect the change without rebooting.

Using Your Network

OK, you got all the hardware up and configured, the cables are in, the whole thing is connected, and now you actually want to do something with your network like sharing files or, in Windows 95-speak, documents.

Sharing and Mapping Drives

The simplest way to share files on your new network is to first share the drive or drives they reside on. Others on the network can map your drive to look like a local drive on their own computer.

To share a drive with others on your network, follow these steps:

1. Right-click on the drive letter in the Explorer or in My Computer, and you get the familiar menu.

2. When you select Sharing from the menu, you get the Properties page for the drive, with the Sharing tab in front, as shown in Figure 14.10.

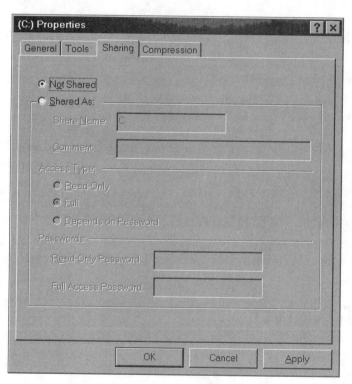

FIGURE 14.10:
You control whether the drives on your computer are available for others to share.

3. Just click on the Share As button and the rest of the options on the tab become available, as shown in Figure 14.11.

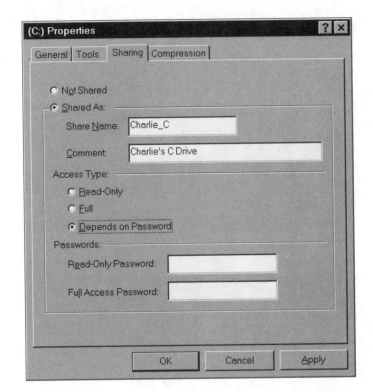

FIGURE 14.11:
You can let some users have full access to your drives while others have read-only access.

4. By specifying different passwords for the different access levels, you can let some users have full access to your drives, while others can read files on the drives but can't change anything.

5. Once you've got things set up the way you want them, someone can use one of your drives as if it were on his or her own computer by double-clicking on the icon that represents your computer in Network Neighborhood. This brings up a window (like the one in Figure 14.12) showing the drives or folders you are sharing with others.

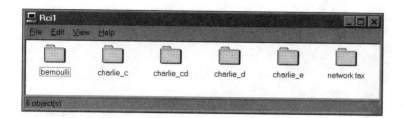

FIGURE 14.12:
The Network Neighborhood lets you see what drives are available on other computers.

6. The user completes the process by right-clicking on the drive to be used and selecting Map Network Drive from the menu to get the dialog box shown in Figure 14.13.

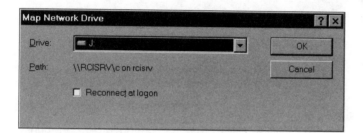

FIGURE 14.13:
Here's where you map drives on other computers to look just like another drive on your computer.

Sharing Printers

Sharing printers is another important reason for a network. You can give everyone access to a printer without having to shell out the money to put a laser printer next to everyone's desk. Windows 95 makes this easy and painless. The person who has the printer attached to a PC simply shares it the same way they would share a drive or folder.

From the remote user's standpoint, using someone else's printer is no different from using one attached to your computer. Here's how to set it up:

1. First you add it as a new printer. (Like most things in Windows 95, you can do this from several different places.) One easy way is off the Start button. Select Settings ➤ Printers to open the Printers folder, and then double-click on the Add Printer icon.

2. This opens the Add Printer Wizard. You'll end up with something like Figure 14.14 after you select Network Printer. Type in the location for the printer if you know it, or just use the Browse button to find the printer on the network.

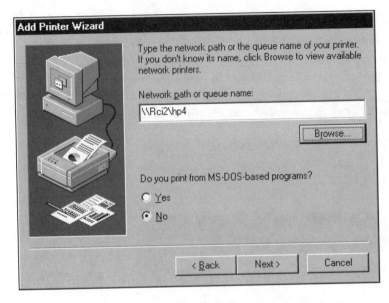

FIGURE 14.14:
Adding a network printer is as easy as adding a local printer.

3. If you think there's any chance you'll ever need to print something produced by a DOS program, make sure you click on the Yes button for "Do you print from MS-DOS programs?" Click on the Next button again and select a printer port to capture for your DOS programs, since most of them are going to need to think they are printing to a specific port.

4. Give the printer a name, and you're done.

Now you can use this printer exactly as if it were directly connected to your computer, as long as the computer with the printer attached is up and running.

Sharing a Network Fax

So you can share printers, files, folders, and such, but how else can you take advantage of your network? Windows 95 can't yet let you share some of those expensive peripherals you might want to share—like color scanners or high-speed network modems—but you can share the fax part of a fax modem across the network.

The fax modem is seen by the operating system and by applications as a printer, so sharing it is just like sharing a printer. When you go to fax something to someone, you simply print to the fax just as if the fax were a printer attached to your computer.

NOTE For more on setting up Microsoft Fax software, see Chapter 15.

You can add Microsoft Fax to your computer and compose a fax on your local workstation as follows:

Mail and Fax

1. First, run the Mail and Fax applet from the Control Panel.

2. This will bring up the MS Exchange Settings Properties dialog box shown in Figure 14.15. If you don't yet show a Microsoft Fax service, just click on Add to add one.

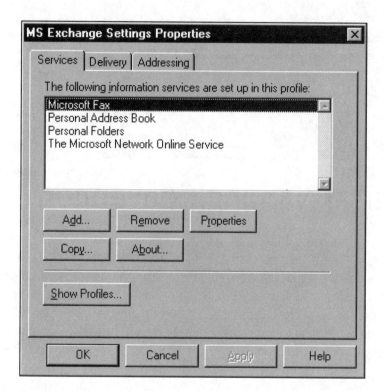

FIGURE 14.15:
Fax services are handled by the Microsoft Exchange, whether local or over the network.

3. Once you have added the fax, you merely have to select it as your printer, and print your document to it. This will cause Windows 95 to pop up the Compose New Fax dialog box shown in Figure 14.16.

4. This Wizard guides you through the steps to create and send a fax, including adding a cover sheet and picking an "address" (fax phone number) for the document. You won't even be aware that the fax modem is on another machine on the network.

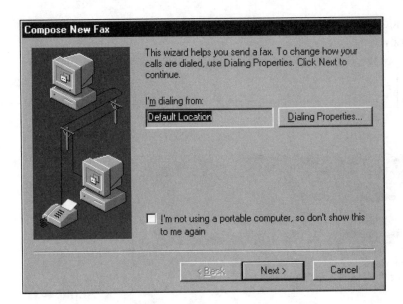

FIGURE 14.16:
Printing to a network fax starts up the Compose New Fax Wizard.

The Universal Naming Convention

Drive letter mapping provides complete compatibility with applications written before Windows 95, but it goes against the concept of documents and folders as being the central things we work with—not drives and files. After all, I don't really care where the document representing the outline for this book is stored. What I care about is getting at it when necessary, even if it's stored on someone else's machine. Double-clicking on it starts the application that created the outline, and then opens the outline so I can update it.

This method doesn't require any drive mappings at all, thanks to something called the Universal Naming Convention (UNC). Under this convention, the outline is known as: \\Rcisrv\ABCS\OUTLINE.DOC. The UNC will be used more and more in the future. It will enable any machine added to the network to find \\Rcisrv\ABCS\OUTLINE.DOC on the network without having to know anything else about it.

All About Passwords

An important network topic not yet discussed is passwords. Everyone hates passwords. They're a pain. We know that. And if you don't want a password on your PC, that's your call.

But you really need a password if:

- There are ever more than two people on the network
- You ever intend to make a direct connection to the outside world, or
- You ever have business-critical data stored on any of the machines on your network

If your needs are minimal, you can make the password easy to remember; but the best password is one that can't be easily guessed. If you will be directly connecting your computer to the Internet, we strongly urge you to adopt strict password guidelines, and stick to them.

> **NOTE** For more on passwords in general, see Chapter 13.

Here are some *bad* ideas for passwords:

- Your name, nickname, or logon name
- Your spouse's, child's, or parent's name
- Your pet's name
- Your license plate or Social Security number
- Common swear words or combinations of them
- Any of the above, spelled in reverse

Ideal passwords are a mixture of upper- and lowercase letters and numbers or other non-alphabetic characters that don't spell anything, yet are easy to read, pronounce, type, and are at least six characters in length. Something like "SoAfa4!".

> **TIP** If you don't use a password and you're endlessly annoyed by the network password logon each time you boot your machine, you can get rid of it. Open the Network applet in the Control Panel. On the Configuration page, look for Primary Network Logon. Open the drop-down list and select Windows Logon. Now you can boot your machine without having to enter a password.

Direct Cable Connections

You may not need a network if all you need is to occasionally connect two computers. For example, if you use a laptop at home or on the road, you need to transfer files back and forth. For the cost of a simple cable, maybe $10-20, you can easily connect two computers for this purpose.

Choosing a Cable

The cable you want is like a parallel printer cable—except that a printer cable has one end made to attach to the computer and the other end to attach to the printer. The cable you need has the computer end on *both* ends. The cable can be described variously as a File Transfer Cable, a LapLink Cable, a DOS6 Interlink Cable, or, to be absolutely correct, a Parallel DB25 Male/Male cable.

A serial cable can also be used, if necessary (though they're not as fast as parallel cables). Look for one of the special four-headed cables that have both 25-pin and 9-pin connections at each end. That way you'll be sure to have the right connector no matter what your serial ports look like. These serial cables will have similar names to the parallel port version, but will have "serial" in the name and will have female connectors at each end.

The Direct Cable Connection Wizard

Once you have the cable, all it takes to connect your two computers is to open up the Direct Cable Connection Wizard shown in Figure 14.17. This is located on the Accessories menu of the Start menu.

> **NOTE**
>
> No Direct Cable Connection on the menu? You'll have to install it from Add/Remove Programs ➤ Windows Setup ➤ Communications, then come back.

Once started, the Wizard prompts you through the steps to connect the two computers. One side will be the host—sharing its resources with the guest computer:

1. Start the Wizard on both computers, and select one as the host and the other as the guest.

2. Click on Next and choose the port to connect the two computers as shown in Figure 14.18. Choose the same type of connection on both the host and guest computer.

| NOTE | If some critical parts aren't installed, you'll get a message when you click on Next that tells you to first install the Dial-Up Adapter and then rerun the Direct Cable Connection Wizard. Follow the instructions on the screen and come back to this point. |

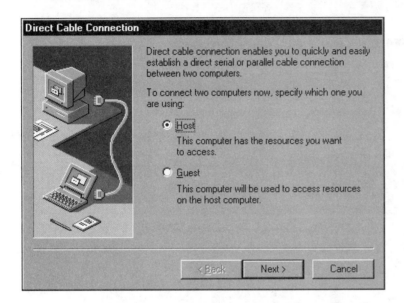

FIGURE 14.17:
The Direct Cable Connection Wizard lets you easily connect two computers over a simple cable.

3. Plug in the cables if you haven't already, and click on Next again.
4. On the host computer, as shown in Figure 14.19, you choose if you want to require a password for this access. (Kind of seems like overkill to me.)
5. Click on Next again on both computers and Windows 95 will try to connect the two computers together. And, assuming you have the right cable, it shouldn't have any problem at all.
6. On the host side, you'll see a confirmation that the two computers are connected. On the guest side, you'll see a typical Network Neighborhood window like that in Figure 14.20 showing all the shared and accessible folders on the host computer.

WARNING If the guest computer, which should generally be the laptop, is connected on a network at the same time you're connecting over a direct cable connection, you may lose the network connection. Close down any network applications you are running on the guest machine before firing up the direct cable connection.

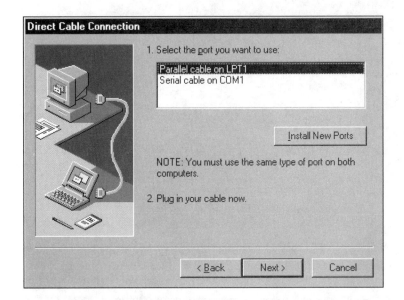

FIGURE 14.18:
You can use either a serial or parallel connection between the two computers.

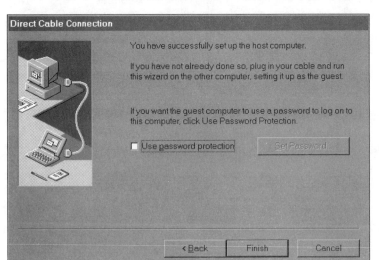

FIGURE 14.19:
You even have the option to require a password to connect the two computers.

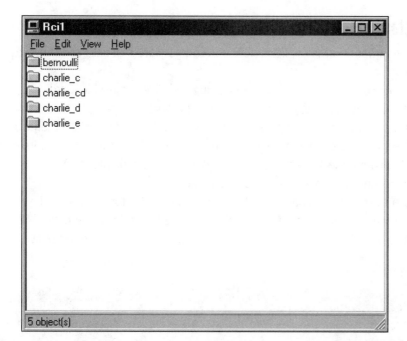

FIGURE 14.20:
The guest computer can use the drives the host has shared just as if they were a network connection.

Networking for *Anyone*

Even a year or two back, building the simplest network called for an expert to be imported, because only a few (very expensive) people knew the magic incantations to construct a network—and more importantly, to *keep* it running. This expert cost the earth and you were totally at his or her mercy. When the network failed, you had no choice but to call in this human money-drain.

Complex networks still call for complex solutions, but most people don't need a complex setup. Most people just need to share files and programs and maybe a printer. If this is what you want to do, here's how you can, in a few easy steps, set up a fully functional network.

Buy the Hardware

A minimum amount of hardware is needed. Go to a store that sells computer equipment and buy:

1. Two network cards. Make sure they're Plug-and-Play compatible. Cards are circuit boards that fit into slots inside your computer.
2. Cable to connect the computers. You'll need RG58 Thin Ethernet (Ethernet) cable with BNC connectors at either end. (This cable looks a lot like the wire used to run cable TV into your house, but it's not interchangeable.)
3. Two 50-ohm terminators. One for each machine.

You can get the cards, terminators, and cable for under $100 total. However, if you can afford to pay more, you'll get better quality. But even really good cards and cable should add up to less than $300. Shop around for the best prices on the more expensive cards and cable.

> **NOTE**   Make sure you get enough cable to connect the two computers without the cable itself becoming a tripping hazard. You don't need to worry about length limitations—Thin Ethernet can be run up to several hundred yards!

Install the Hardware

To install the pieces, you'll need a small Phillips screwdriver and possibly a slotted screwdriver as well. Also have a cup or other container for the screws you'll otherwise remove and immediately lose.

1. With the computers turned off, install a network card in an available slot in each computer.
2. T-shaped connectors (called, not surprisingly, T-connectors) come with the cards. You attach one point to the cable, the second point to the network card, and the third gets a terminator. Check the instructions that come with the card to see which goes where.

Configure the Network

Now you need to follow several (uncomplicated) steps on each computer:

1. Restart the computer and let Windows 95 detect the new card. (If it's not detected, try Add New Hardware and specify the card you have.)

2. Double-click on the Network icon in the Control Panel.

Network

3. Highlight your network card in the list of network components and then click on the Properties button. Select the Bindings tab.

4. Select either NetBEUI or IPX/SPX. The one you "bind" with will act as your networking protocol. Choose the same protocol on each machine. (You can even choose both, but there will be a cost in memory and you don't *need* both.) Click on OK.

> **NOTE** TCP/IP may be one of the choices, but you don't want to include it for this kind of network because it's much more complex to set up.

5. On the Configuration page, click on the File and Print Sharing button and enable sharing.

6. Click on the Identification tab. Each computer should have a different name but the same workgroup name. Click on OK.

7. Shut down and restart both computers.

Share the Resources

To make drives or individual folders on one computer available to the other computer, open Explorer and right-click on the drive or folders and select Sharing from the pop-up menu. Configure the sharing properties.

To share a printer, open the Printers folder (in My Computer or the Control Panel) and do the same.

You can also have one or more of the drives on the other computer show up in your computer's Explorer, so you can access files and folders easily. To *map* another computer's drive to your computer, follow these steps:

1. Double-click on the Network Neighborhood icon, then on the Workgroup name and finally on the name of the other computer. All the drives that have been shared by the other computer will appear in the window.

2. Right-click on the first drive you want to appear on your computer and select Map Network Drive. A window like the one shown in Figure 14.21 will open. In this case, the drive called C: on the other computer will be mapped as E: because the computer doing the mapping already has a drive C: and drive D:.

3. Click on Reconnect at Logon only if you'll be accessing this drive a lot. If you leave it unchecked, your computer will connect only when you request access to drive E: by selecting it in Explorer (or My Computer).

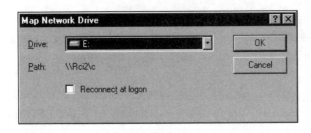

FIGURE 14. 21:
Mapping a drive on another computer so you can see it in your Explorer window

4. Click on OK when you're finished.

You can map any or all of the drives on the other computer. Resources you've shared with the other computer will have an icon with a hand like this.

The same resource from your computer will appear on the *other* computer with this type of icon.

This kind of network will work quite well. If you need a more complicated setup, one with many computers or one that requires a server, you'll need the advice of an expert or you can study and become an expert yourself.

Next Step

Now that you have an idea how to connect the computers you have to one another, we'll move on to connecting to the outside world. This includes sending and receiving faxes, Internet mail, and the use of the Microsoft Network.

Chapter 15

CONNECTING TO THE OUTSIDE WORLD

- **Setting up Exchange**
- **Getting Internet access**
- **Faxing: the ins and outs**
- **Connecting to the Microsoft Network**

During the first decade in the history of the PC most people who had computers—whether at work or at home—used them as independent, stand-alone machines. But in the last few years, there's been a lot of noise about what's called *connectivity*. This can mean everything from e-mail and Internet connections to networks of varying degrees of complexity.

Windows 95 incorporates several different types of connectivity functions, including built-in fax capability (providing you have a fax modem), the Microsoft Network (providing you subscribe), and Internet access. All these are covered in this chapter.

Exchange Basics

The Exchange is a new concept in Windows 95—the idea being to centralize all mail, messaging, and fax activities in one location. You start Exchange by double-clicking on the Inbox icon on your Desktop.

The Exchange is going to be a very powerful tool, but right now it's a bit ahead of its time. For example, it requires a pretty fast processor (486-66 at least) and a lot of memory to load quickly enough. If you click on the Inbox and a minute later you're still twiddling your thumbs and staring at the screen in disbelief, you're better off sticking with your old fax and communications software for the time being.

If you *are* able to use Exchange, you'll probably come to see its many advantages as well as its few disadvantages. Exchange does have one remarkable feature that isn't used much now but will be very common in a year or less. It's a new standard called TAPI.

It's TAPI Standard Time

TAPI is yet another in the continuing series of cryptic computer acronyms. It stands for Telephony Applications Programming Interface. What that means (short version) is that new communications programs will be able to adopt the settings you've already made on your system: modem type, port, and that sort of stuff. Up until now, you've had to tell each communications program what kind of modem you have, where it is on your computer, and sometimes even the dread initialization string. And if you buy a new modem, you have to do all that stuff all over again for every program.

TAPI puts a stop to that nonsense. All programs written to the TAPI standard will be able to detect the settings of your modem. If you change modems, you just go to the Modem icon in the control panel, delete the old modem, and install your new one. Another aspect of TAPI is that you can set up various locations you're calling from and when you select one, any TAPI application can use that information to properly dial the number—whether it's a local call, a long distance call, or charged to a particular credit card.

TAPI-compliant software can also share a single phone line. You can have fax software on auto-receive all the time. Want to check your e-mail? The fax software will politely step aside and, after the call is finished, reinstate itself on auto-receive.

The communications capabilities built into Windows 95—such as the fax software, HyperTerminal, and Phone Dialer—are all TAPI-compliant. The bad news is that your other software is probably not, though most programs released *after* Windows 95 will be adopting the TAPI standard.

Internet Access with Windows 95

If you already have an account with an ISP (Internet Service Provider), you can continue to use the e-mail software and Web browser that you had before. Just install them as you'd install any other software. (See the section "Add/Remove Programs" in Chapter 13.)

Or you can use the Windows 95 Internet tools. These tools do not come with the basic Windows 95 package. This is because Windows 95 will "sort of" work on older machines (computers with less than a 486 processor or less than 8MB of RAM), but a World Wide Web browser and Exchange are too dead-slow on those kinds of computers.

To get the Web browser and Internet mail software, you can:

- Buy the Plus! for Windows 95 package that includes the Internet Jumpstart kit. Plus! includes a lot of extra sounds and screen savers, advanced compression tools, and other utility programs. It retails for $50 or less.
- Download the Internet tools from the Microsoft Network (MSN). You'll have to enroll in MSN first—covered later in this chapter.

To download the software, connect to the Microsoft Network and follow these steps:

1. Click on the Start button and select Find ➢ On the Microsoft Network.
2. A window will open like the one shown in Figure 15.1. Type in **Internet Explorer Web Browser** in the Containing field.
3. Next to the field labeled Of Type, select Folders and Forums. Then click on the Find Now button.
4. Double-click on the Internet Explorer Web Browser folder that's found and double-click again on the file icon of the same name. The file will be downloaded and, once you assent, will install itself.

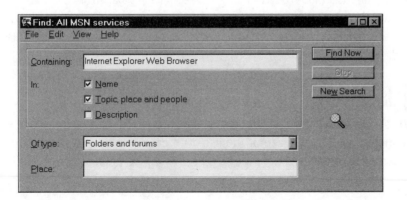

FIGURE 15.1:
Finding the Internet tools on the Microsoft Network

TIP — If you're fairly knowledgeable about Internet matters, you can also find the Internet Explorer at Microsoft's Internet site. Use **ftp.microsoft.com** to get to the site and download it.

Setting Up Exchange

Setting up Exchange is started by double-clicking on the Inbox on your Desktop. The Inbox Setup Wizard runs when you first opt to install the mail and/or fax services. This happens usually at installation of Windows 95 but it can always be done later by using Add/Remove Programs in the Control Panel.

Before You Go Farther

There are a couple of terms used in the Exchange that are not familiar and not really explained. So here are the definitions:

Services In Windows 95, a service is any of the various ways you connect to the outside world using the Exchange. This includes:

- Mail to another Microsoft Network member
- Sending and receiving faxes
- Internet mail going by way of the Microsoft Network
- Internet mail going by way of your Internet provider
- Microsoft Mail messages going to others on your network

Profiles Profiles are made up of combinations of services. You'll probably have only one profile on your computer. This profile will consist of the various services you've installed and the configurations for each. The default profile is called MS Exchange Settings. You may need multiple profiles if more than one person uses the computer or you have more than one e-mail account at a particular provider. (Information on how to do this is in the section called "Creating Additional Profiles" later in this chapter.)

Running the Wizard

Even though getting everything set up requires a lot of steps, each step is quite easy, so don't be intimidated by the size of the list. With each item, I've also included an explanatory sentence or two. Here are the steps that you'll be presented with (you may not see every step, depending on what services you select) after double-clicking on the Inbox for the first time:

1. **You'll see a list of what the Wizard calls *services*.** These include fax, Microsoft Mail, and the Microsoft Network (Figure 15.2). You check the boxes in front of the services you want to use.

NOTE   If you have the Plus! for Windows 95 package, Internet mail will also be an option on the list. If you don't have Plus!, you can download the Internet Explorer from the Microsoft Network and that will also give you Internet mail.

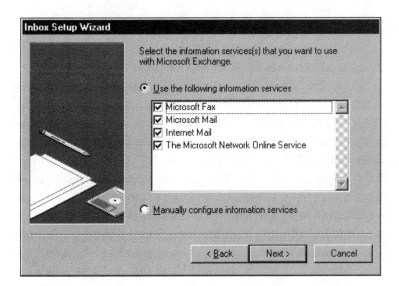

FIGURE 15.2:
The Inbox Setup Wizard asks you to choose the services you want to use.

2. **Select a fax modem.** Your modem should be highlighted in the window. Click on Properties to set the Answer mode, speaker volume, and other settings (see Figure 15.3).

TIP   Remember, you can always take advantage of the Windows 95 help system. For dialog box items: Right-click on the item you need help with, then click on the What's This? box that appears.

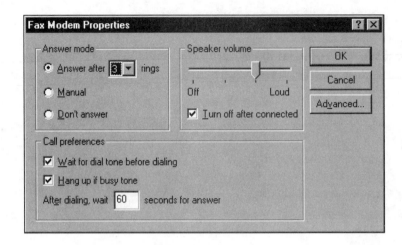

FIGURE 15.3: The Fax Modem Properties dialog box lets you decide how you want the fax system to answer.

3. **Do you want Microsoft Fax to answer every incoming call?** You get this window even if you've answered in the previous step. Usually, the answer is No, unless the modem on your computer is connected to a dedicated line. With a No setting here, a fax icon will still appear on your Taskbar. You can right-click on it when a fax call comes in, and then select Answer Now.

4. **Enter your name and fax number.** This is needed for your fax headers as well as for determining local versus long distance calls.

5. **Microsoft Mail postoffice location.** If you are on a network that has Microsoft Mail, you'll need to supply the path to the postoffice. Ask your network administrator where the postoffice is. (If you're the administrator, just click on the Browse button and put the postoffice wherever you darn well want to.)

6. **Select your MS Mail name from the list.** For an ongoing MS Mail system, there'll be a list of names. Select yours.

7. **Supply password.** On this screen is your name, mailbox, and a place for your password. Type it in.

8. **Select Internet mail connection.** If you connect to an Internet provider using a modem and a phone line, select Modem. That means you have what's called a dial-up connection. If your connection is made through an adapter on your network, select Local Area Network.

9. **Phone Connection for Internet mail.** For a dial-up connection, the next window asks for the name of the computer you're dialing. This isn't anything official, just a name you give to identify the service. (You may have other dial-up services now or later—perhaps connecting from home to your work site—that will also require a name.)

10. **Phone number for Internet access.** Here you provide the phone number for a dial-up connection. The next window informs you of your success at creating a connection. This newly made connection will be placed in your Dial-Up Networking folder where you can later double-click on it to start the connection.

11. **Mail server name or IP address.** No matter how your Internet mail connection is made, you'll need to provide the name or IP address of the computer that receives your Internet mail (see Figure 15.4). Your Internet Service Provider supplies this information.

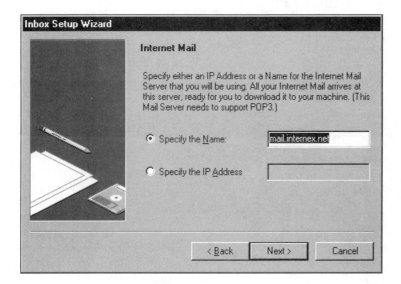

FIGURE 15.4:
Here's where you provide the Internet address for your mail server.

12. **Selective or automatic mail transfer.** How much Internet mail do you get? Use Selective if you want to filter out some of the stuff you get using Remote Preview, Automatic if you want the system to automatically establish the connection and transfer all your mail whenever you open the Exchange.

13. **E-mail address and full name.** Enter your Internet e-mail address in the format *name@domain* and your full name (as you want it to appear on your e-mail).

14. **Mailbox name and password.** Your mailbox name is provided by your Internet Service Provider. It's how the mail server identifies your mail location and it's not the same as your e-mail address.

15. **The path to your personal address book.** The system will create a location for your address book. This is where you'll enter the e-mail addresses and fax numbers you use.

16. **The path to your personal folder file.** This is the storage spot for incoming and outgoing messages and faxes. More than one personal file (as well as address book) can be created if you have need for them.

17. **Want the Exchange in the Startup group?** There are good reasons both to have and to not have the Exchange in the startup group, but they don't make sense until you know more about how the Exchange works. If you do plan to receive faxes on this computer, you should have the Exchange in Startup.

Looking at What You've Done

Now you get a list of the services that are ready to use (see Figure 15.5). Most of the settings you make during this installation are done without any real knowledge of how the choices will work out in actual practice. Fortunately, all of them can be changed—in fact, the whole next part of this chapter is about how to make those fine-tuning adjustments.

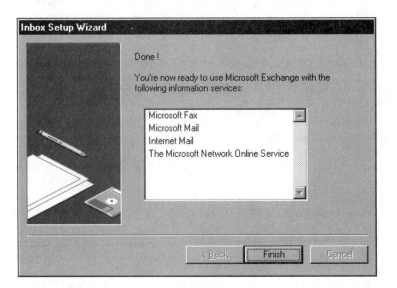

FIGURE 15.5:
Now you're ready to use any and all of the Exchange services.

Working with Messages

By default, the message (and fax) addresses are kept in a file called MAILBOX.PAB in the Exchange directory. This file is referred to in and around the Exchange as your Personal Address Book.

Adding Addresses

To add someone's address to the Personal Address book, follow these steps:

1. Click on the Inbox icon on your Desktop.
2. Select Address Book from the Tools menu.
3. Select New Entry from the File menu. This will open the New Entry box shown in Figure 15.6. The entry types listed will depend on the types of services you have installed.

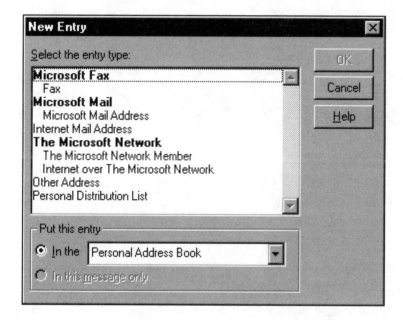

FIGURE 15.6:
Select the entry type from this list.

4. Select one of the services based on whether the address is an Internet address or a fax number or whatever, and then click on OK.
5. Provide the information requested, and click on OK when you're done.

Now, whenever you select New Message from the Compose menu, you can click on the To button. This takes you to your Personal Address Book where you can select a recipient or add a new one.

The bad news is that if your old pal Bill has a fax number, plus an Internet mail address, *and* an MSN address, you'll have to make a separate entry for each one. And when you click on the To button on a new message, you'll see your friend's name three times with no indication of which address is which.

Admittedly, this is the dumbest idea anywhere in Windows 95, but you can bypass it somewhat. Plan ahead and when you add a new name to the address book, include a notation to help you later (as shown in Figure 15.7).

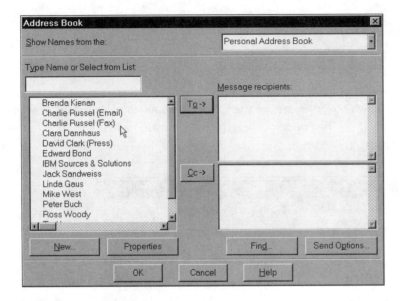

FIGURE 15.7:
Adding a notation
to names that have
multiple listings
can be of help
later.

Sending Messages

To send a message, click on the Inbox on your Desktop to open the Exchange. Select New Message from the Compose menu. Address and type your message (see Figure 15.8), and then select Send from the File menu.

> **TIP**
>
> If you have Remote Mail enabled, you'll have to select Deliver Now Using from the Microsoft Exchange Tools menu to send mail.

Receiving Messages

When you open the Exchange, the way new mail will appear in your Inbox depends on the mail's source. The following sections describe the ways.

> **TIP**
>
> The Exchange is a little easier to understand if you select View ➢ Folders. It makes it easier to see what you've sent, what's been received, and so forth.

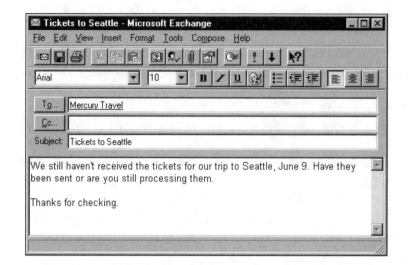

FIGURE 15.8:
When typing a message in the Exchange, the subject line becomes the name of the message.

Microsoft Network Mail

Connect to the Microsoft Network, and if you have mail, you'll see a message advising you of that fact and asking if you want to open your Inbox so you can see it now. Click on Yes, the Exchange will open, and the message will be delivered to your Inbox. Say No, and the message will be held at the MSN. To see it later, click on E-mail at the MSN Central window.

Internet Mail

How Internet mail is delivered to your Inbox depends on whether your Internet connection is a so-called dial-up connection (you use a modem and a phone line) or a LAN connection (the modem is somewhere on your network and the connection is made there). Either way, you can go get your mail when you want it or you can have it done automatically.

With an automatic connection, your Internet mail server is queried as soon as you open the Exchange and then as often thereafter as you specify. For a dial-up connection, that means Exchange will open the phone line, dial your Internet service provider, and connect to your mailbox. To set up an automatic connection, follow these steps:

1. Open the Exchange and select Services from the Tools menu.
2. Highlight Internet Mail and click on Properties.
3. Click on the Connection tab, make sure you have Automatic showing in the lower drop-down box, and then click on Transfer Options.
4. Select how often you want the network to check for mail messages. Select OK three times.

Setting Up Remote Mail Preview

With remote mail preview, the Exchange will call your mail server and show you the headers for any messages waiting there. You can then select the ones you want to read and transfer them to the Exchange Inbox.

To set up remote preview:

1. Open the Exchange, select Services from the Tools menu, highlight Internet Mail, and click on Properties.
2. Click on the Connection tab. Make sure you have Selective showing in the drop-down windows.
3. Click on OK twice. Close and then restart the Exchange.
4. When you want to check for mail, select Remote Mail from the Tools menu.
5. From the Tools menu for Remote Mail, choose to Connect, Connect and Update Headers, or Connect and Transfer Mail.
6. If you connect to select particular mail, highlight the messages you want to transfer to your Inbox and select Transfer Mail from the Tools menu.

Reading Messages

To read a message in your Inbox, just double-click on it. For a mail message, a window like the one in Figure 15.9 will open. If you want to know what any of the buttons mean, just position your pointer over one and a descriptive box will pop open.

> **TIP**
>
> If you're used to getting Internet mail using other software, you'll notice that the Microsoft Network window shows only the name of the person sending you the mail with no clue as to the origins. Most of the time this doesn't matter, but if you need to see the entire Internet header, select Properties from the File menu, and then look at the Internet tab.

Working with Faxes

There are at least two ways to send a fax: double-click on the Inbox icon on your Desktop and select New Fax from the Compose menu; or prepare the fax in your word processor or

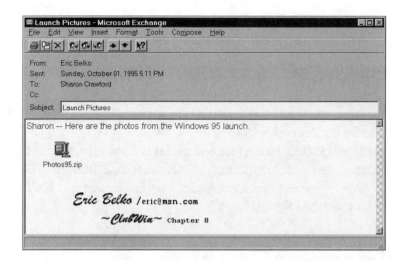

FIGURE 15.9:
Here's a message
received over the
Microsoft Network.

other application, and then select Microsoft Fax as your printer. You can receive a fax either
by having the MS Fax system set to Auto-Receive or by receiving manually.

Sending Faxes

The first time you send a fax, a Compose New Fax Wizard opens and guides you
through the process. The first window lets you change the location you're dialing from—if
you're not using a portable machine, put a check in the box to tell the system you don't
need to see this window again.

Follow these steps:

1. In the Compose New Fax window, type in the name of the addressee and fax
    number or click on Address Book to get a listing from there.
2. If you typed in the name and fax number, click on Add to List. (Add additional
    names if you want this fax sent to multiple recipients.)
3. Click on Next.
4. Indicate whether you want a cover page sent with this fax and if so, what kind.
5. Click on Options to change when the fax should be sent, the message format,
    and other properties for this message.
6. Type in a subject header, and then the contents of the fax message. If you're
    faxing from a word processor, leave this page blank.
7. Next you'll be given the opportunity to include a file with this fax. The file you
    choose will be opened in the application that created it and then "printed" to
    the fax. Use the Add File button to locate the file.

8. When you're done, the fax will be sent immediately unless you've made a change under Options to schedule a different time for sending.

A Fax That Fails

Occasionally, you'll have a fax that fails to go where it's supposed to. Maybe you had to cancel in mid-stream, or maybe the connection was broken or the fax at the other end dumped you before the transfer was complete.

The transfer will appear to have taken place and the fax will end up in the Sent folder of Exchange. Within a few seconds, though, a new message from the "System Administrator" will appear in your Inbox. Double-click on the message and you'll see a report on why the fax failed (see Figure 15.10).

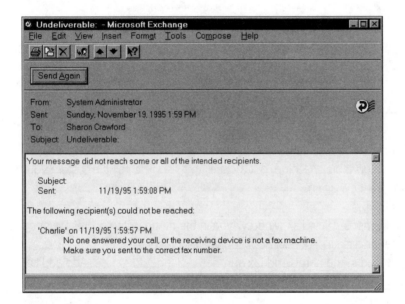

FIGURE 15.10:
A report on a failed fax transmission

 Click on the Send Again button and then the Send icon at the left of the toolbar in the next dialog box.

Receiving Faxes

To reset the fax answer mode after installation, open the Exchange by double-clicking on the Inbox. If the fax service is installed, a miniature fax machine will appear at the end of the Taskbar. Right-click on this icon and select Modem Properties. Figure 15.3 shows the same Fax Modem Properties window. Here you can select one of the three options:

- Answer After (select the number of rings)
- Manual
- Don't Answer

If you select Manual, you'll hear the phone ring when a fax is coming in and it will be up to you to right-click on the Fax Modem icon on the Taskbar and select Answer Now from the pop-up menu.

> **NOTE**
>
> While you have automatic answer or manual enabled, you won't be able to use other communications programs to dial out unless the programs are TAPI-aware. Most "legacy" software (in other words, the stuff you already own) is not TAPI-aware, so you'll have to change the setting to Don't Answer when you want to call CompuServe or a local BBS.

Reading Faxes

When you receive a fax, you can double-click on it to open the Fax Viewer (Figure 15.11). From this window, you can zoom in or print the fax. If you want to forward the fax to someone else, highlight the fax in the Inbox and select Forward from the Compose menu.

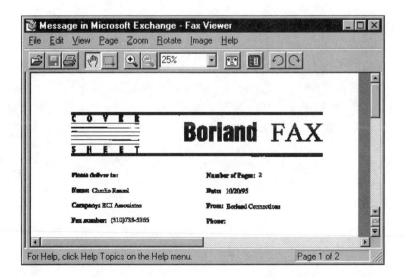

FIGURE 15.11: Here's the first page of an incoming fax. You can use the Page menu to move from page to page.

Forwarding a Message or Fax

When you receive a message or a fax, the Inbox window will have a button for forwarding the message on to another recipient. But what if it's a fax you want to send by e-mail or e-mail that you'd like to fax to someone? Click on the item's icon on the Inbox window and drag the item to a Message window (see Figure 15.12) or to your Desktop (so you can put it in a message later). You can then send the message using Microsoft Fax, containing the icon in any way you choose. If you're faxing a document made in another application such as Word or WordPerfect, the embedding of e-mail messages won't work. Yet. (Someday it will—in Windows 2000 or WordPerfect 10—but not today.)

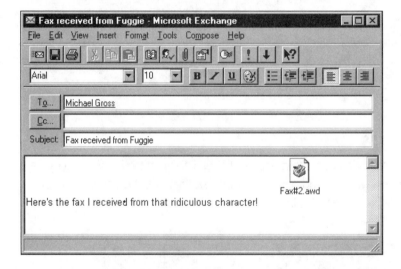

FIGURE 15.12:
You can forward a fax via electronic mail.

TIP

Those unfortunates who are not yet using Windows 95 won't be able to open and read a fax file in the .AWD format sent in an e-mail message. For those backward souls, you'll need to forward the fax as a fax (highlight the name in the Inbox and click on the Forward button). The fax system will deliver the fax to the recipient as a printed document.

More on Profiles

As discussed earlier in this chapter, a *service* is any of the various ways your computer connects to the outside world using the Exchange. This includes: local network mail, faxes, Internet mail, and Microsoft Network mail. A *profile* is made up of a combination of services you have installed and their configurations.

The following sections show you how to set up more than one profile on your computer, how to use multiple profiles, and how to customize them.

Creating Additional Profiles

The default profile for the Exchange is MS Exchange Settings; but if you have multiple e-mail accounts at the same Internet provider or multiple people using the same computer, you'll need to set up one or more additional profiles. Here's how to do one:

1. Double-click on the Mail and Fax icon in the Control Panel, and then click on Show Profiles.
2. Click on the Add button to open the window shown in Figure 15.13.
3. Select the services you want to use in this profile.

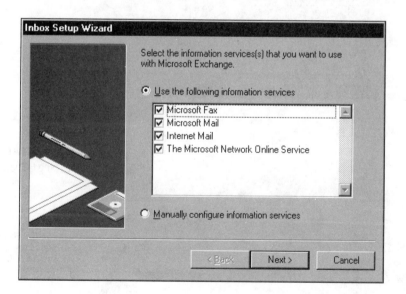

FIGURE 15.13:
Select whatever services you want to include in the new profile.

4. Enter a name for the profile. I suggest something descriptive (that is, something more memorable than MS Exchange Settings 1).

5. From here on, the Inbox Setup Wizard steps you through the same process you went through for the first Exchange setup. For a refresher course, consult the first part of this chapter.

Selecting the One to Use

By default, the MS Exchange Settings profile will be the one loaded when you start the Exchange. To use another profile on a regular basis, you'll have to open Mail and Fax in the Control Panel, click on Show Profiles, and select the one to start up with (see Figure 15.14).

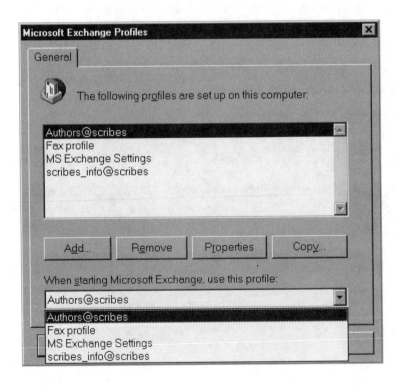

FIGURE 15.14:
You can choose the profile you want to start the Exchange with.

If you switch back and forth often enough for that to be a nuisance, you can set things up so you get a prompt each time you open the Exchange. Just follow these steps:

1. Double-click on the Inbox icon on your Desktop.
2. Select Options from the Tool menu.
3. On the General page, select Prompt for a profile to be used.
4. Click on OK when you're done.

The next time you start the Exchange you'll see a window like the one shown in Figure 15.15. Just click on the arrow next to the name and choose the profile you want to use.

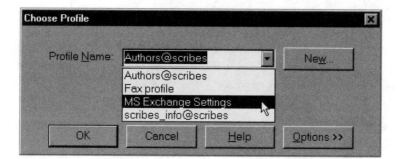

FIGURE 15.15:
Choose the profile that's best for the job at hand.

Customizing Your Profiles

Unless you make some changes, all your profiles will use the same address book and the same set of folders for incoming and outgoing messages. This can be a bit of a problem if you don't want all your incoming (and outgoing) messages to be mixed together.

To make separate sets of folders for your profiles, follow these steps:

1. Double-click on the Mail and Fax icon in the Control Panel. Click on the Show Profiles button.
2. Select the Profile you want to give the new folders to and click on Properties.
3. Highlight Personal Folders and click on the Remove button. After it's deleted, click on the Add button.
4. In the Add Service to Profile window (Figure 15.16), highlight Personal Folders and click on OK.
5. Personal folder files all have the extension .PST. You can make a new one for this profile with any name you want as long as the extension is .PST. Enter a name that you can identify as belonging to the profile, like Antoinette's Mail.PST (don't you love those long file names!).
6. In the Create Microsoft Personal Folders dialog box, you need to address several settings besides just giving a name to the Folders.

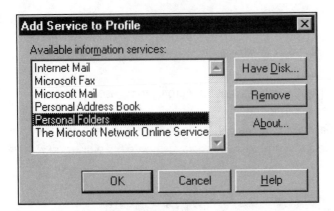

FIGURE 15.16:
You can add and remove services using this window.

Encryption Setting Even when password protected, .PST files can be opened and read in other applications (like word processors). If security is an issue, select Compressible Encryption, and if security is very important, select Best Encryption—the file can't be compressed but there's greater protection with this option.

Password Whether or not the file is encrypted, you can add a password to keep out the casual snoop. If you check the box for saving the password to your password list, you won't be prompted for the password every time you connect to this set of personal folders.

Now this profile will have a completely separate set of Inbox, Outbox, Sent, and Deleted folders. To make a new address book for the profile, follow these same steps (except in step 5 the address book file has the .PAB extension).

Adding or Deleting Services

Although your Exchange services are initially configured when you run the Microsoft Exchange Setup Wizard, settings for services can be changed in several ways—the easiest being to double-click on the Mail and Fax icon in the Control Panel. From there, here's what to do:

- To remove a service just highlight it and click on the Remove button.
- To add a service click on Add, select from the available information services, and then click on OK.

To configure a service, highlight it and click on Properties. The information you will need to supply varies depending on the service. (If it's Internet mail, for instance, you'll need to supply the name of your Internet mail service, account name, and so forth.)

The Microsoft Network

The Microsoft Network (MSN) is another step toward getting every last person on the planet hooked up to the online world. If you've already looked at the Internet, you know what a pain it is to type in those horrible http:\\ addresses or navigate through layers and layers of directories at a gopher site. MSN aims to make all that a lot easier.

MSN comes with the full complement of news, sports, weather, software libraries, bulletin boards, and chat areas you'd expect in any online service, but with a twist—access to the network is built into the operating system itself.

Introducing the MSN

The Microsoft Network

If you opted to install the Microsoft Network when you installed Windows 95, the MSN icon will already be on your Desktop.

Double-click on the icon to start setting up your membership.

After an introductory screen, you'll be asked to supply your area code and the first three digits of your telephone number. MSN will use this information to call a local number and download the current information on signing up.

Getting on Board

After you make the phone connection and the information is downloaded, you'll see a screen like the one in Figure 15.17.

The procedure is a familiar one—especially if you already belong to another online service. Even if you don't, you won't be surprised at the sequence:

1. First you provide your name, address, and home phone.

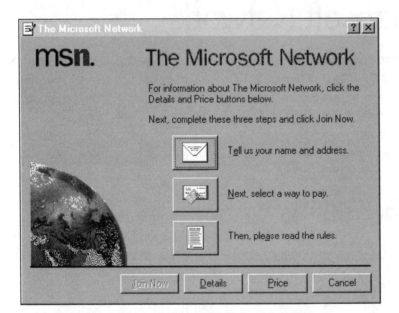

FIGURE 15.17:
This screen aids you in completing the sign up.

> **NOTE**
>
> The MSN also asks if you want to receive "communications and special offers" from Microsoft and others. If you agree, you'll undoubtedly receive a whole lot of messages that are the electronic equivalent of junk mail. And if you don't agree, you might miss out on some interesting (and even valuable) information. It's your call.

2. Next is how you'll pay. Select a payment method and then fill in the details.
3. You should read the rules. These are always good to know in any place you spend some time (not to mention money).

4. And speaking of money, don't forget to click on the Price button (shown in Figure 15.17) to see what you just agreed to have charged to your credit card!

5. When all this is done, click on Join Now and the software will dial and transmit your account information.

6. Finally, you'll be asked to provide a member ID and a password (see the next section). And that's it—you're a member.

> **TIP**
>
> If you have trouble connecting, try the MSN Signup and Access Troubleshooter. To get at it, right-click on the Microsoft Network icon on your Desktop, select Connection Settings from the pop-up menu, and then click on the Help button.

Member IDs and Passwords

The Microsoft Network is somewhere between CompuServe and America Online when it comes to how you're identified online. With CompuServe you use your full name in most places—though there are provisions for using nicknames in the CB area and in some forums. AOL members sometimes use their full names (if they're short enough), but they're greatly outnumbered by people using whimsical handles like STUDMUFIN or HUNYBUNY.

On the Microsoft Network, you can go either way. It all depends on how you want to present yourself. But if you think you might be doing business there, you should probably forego signing yourself as KUTESTUF.

Passwords are another matter—you can be as silly as you want as long as the password is one you'll remember (but would be hard for someone else to guess). Passwords must be from eight to 16 characters long, and using combinations of letters and numbers is best.

The opening screen for the Microsoft Network has an option to have the software remember your password. This is handy if you're in a situation where security isn't a big concern.

What's There Now

It's difficult to get too specific about what's on the Microsoft Network, because there's a lot of stuff and because MSN is constantly changing and adding more. Currently however, the services are divided into five main categories (see Figure 15.18).

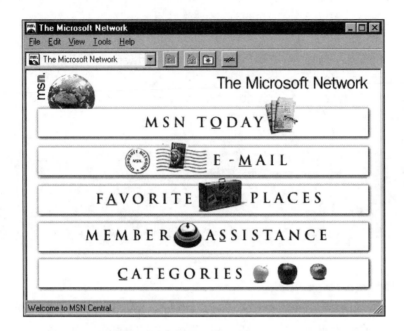

FIGURE 15.18: The main divisions for the Microsoft Network are displayed at MSN Central.

MSN Today The screen that greets you when you first sign on. News of interest to all members and announcements of special events are shown here. Look for hypertext links to further information.

E-Mail Click here to see any incoming electronic mail. (Exchange will be opened automatically.)

Favorite Places As you navigate the network, you'll undoubtedly find spots that you'd like to visit again. To make this easy, you can put a link in Favorite Places to any place you've found. Next time you want to go back, you'll just open this folder and click on the icon for the spot you want to visit.

Member Assistance Problems with connections, questions about billing, account changes, and stuff like that are all addressed here.

Categories This is a visual table of contents for the entire Microsoft Network and it's a good place to start your exploring.

Right-click on the MSN icon at the end of the Taskbar to get this menu.

This is the quickest way to sign out as well as to jump to other functions including MSN Central, the page shown in Figure 15.18.

Navigating the Network

Navigating around the Microsoft Network is easy, especially if you think of it as an extension of Windows 95 and not as some "other" place. That is, you click on folders to open them, a right-click almost always produces a menu, and drag and drop is alive and well.

Things You'll See

As you move around the Microsoft Network, you'll encounter objects both familiar and unfamiliar. Here are some definitions for things you may see:

Folders When you click on Categories, for example, you're opening a top-level folder. Click on a topic, and you enter the subfolder. It's just like navigating through a series of folders in the Explorer.

Kiosks Click here to get the subject matter of a forum, identify who's managing the forum, and view the latest updates on forum activities.

> **NOTE**
>
> **Forums are special interest areas covering particular subjects. A forum usually includes a bulletin board where you can read and post messages, perhaps a chat room, and some files or other information relevant to the subject matter.**

Chat rooms Places for real-time discussions. The appeal of these areas is the immediacy—you're actually talking live to others who are online in the same moment. The disadvantage is that discussions can be slow and hard to follow when there are multiple participants (see Figure 15.19).

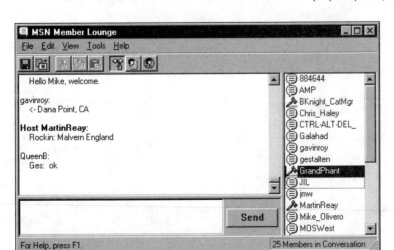

FIGURE 15.19:
A "chat" is going on in the MSN Member Lounge.

Newsgroups These are special interest discussion groups on the Internet. These groups are used by everything from the Human Genome Project to comic book collectors all over the world. Thousands of these groups exist. All of them can be read through MSN but some are read-only, which means you can't post your own message.

BBS Special interest areas on MSN where you can post and read messages.

Not every folder will have a clear labeling as to what's inside, so you'll have to do a bit of poking around.

And Favorite Places

Because there are so many categories with multiple layers of folders inside, you'll want to keep track of the places you want to visit again. One way to do this is to right-click on a folder and select Add to Favorite Places.

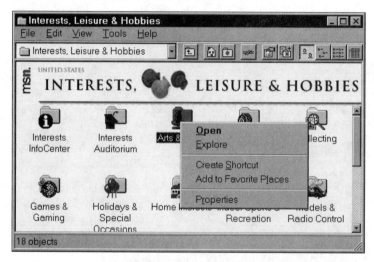

The next time you sign on to the Microsoft Network you can click on the Favorite Places folder and a shortcut to the place you selected will be inside.

TIP

For those *really* special places, right-click on the file or folder in the MSN, drag it to your Desktop, and select Create Shortcut Here. The shortcut contains all the information needed to reconnect later and take you right back to that spot. You can also copy shortcuts into messages you send via the Exchange to point your friends to your favorite MSN resources.

Next Step

From communications in this chapter, we'll move on to the other little programs that come with Windows 95. This includes a word processor, a paint program, and several others that you'll undoubtedly find handy from time to time.

Chapter 16

A BUSHEL OF APPLETS

- **Communications: HyperTerminal and Phone Dialer**
- **Text Editors: WordPad and Notepad**
- **Clipboard Viewer**
- **Character Map**
- **Calculator**
- **Briefcase**
- **Paint**

From the first, graphical operating systems have come with a complement of small-ish programs like calculators and paint programs. Because of their usually limited capabilities, these programs are called applets rather than applications. In many cases, these programs are just as big as they need to be, so they actually *are* full applications. But the name applet has stuck and generally applies to programs that come with an operating system.

In this chapter we'll discuss all the applets that aren't covered elsewhere. The basic use of many of these programs is very simple, so I'll touch on some of the not-so-obvious functions (if there are any).

Communicating with HyperTerminal

HyperTerminal provides the same functions as the Windows 3.1 applet called Terminal. It provides access through your modem to other computers, bulletin boards, and online services. The difference HyperTerminal offers is that it automates most of the process.

Where to Find It

Here's how to find HyperTerminal:

1. Click on the Start button on the Taskbar.
2. From the menu that appears, select Programs and then Accessories.
3. On the Accessories menu, select HyperTerminal. You'll see the HyperTerminal program group.
4. Double-click on the HyperTerminal icon (marked Hypertrm). You will see something like the screen shown in Figure 16.1.

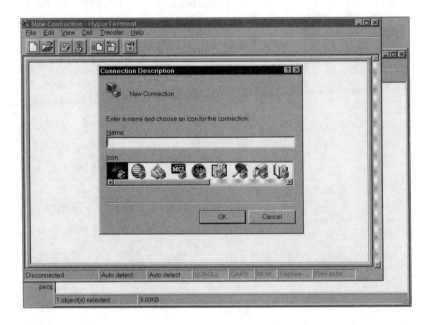

FIGURE 16.1:
The HyperTerminal window and the Connection Description dialog box are where you get started.

How to Use It

When you use HyperTerminal, each connection you make can be named and provided with an icon. That allows you to quickly identify connections so you can make them again.

Let's create a fictional connection that will allow us to fill out the dialog box. Imagine you're a journalist working for a newspaper called the *Past Times* and you need to log on to the paper's BBS to file stories and columns.

1. Type **Past Times** in the Name text box.
2. Scroll through the icons until you locate an icon that resembles a briefcase and umbrella—what better icon for a reporter?
3. Click on the OK button. You will see the Phone Number dialog box shown in Figure 16.2.

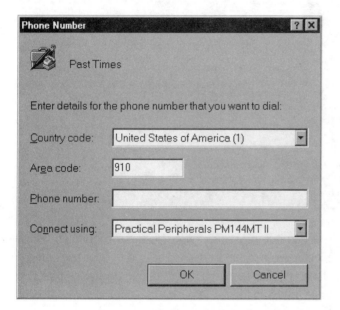

FIGURE 16.2:
The Phone Number dialog box asks you where you want to connect.

4. If the number you want to dial is located in a country other than the one listed in the Country Code list, click on the downward-pointing arrow at the right end of the list box and select the correct country.
5. Enter the area code and phone number of the BBS in the appropriate text boxes. (For our example, enter **555-2122** as the number and click on the OK button.)
6. The Connect dialog box opens, but since this is the first time we've run this application, the Dialing Properties dialog box (Figure 16.3) appears immediately to make sure that the connection is made properly. Look over the options in this dialog box and make sure that they're correctly set.
7. If you click on the check box next to Dial Using Calling Card, a dialog box will open for you to enter your telephone credit card number.

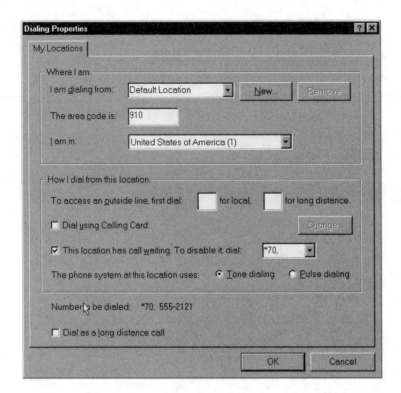

FIGURE 16.3:
The Dialing Properties dialog box lets you check your options.

8. If you have to dial a number to get out of your business or hotel phone system (typically 9 or 7), enter this number in the text box next to the text that reads "To access an outside line, first dial" and enter the number (or numbers) you dial for long distance access in the text box next to it.

9. If this is a long-distance call, click on the check box next to "Dial as a long-distance call."

10. When you are through filling out this dialog box, click on OK. You will see the dialog box shown in Figure 16.4.

11. At this point, all you need to do is click on Dial to make the connection. If all the settings you made in the previous dialog boxes are correct, the call will go through and you can use the BBS software to upload your story to the newspaper. We'll cover file transfers in a moment.

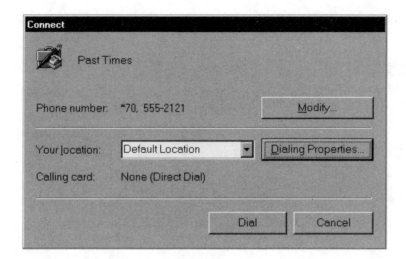

FIGURE 16.4:
The Connect dialog box is where you finally make your connection.

12.   When you're through placing your call, pull down the Call menu and select Disconnect or click on the icon that looks like a handset being hung up, and the connection will be broken.

13.   When you close the window, you will be prompted to save the session.

Sending Files

Once you have connected with a remote computer, you will probably want to upload or download files. This is the principal reason for making this sort of connection. The file-transfer protocols supported by HyperTerminal are:

- Xmodem
- Ymodem
- Ymodem-G
- Zmodem
- Kermit

Binary Files

To send a binary file, follow these steps:

1.   After the connection is made, pull down the Transfer menu.

2.   Select Send File. A dialog box will open.

3.   Using the options in this dialog box (see Figure 16.5), specify the file to send. (Click on the Browse button to locate and identify the file to be sent.)

4.   Select the protocol for file transfer. Zmodem is the best choice because it combines speed and good error correction.

5. Click on the Send button. The file will be transferred.

FIGURE 16.5:
Here's where you select a binary file and the protocol to send it.

Text Files

Text files are a little different from binary files. Most file transfer software distinguishes between binary files and text files—sending one in Binary mode and the other in ASCII mode or Text mode. HyperTerminal is no different.

To send a text file, follow the steps for a binary file except choose Send Text from the Transfer menu. When you specify the file to send and click on the Open button, the file will be sent as if you had typed it into the terminal program.

> **TIP**
>
> Unless you're transferring files to a UNIX system, you're usually better off sending every file as a binary file. Even a little bit of formatting in the file can cause a text file transfer to fail, while *any* file can be sent as a binary transfer.

And Receiving Them Too

To receive a file being sent from another computer, follow these steps:

1. Pull down the Transfer menu and select Receive File. That will open a dialog box that looks like the Send dialog box shown in Figure 16.5.

2. Click on the Browse button to specify a file name and location for the received file.

3. Select a file transfer protocol.

4. Click on the Receive button to start receiving the file from the remote location.

> **NOTE**   Take the above steps when you hear the incoming call from the other computer. You have to do this yourself, because HyperTerminal is not smart enough to answer the phone.

Saving a Session

To help you remember how to navigate the complexities of a service you don't use very often, terminal programs provide *logging*—a way to save everything you do in a particular session to disk and/or print it on paper.

To save everything to disk:

1. Pull down the Transfer menu and select Capture Text.
2. By default, all the screen information in a session will be saved in a file called CAPTURE.TXT in the HyperTerminal folder inside the Accessories folder. Of course, you can use the Browse button to save the file in a different location. Click on Start when you're ready.
3. Pull down the Transfer menu again. Now you will note that there is a tiny triangle next to the Capture Text option. Select it, and you will see a submenu with Stop, Pause, and Resume options to give you control over the capture.
4. If you prefer to send the session to the printer rather than to a file on your disk, pull down the Transfer menu and select Capture to Printer.

Using a Connection

As you recall, when we started using HyperTerminal, we created a connection with a name and an icon. This connection appears in the HyperTerminal program group. Any time you want to use this connection in the future, simply double-click on its icon, and all the settings (telephone number and so forth) will be in place for you.

Any time you want to change the settings in a particular connection, open the connection, pull down the File menu, and select Properties.

Getting Your Phone Dialed

Do you frequently have to make a lot of telephone calls? Has your dialing finger ever felt as if it were going to fall off? If you have Windows 95 (and if you don't, what the heck are you doing reading this?), you can turn over the grief of dialing to its capable, if virtual, hands. Phone Dialer is a handy little program that doesn't do a lot, but if you need it, it's terrific to have.

NOTE

Essentially, Windows uses your installed modem to dial your telephone. In order for this scheme to work, you need to have a telephone on the same line you're using for your modem. If you have a separate phone line for data, you'll need an actual telephone on that line to use Phone Dialer.

Here's how to access Phone Dialer:

1. Click on the Start button at the left end of the Taskbar.
2. Select Programs from the resulting menu.
3. Select Accessories from the Program menu and click on Phone Dialer. You'll see the window shown in Figure 16.6.

FIGURE 16.6:
The Phone Dialer window can help you put an end to the heartbreak of "Digititis."

The Phone Dialer gives you two simple ways to make phone calls using your computer.

Speed Dialing If you have a number you need in an emergency or one you call constantly, you can enter it in the Speed dial list.

The Telephone Log If you have a long list of numbers you call periodically, you can simply type those numbers into the Number to Dial text box and they will be added to a telephone log. You can access your log by clicking on the downward-pointing arrow at the right end of the Number to Dial box.

Speed Dialing

To create a speed dial number, pull down the Edit menu and select Speed Dial. You will see the dialog box shown in Figure 16.7.

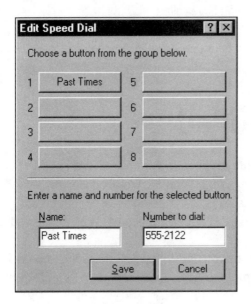

FIGURE 16.7:
The Edit Speed Dial dialog box puts you on the telephone fast track.

Here's how to set it up:

1. Click on the speed dial button you want to assign.
2. In the Name text box, type the name of the person or place that you will dial with that button.
3. Type the number to dial in the Number to Dial text box.
4. Click on Save. (You'll be returned to the Phone Dialer dialog box and the name you entered in the Edit Speed Dial dialog box will appear on the speed dial button you selected.)
5. To speed dial the number, just click on the button and lift your telephone handset.

The Telephone Log

As mentioned at the top of this section, there are two ways to use the Phone Dialer. The quick and easy way is to use the speed dialer, but as you'll have noted, the speed dialer is limited to eight numbers. If you have more than eight numbers that you call on a regular basis, you'll have to use your log. Here's how:

1. Either type the number in the Number to Dial box or use the telephone keypad to punch in the number.

2. When the number's completely entered, click on the Dial button and pick up your telephone. In a moment, you will be connected with the voice mail system at the number you are calling. (No one ever talks to real people anymore.)

3. To call the number again, pull down the Tools menu and select Show Log. This displays a list of all the numbers you have called.

4. To redial one of these numbers, double-click on its entry in the log.

You can see how the Phone Dialer can be a terrific convenience if you spend a lot of time making calls.

Working with WordPad

WordPad is the successor to the Write program in Windows 3.1, and how you felt about Write may determine how you feel about WordPad. WordPad is an odd duck. It's more elaborate than Notepad but still falls way short of being a real word processing program. WordPad will read Write and Word for Windows 6 documents as well as text and Rich Text formats.

To open WordPad, click on the Start button and follow the cascading menus from Programs to Accessories. At the bottom of the Accessories menu you'll find WordPad.

> **TIP**
> WordPad can be uninstalled using the Add/Remove Programs function in the Control Panel. However, if you use Microsoft Fax you'll need WordPad because it's the fax operation's text editor. If you use a different fax program such as WinFax or you don't fax from your computer at all, you can remove WordPad without worry.

Opening It Up

When you open WordPad (see Figure 16.8), it looks like most other editors and on the menus you'll find the usual things one associates with text editors. Pull down the menus to see the various options.

WordPad is different because it's completely integrated into Windows 95. You can write messages in color and post them to the Microsoft Network so recipients see your messages just as you wrote them—fonts, colors, embedded objects, and all. WordPad also has the distinct advantage of being able to load really big files.

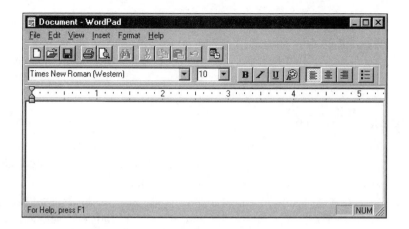

FIGURE 16.8:
This is the opening screen for WordPad.

Making and Formatting Documents

You can always click on a document and drag it into WordPad. Documents made by Microsoft Word (.DOC) and Windows Write (.WRI), as well as text (.TXT) and Rich Text format (.RTF) documents, are all instantly recognized by WordPad. You can also just start typing.

Formatting Tools

The toolbar (Figure 16.9) and format bar (Figure 16.10) are displayed by default. You can turn either of them off by deselecting it from the list under the View menu.

FIGURE 16.9:
Here are the various functions on the WordPad toolbar.

FIGURE 16.10:
The WordPad format bar lets you manipulate text in all the basic ways.

Tabs are set using the ruler. Click on the ruler at the spot where you want a tab. To remove a tab, just click on it and drag it off the ruler.

Other Options

Other formatting tools are under Options on the View menu. This is where you can set measurement units as well as word-wrap and toolbars for each of the different file types that WordPad recognizes.

Page Setup and Printing

The File menu has the usual Print command, but there's also a Page Setup item that you can use to set margins as well as paper size and orientation. Unlike its predecessor, WordPad can print envelopes as well as varying sizes of paper.

It may take some fooling around to get envelopes lined up correctly, but fortunately there's a Print Preview choice (also on the File menu). There you can see how the envelope or paper is lining up with your text. Adjust the margin in the Page Setup dialog box until you get it the way you want.

> **TIP**
>
> To change printers, select Page Setup from the File menu. Click on the Printer button and you can select any printer currently available to you.

Using Notepad

Notepad is a simple text editor with very few charms except speed. Double-click on any text file and it will immediately load into Notepad (unless, of course, it's bigger than 64K, in which case you'll be asked if you want to load it into WordPad instead).

What It's Got

Notepad has the bare minimum of facilities on its menus. You can:

- Search for characters or words
- Use Page Setup to set margins, paper orientation, customize the header and footer, and select a printer
- Copy, cut, and paste text
- Insert the time and date into a document

What Clipboard Viewer Does

The Clipboard Viewer is not much different than the one shipped with Windows 3.1. When you copy or cut something, Windows needs to have a place to store it until you decide what to do with it. This storage place is called the Clipboard.

Sometimes you want to see what's on the Clipboard and maybe save its contents. Clipboard Viewer makes it possible for you to do this.

Taking a Look

To see the Viewer, click on the Start button, then select Programs ➢ Accessories ➢ Clipboard Viewer. You'll see a window like the one shown in Figure 16.11.

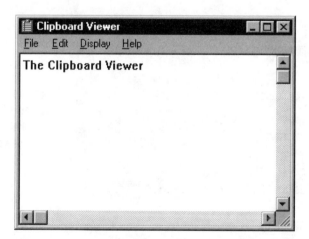

FIGURE 16.11:
The view of the Clipboard Viewer

Saving the Clipboard's Contents

To save the current contents of the Clipboard, pull down the File menu and select Save. You can save files under a proprietary format identified by the .CLP extension. These files are (as far as I've been able to tell) only used by the Windows Clipboard Viewer.

Once you've saved the contents, you can use the Clipboard to copy and paste other material, and later, you can reload what you saved by pulling down the File menu and selecting Open. Pull down the Display menu and you'll be able to see all your options for viewing the data on the Clipboard.

Making the Most of Character Map

The fonts that show up in your word processor are very nice but they often don't go beyond the characters found on your keyboard. What about when you need a copyright sign (©) or an e with an umlaut (ë)? With the Character Map you have access to all kinds of symbols including Greek letters and other special signs.

To start up the Character Map, click on the Start button in the Taskbar at the bottom of your Windows 95 screen. Select Programs ➤ Accessories ➤ Character Map to see the window in Figure 16.12.

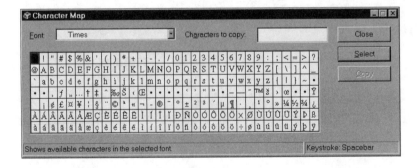

FIGURE 16.12: The Character Map shows all.

Entering Characters

Select the font you want to use by clicking on the downward-pointing arrow at the right end of the Font list box. To enter a character, double-click on it in the window. It will appear in the text box at the top right of the window. Continue double-clicking until you have the entire string of characters you want in the text box. When you have all the characters you want in the text box, click on the Copy button halfway down the right side of the window.

Then return to your application using the Taskbar or by pressing Alt+Tab until your application is selected.

Position the cursor on the spot where you want to place the character and select Paste from the Edit menu or just press Ctrl+V.

Using the Calculators

You actually have two calculators in Windows 95: a standard calculator, the likes of which you could buy for $4.95 at any drugstore counter, and a scientific calculator.

Just the Basics

To start the standard calculator, click on the Start button in the Taskbar, then select Programs ➤ Accessories ➤ Calculator to display the calculator shown in Figure 16.13.

Using the mouse, click on the numbers and functions just as if you were pressing the keys on a hand-held calculator. Or if you have a numerical keypad on your keyboard, press NumLock and you can use the keypad keys to enter numbers and basic math functions.

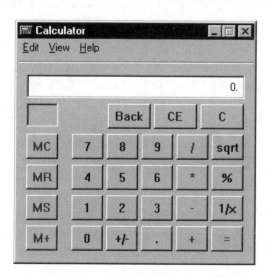

FIGURE 16.13:
The standard calculator is pretty basic.

Or One Step Beyond

To access the scientific calculator, pull down the View menu on the Calculator and select Scientific. That displays the item in Figure 16.14.

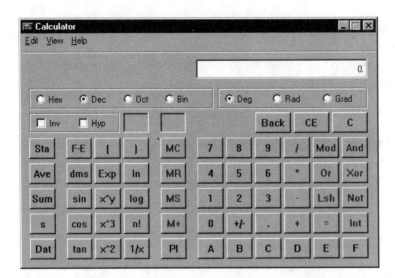

FIGURE 16.14: The scientific calculator is a whole different beast.

TIP If you're unsure of the use for a function, right-click on its button. You'll see a rectangle containing the words "What's This?". Click on the text to see a short explanation of the function.

Getting Statistical

As a sample of what the scientific calculator can do, let's enter a list of data for deriving statistical results:

1. Enter the first value in the series.
2. Click on the Sta button.
3. Click on the Dat button.
4. Enter the second value in the series.
5. Click on Dat.
6. Repeat steps 4 and 5 until you have entered the last value in the series.
7. Click on Sta.
8. Click on the function key that corresponds to the statistical command you want to enter.

Pasting in the Numbers

Both calculators can be used in conjunction with the Clipboard. Type a number in any application, and select it by dragging through it. Press Ctrl+C (for Copy). Press Alt+Tab until the calculator is selected (or click on it in the Taskbar) and press Ctrl+V (for Paste). The number will appear in the number display of the calculator as if you had entered it from the calculator keypad.

Work your magic: adding, subtracting, multiplying, or deriving the inverse sine. You can pull down the Edit menu and select Copy, which places the contents of the display on the Clipboard—ready for you to paste into your document.

Packing a Briefcase

The Briefcase is not an applet in the usual sense. You won't find it listed under Accessories, for one thing. But you can always right-click on the Desktop and select New ➤ Briefcase to create a new instance. Or a Briefcase may be on your Desktop from the original installation of Windows 95.

Briefcase is designed to help those with multiple computers keep a set of files synchronized. It may be your computer at work and your computer at home. Or maybe you have a desktop computer and a laptop where the same files are worked on. When two computers are involved it's only a matter of time before things get confused as to which version of a memo or a speech is the *most current* version.

How It Works

When you open a Briefcase and copy a file into it, a link is made between the original and the copy in the Briefcase. This is called a *sync link*. After the link is made, you can work on the copy in the Briefcase or the original file and select Update (from inside Briefcase), and the latest version will be copied over the earlier version, keeping both in sync.

To move to the other computer, you copy the Briefcase to a floppy disk. At computer #2, open the Briefcase on the floppy. Copy the files from the Briefcase on the floppy (*not* the Briefcase itself) to the Desktop or another folder on computer #2. Work on the files and update the Briefcase when you're done. When you go back to computer #1, you can use the Briefcase on the floppy to update the files on computer #1.

Basic Steps

Here's how to make use of Briefcase:

1. Open the Briefcase on the Desktop of computer #1. (Rename it if you wish.)
2. Copy the files to the Briefcase. Then copy the Briefcase to a floppy disk.
3. Take the floppy to computer #2. Open drive A: either in the Explorer or My Computer.

4. Open the Briefcase. Work on the files inside the Briefcase on computer #2.
5. When you're finished, save and close the files in the usual way.
6. Return the floppy to computer #1. Open the Briefcase on the floppy disk and select Update All from the Briefcase menu. That will open a window like the one in Figure 16.15.
7. Click on the Update button.

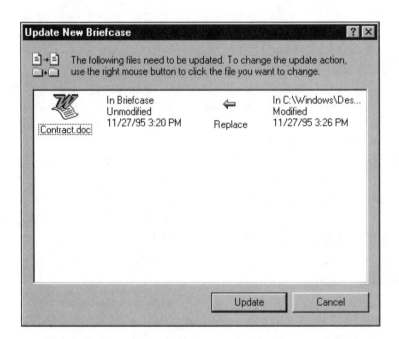

FIGURE 16.15:
Briefcase finds differences between the file on the hard disk and the file in the Briefcase.

What's Wrong About Briefcase

Briefcase has lots of weaknesses, as if it's just a test for a better version further down the road. Could be. Anyway, at this time, Briefcase has weaknesses along these lines:

- A Briefcase cannot be bigger than the size of the floppy disk you're copying to and since you have to use copies and not shortcuts, the floppy fills up real fast.
- The floppy can be synchronized with the files on only one computer, not both. That's why you have to work *inside* the Briefcase on the floppy drive of computer #2.
- Synchronization is not automatic. You must choose Update from the Briefcase menu.
- Briefcase is *not* easy to use. After a lot of practice, I still have problems getting it to work the first time.

Painting a Picture

As a drawing and painting program, Paint has its limitations, but it's nevertheless much improved over the Paintbrush included with Windows 3.1. To find Paint, look under the Accessories menu. It's not installed by default, so if you don't see it, use the Add/Remove Programs function in the Control Panel. (It's under Accessories on the Windows Setup page.)

What's New in Paint

If you've used the paint program in Windows 3.1, there are some improvements in this version:

Zooming Much better zooming capability from 100 percent up to 800 percent.

Opaque as well as transparent drawing With opaque drawing, your additions cover the existing picture; transparent drawing lets the existing object show through your additions.

More options for manipulation The new Paint has more choices for stretching, skewing, flipping, and rotating the object being drawn.

Committing Original Art

Open Paint and, using the tools down the left side of the window, make a drawing and/or painting. When you're done, you can:

- Select File ➢ Save and give the picture a name. You can save it as one of several different kinds of bitmaps (see the Save as Type list).
- Select File ➢ Send, which will open Exchange and let you select an e-mail recipient worthy of receiving your work.
- Select File ➢ Save as Wallpaper. This will let you tile or center your work of art as the wallpaper on your screen.

Modifying the Work of Others

Any file with the extension .BMP or .PCX or .DIB can be opened in Paint. Use the tools to make any modifications you want and then do any of the things listed in the section above. Modified files are all saved as bitmaps (.BMP).

> **TIP**
>
> For a really good painting program at a very reasonable price, check out the excellent shareware program Paint Shop Pro. It's available for download on the major online services as well as the anonymous ftp site: **ftp ftp.winternet.com.** The file name is **PSP30.ZIP** in the **users\jasc** directory at the site. Or you can call **(612) 930-9171.**

Next Step

As you can see, some applets are very valuable and others you'll never use. In the next chapter, we'll deal with other small applications that come with Windows 95. But in this case, they're known as system tools. No one uses them for fun, but like a smoke alarm in your house, they're not only necessary but also comforting to have.

Chapter 17

TOOLS TO KEEP YOUR SYSTEM HEALTHY

- **Disk maintenance with ScanDisk**
- **Faster hard drives with Disk Defragmenter**
- **Saving files using Backup**
- **Compressing drives to gain more space**

The basic disk tools needed for your system are included with Windows 95 so you really don't need to go out and buy extra programs. Of course, if there are special things you want, like Norton Utilities or a particular backup program, feel free to buy what you like. Just make sure any utility programs you use are Windows 95-compatible so you don't damage any of your data.

In this chapter, we'll talk about disk tools, what they do and how best to use them. You'll find your list of installed tools by clicking on the Start button and then selecting Programs ➤ Accessories ➤ System Tools.

Taking Care of Your Drive with ScanDisk

A computer is a very complex system. There's lots of stuff going on all the time that you never know about. Like most complex systems, errors are made by the system itself, and if not corrected, will pile up into serious problems.

ScanDisk is protection against the accumulation of serious problems on your hard drive. It's a direct descendant of the CHKDSK utility in DOS with added features like those in the justly famous Norton Disk Doctor.

> **NOTE**
> You may have seen ScanDisk if you installed Windows 95 yourself, because in the installation routine ScanDisk does a quick check of the hard drive to look for errors.

Running ScanDisk

To run ScanDisk, follow these steps:

1. Select ScanDisk from the System Tools menu under Accessories. This will open the window shown in Figure 17.1.

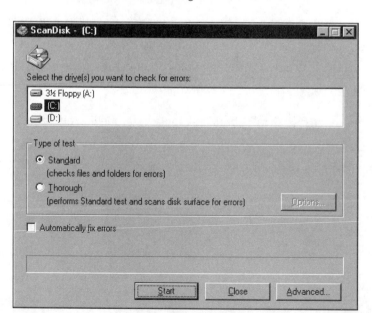

FIGURE 17.1:
Here's the basic ScanDisk window.

2. Highlight the drive you want tested.
3. Select the type of test and whether you want ScanDisk to automatically fix all errors or prompt you.
4. Click on Start to run.

NOTE

If the Automatically Fix Errors box is checked, ScanDisk will repair most errors without consulting you again. Such corrections are made based on settings you can review by clicking on the Advanced button.

Changing ScanDisk Settings

Click on the Advanced button to see (and change) the settings that ScanDisk uses.

Display summary This setting controls when you see the summary of ScanDisk's findings after a check (see Figure 17.2).

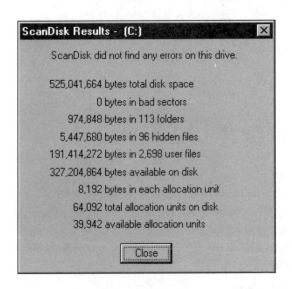

FIGURE 17.2:
This is ScanDisk's summary report on the drive just scanned.

Log file By default, ScanDisk creates a new log detailing its activities every time it's run. If you want one long continuous log or no log at all, change the setting.

Cross-linked files A cross-link occurs when more than one file tries to use the same area (cluster) on the hard drive. Whatever information is in the cluster is probably correct only for one file (though it might not be correct for either of them). The default setting attempts to salvage order out of the mess by copying the information in the cluster to both files contending for the space. This is the best of the three settings—it may not save any of your data but the other two options definitely won't.

Lost file fragments File fragments are a fact of computer life. You can leave the default setting to convert them to files. They'll be given names like FILE0001 and FILE0002 and deposited in your root folder (that's the C: folder which contains a lot of folders but some files too). The odds are very high that these fragments aren't anything useful, and they do take up valuable disk space. We've changed our default setting to Free but you can be extra cautious and leave it at Convert to Files. (Just remember to look at these files periodically and delete the junk.)

Check files for The default is to look just for invalid names, though you can add dates and times if you want. It will slow down ScanDisk's progress but not dramatically.

Check host drive first If you have a compressed drive, errors are sometimes caused by errors on the host drive. Leave this box checked so the host drive will be examined first.

> **TIP**
>
> You should run ScanDisk frequently. Once a week is a good idea. And at least once a month you should run its Thorough testing procedure, so the hard disk surface is checked for problems in addition to the standard checking of files and folders.

Defragmenting Your Disk

Windows 95 is much like the operating systems that preceded it in that when it writes a file to your disk, it puts it anywhere it finds room. As you delete and create files, over time files start to be a piece here, a piece there, another piece somewhere else.

This isn't a problem for Windows 95—it always knows where the pieces are. But it will tend to slow down file access time because the system has to go to several locations to pick up one file. When a file is spread over multiple places, it's said to be fragmented. The more fragmented files you have, the slower your hard drive will run.

As a matter of good housekeeping then, Disk Defragmenter should probably be run about once a month. Here's how it's done:

1. Select Disk Defragmenter from the System Tools menu.
2. Use the drop-down list shown in Figure 17.3 to choose the drive you want to defragment. Click on OK.

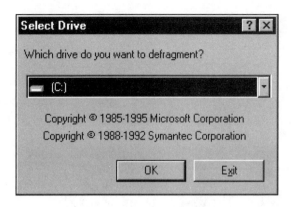

FIGURE 17.3:
Select the drive
you want to defrag-
ment. You can
select All Hard
Drives from the
drop-down list.

3. Disk Defragmenter will provide you with a report on the degree of defragmentation. Click on the Advanced button to see the options box shown in Figure 17.4.
Here's what the options mean:

- By default, full defragmentation is selected. This is the best option because
even though it's a little slower than the other two options, both files and free
space are consolidated. If you just defragment files, the free space is still in
clumps and future files you create are bound to be even more fragmented.
If you consolidate free space only, the files you already have will probably
become even more fragmented.
- If the Check for Errors box is selected, Disk Defragmenter checks the drive
for errors before defragging. If it finds errors, you'll be advised of this fact and
Defragmenter won't continue.

NOTE When Disk Defragmenter has found an error on your disk, run
ScanDisk (described earlier in this chapter) to repair the problem, and
then run Defragmenter again.

- Select whether these options are for this session only or should be saved for
future sessions.

4. Click on Start. You can click on Show Details to get a cluster-by-cluster view of
the program's progress. Or you can just minimize Disk Defragmenter and do
something else. If what you do writes to the hard drive, Disk Defragmenter will
start over—but in the background and without bothering you.

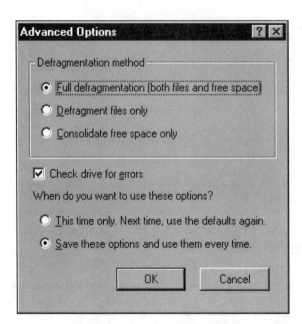

FIGURE 17.4:
The Disk
Defragmenter
has a number of
options that you
can choose among.

TIP   A useful tool in the Plus! for Windows 95 package is a program called System Agent that lets you automate regular runs of both ScanDisk and Disk Defragmenter so you don't forget to do these chores.

Backing Up Your Hard Disk

Your hard disk has (or will soon have) a lot of material on it that's valuable to you. Even if it's not your doctoral dissertation or this year's most important sales presentation, you'll have software (including Windows 95) that you've set up and configured *just so*.

Hard disk crashes are really quite rare these days, but if you are unlucky enough to have a crash, not having a recent backup can change your whole perspective on life. So resolve now to do frequent backups of your important files. If you are lucky and/or cautious enough to have a tape drive or other high-capacity backup system, you should also make less-frequent backups of your entire system.

Getting Started

To start the Backup program, click on the Start button, then select Programs ➤ Accessories ➤ System Tools and finally Backup.

NOTE   If the Backup program isn't on the menu, you'll need to install it. Go to Add/Remove Programs in the Control Panel and use Windows Setup to add Backup.

Figure 17.5 shows the opening window you'll see when you open Backup the first time.

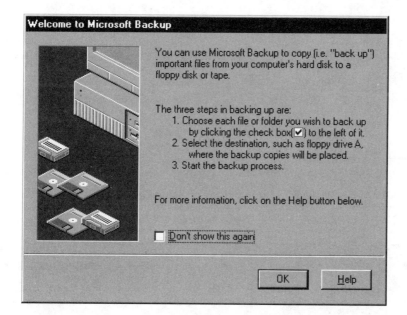

Welcome to Microsoft Backup

You can use Microsoft Backup to copy (i.e. "back up") important files from your computer's hard disk to a floppy disk or tape.

The three steps in backing up are:
1. Choose each file or folder you wish to back up by clicking the check box(☑) to the left of it.
2. Select the destination, such as floppy drive A, where the backup copies will be placed.
3. Start the backup process.

For more information, click on the Help button below.

☐ Don't show this again

OK   Help

FIGURE 17.5:
The Backup opening dialog box has information you should read—at least once.

Once you have read this dialog box, if you don't want to see it again click on the box next to "Don't show this again" and click on the OK button.

Tape Drive or Floppies

If you have a tape drive and it's been installed properly, Backup will find it and prepare to back up to it.

NOTE

Not all tape drives are supported. To find the list of ones that are, click the Help menu and select Help topics. Click on Using Tapes for Backup to see what's compatible with Backup. If your tape drive isn't among those listed, don't give up. Call the manufacturer of the tape drive and see if they have a driver—a program that will enable Windows 95 to use your tape drive. These programs are almost always free.

If Windows 95 doesn't find a tape drive, it'll present you with a message telling you that if you really do have a tape drive, it isn't working and what to do about it. If you really don't have a tape drive, just click on OK. You'll be backing up to floppies (which you already know).

NOTE

If you have two hard drives, backing up from one to the other is as safe as any other method. But you must use two physically separate hard drives, not just different partitions on a single hard drive.

Full System Backups

Next, Backup will create a file set designed to back up everything. This will automatically be called Full System Backup, and, if you use it, it will back up everything, including system files.

TIP

If your hard disk suddenly sounds like it's full of little pebbles, there's nothing more comforting than having a Full System Backup on your shelf. You should make a Full System Backup when you first install Windows 95, after you install new applications, and occasionally thereafter.

Defining a File Set

What is a file set? Backup is based on the idea that you have a large hard disk with perhaps thousands of individual files and perhaps hundreds of different folders. You don't usually want to back up everything on the disk. Usually you'll be backing up a few folders—the folders containing your Corel drawings, your Excel spreadsheets, your WordPerfect documents, your appointment book, your customer database, and so on.

Therefore, you need to tell Backup which folders need to be backed up every day or every week. Once you have a solid backup of your entire hard disk, you'll want to back up only certain folders on a regular basis (that'll be covered a little later). You probably don't need to back up your whole Corel package every week, because if worse comes to worse, you could reinstall it. Backing up a program that large takes forever and these days almost all the major programs are huge. The file set tells Backup which files and folders to back up.

Regular Backups

Regular backups involve less than the entire disk and will probably depend on how valuable certain of your files are, how difficult they would be to re-create, and how often they change.

> **TIP**
>
> You might want to make several file sets for backups of different depths. Back up really important folders at the end of every work day (or at lunch) and less important ones at the end of major projects. How to create a backup file set is covered in the following section.

Creating a Backup

In this section we'll create a backup to demonstrate how it's done. If Backup isn't running, start it now. (See the instructions earlier in this chapter.) Once you get through the initial dialog boxes, you should see the window shown in Figure 17.6.

Clicking on the objects in the section on the left tells Backup which device, folders, or individual files you want to back up.

> **NOTE**
>
> Each of the drives shown in the Backup window has a tiny check box next to it. If you want to back up the entire device—every file and folder from the root to the farthest branch—click on this box to automatically select everything. This in itself may take several minutes.

Backing Up Particular Files or Folders

Here's how you can back up particular files or folders. For the sake of this example, we'll back up a single file, but the principle is the same for a larger selection.

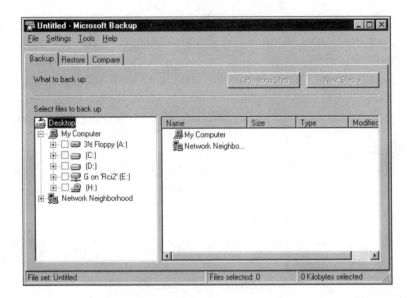

FIGURE 17.6:
The Backup
window lets you
choose what you
want to back up.

1. Click on your hard disk's name in the list. That will make all of the folders in the root folder of your hard disk appear in the list at the right.

NOTE When you look at the Backup window, it looks like simply a list of folders. Where are the files? The folders appear at the top of the list, so they may be the only thing visible to you. If you use the scroll bar at the right edge of the list to move to the bottom of the list, you will see the files in the root folder of the selected device. We'll get down to the file level shortly.

2. Search through the list of folders to find your Windows 95 folder. If you want to back up every file and folder in WINDOWS, you should click on the box to the left of the WINDOWS folder name. Instead, we are going to select a single file to back up.

3. Double-click on the WINDOWS folder. You'll see even more folders; scroll down until you start seeing individual files like those in Figure 17.7.

4. Scroll through the files in the folder until you locate the file called WIN. In the Type column, it will say Configuration Settings.

NOTE If you have file extensions turned on, the file will be listed as WIN.INI.

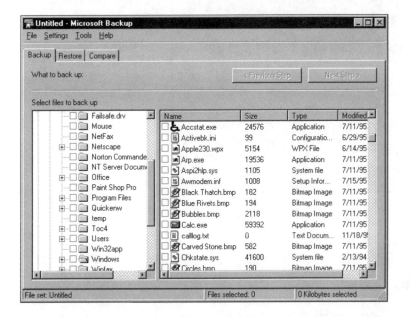

FIGURE 17.7:
Here are the files in the Windows folder—you'll have to scroll down past the subfolders to see individual files.

5. If the files are not in alphabetical order, you can click on the Name block at the top of the list to list them alphabetically. Or you might want to click on the Type block and search through the configuration files for WIN.

6. When you have located the file, click on the tiny box to the left of the file name in the list.

7. Click on the Next Step button at the top-right corner of the Backup window. This will give you a list of devices to use for the backup.

8. Select a device for the backup from the list at the left in the window by double-clicking on it. For our example, we will pick our A: drive.

9. To save the file set, pull down the File menu and select Save.

10. In the resulting dialog box, we'll type the name WIN as the name of the file set.

11. Click on OK. The file set will be saved.

12. Click on the Start Backup button at the upper-right corner of the Backup window.

13. Backup will display a dialog box asking for a name for your backup file. Make sure you have inserted the proper medium in the proper backup device (in this case a 3.5-inch floppy in the A: drive). Type in WIN as the backup file name and click on OK. The backup will begin immediately. As the backup proceeds, you will see the dialog box shown in Figure 17.8.

FIGURE 17.8:
This dialog box lets you know how it's going.

14. The final step is to click on the OK button.

> **TIP** If you want to keep this file set for future use, after you choose a destination for the backup, select Save from the File menu. Specify a name for your file set. When you next want to use it, start Backup and select Open File Set from the File menu.

Backing Up an Existing File Set

Let's do a backup of an existing file set. Since we just created it, let's use the WIN file set. Here's what to do:

1. Begin by shutting down Backup. Click on the X icon at the extreme upper-right corner of the Backup window.
2. Start Backup by following the instructions earlier in this chapter.
3. When you get to the Backup window, pull down the File menu and select Open File Set.
4. In the Open dialog box, double-click on the icon WIN (or whatever you used as the name of the file set we just created). The file set will open.
5. Click on the Next Step button at the top-right corner of the Backup window.
6. Select a device to which you want to save the backup (from the list in the left part of the window) by double-clicking on the device icon. For this example, select drive A: as the destination.

7. Click on the button at the top right marked Start Backup.
8. You will be prompted for the name of the backup.
9. Make sure your backup medium (floppy disk or tape) is in the device selected, and then click on OK to begin the backup process.

TIP Windows 95 has already made a Full System Backup file set. Open and use this file set when you want to back up everything on your computer.

Choosing Backup Options

To use Backup's other options, pull down the Settings menu and select Options. This will display a dialog box showing four tabs: General, Backup, Restore, and Compare. When you click on the Backup tab, you'll see the following options:

- Quit Backup after operation is finished
- Full backup of all selected files or backup of selected files that have changed since the last backup
- Verify files (make sure they were backed up properly)

NOTE Naturally, verifying your backup will be safer than not, but the backup is much slower with verify on.

- Use data compression
- Format tape, if needed
- Erase on tape backup
- Erase on floppy disk backup (erases contents of disk before making backup)

Making Comparisons

The purpose of Compare is to make sure a backup is current. Since we've already completed a backup of a single file, let's compare that file we backed up to the original.

1. Start Backup (see the steps earlier in this chapter).
2. When you get to the Backup window, click on the Compare tab to check the backup against the original.

3. Although it's not at all clear, you are being asked to identify the location of the backup file, so click on the icon for drive A:. A list of all of the backups on drive A: will appear. Select the one you want to compare.

4. Click on the Next Step button. At the top of the left list box you should see WIN (the name of the backup set), From Drive C: (the origin of the files in the set), and then WINDOWS (the name of the folder from which the file was backed up—all these will differ if you're using a different backup set). Click on the check box to the left of the Windows folder.

5. In the right list box you will see the files from the Windows folder that are part of this backup set. If you are using the backup set you created earlier, this will be the single configuration settings file called WIN. The check in the box to its left indicates it will be included in the compare operation.

6. Click on the button marked Start Compare in the upper-right corner of the Backup window, and the comparison will proceed.

Error Messages

If there are differences between the backup file and the file on your disk, you will be notified. In this case, after doing the backup of WIN.INI to the floppy, I loaded the WIN.INI file on the hard drive into a word processor and added an extra carriage return to the file so it would be different from the file backed up. I ran Compare and was notified there was a difference and then was asked if I wanted to see the report shown in Figure 17.9.

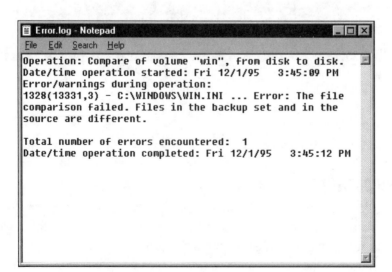

FIGURE 17.9:
The error report tells you about errors found.

Compare Options

Pull down the Settings menu, select Options, click on the Compare tab, and a dialog box shows you the following options:

- Quit Backup after operation is completed.
- Compare to file in original location, in an unspecified location, or in a specific alternate location—a single folder.

Restoring Files Later

Restore is useful for more than recovering from disaster. It's a good way to move large files off your hard disk when they aren't immediately needed, and then restore them at a later date.

How to Do It

We'll use Restore to restore the WIN configuration file we backed up earlier. (On the disk, it's called WIN.INI.)

1. Start Backup.

2. When you get through all the introductory dialog boxes, click on the tab at the top of the Backup window marked Restore.

3. In the list at the left side of the window, click on the device from which the restore is to be made—floppy drive A:. A list of the backup files on drive A: will appear in the right side of the Backup window.

4. Select the backup from which you want to restore.

5. Click on Next Step. As with compare, use the left pane to select the folder whose files you want to restore. In the right pane, select the specific files you want to restore if you don't want to restore all the files in the selected folder.

6. Click on the Start Restore button, and the restoration will proceed.

Dealing with Problems

If there are problems with the restore, you'll see a dialog box giving you the option of seeing a report something like the one in Figure 17.10.

The error here was caused by the insertion and then deletion of a single carriage return. After changing the file on the hard disk, I saved the file. This made the time/date stamp on the file on the hard disk more recent than the stamp on the backed up file. So there's an error when attempting to restore the backed up file because it's now older than the one on the hard drive. Allowing the restoration of an older file over a newer one is not usually a good idea.

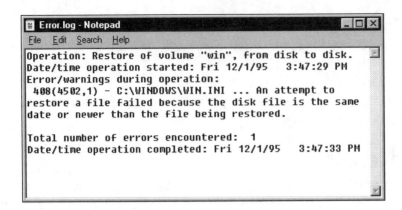

FIGURE 17.10:
This report lets you know what went wrong.

Options for Restoring

Pull down the Settings menu, select Options, and in the Options dialog box, click on the tab marked Restore. These are the options you're given:

- Quit Backup after operation is completed
- Restore to the original location, an alternate location, or to a specified folder in an alternate location
- Verify restore (which exacts a price—it adds to the length of time of the restore, but also makes it more reliable)
- Never overwrite files
- Overwrite older files only (this option is set on my system, in order to generate the error shown in Figure 17.10)
- Overwrite files (if this is selected, you have the additional option of being prompted before the files are overwritten)

Some Additional Backup Options

The Tools menu in Backup contains three options: Format Tape, Erase Tape, and Redetect Tape Drive. If you have a tape drive, you will need to format your tapes before using them. If you have an old tape, you may want to erase it before using it again to prevent problems with Backup overwriting existing files on the tape. If you install a tape drive after you have run Backup the first time (or if Backup failed to recognize an existing tape drive), you will want to run Redetect Tape Drive.

Drag-and-Drop Backup

On the Settings menu there is also an option called Drag and Drop, which lets you place Backup on your Desktop as an icon. You can then back up a file set by dragging it to the Backup icon and dropping it. If you want to use this option, select it from the Settings menu and confirm the settings in the dialog box: Run Backup minimized, Confirm Operation before Beginning, and Quit Backup after Operation Is Finished. By default these are set On.

Here's how to place Backup on your Desktop as an icon:

1. Right-click on the Start button and select Open.
2. In the window that opens, double-click in turn on Programs ➤ Accessories ➤ System Tools.
3. Right-click on the Backup icon and drag it to the Desktop.
4. Release the mouse button and select Create Shortcut(s) Here from the pop-up menu.

When you're ready to back up a particular file set, you can find it in the Program Files ➤ Accessories folder and then drag and drop it on the Backup icon on the Desktop. An easier way is to make a folder called Backup. Put shortcuts to your file sets and to Backup inside. If you want, put a shortcut to the folder on your Desktop. Then all you have to do is open the folder and drag the appropriate file set to the Backup icon to start a backup.

Making More Room on Your Hard Disk

Five or six years ago when hard drives were running up to $5 for each megabyte of storage space, the first disk compression programs were born. They were slow and not all that reliable. Now that hard drives are selling at maybe 20 cents per megabyte and compression is no longer a big issue, compression is very fast and very reliable. Compression just means that all or a portion of your hard drive can be made to appear much larger than it actually is.

Windows 95 supports two varieties of disk compression: DoubleSpace and DriveSpace. DriveSpace is the program supplied with Windows 95. DoubleSpace is a slightly different, older version that had its first incarnation with MS-DOS 6. Windows 95 creates only DriveSpace compressed drives.

NOTE Windows 95 works with drives that are compressed with Stacker, SuperStor, and AddStor, in addition to DriveSpace and DoubleSpace.

How Compression Works

Let's say you have one hard drive labeled C: and use DriveSpace to create a compressed drive D:. The compressed drive is not a separate partition of your hard drive. It's actually a file referred to as the CVF (compressed volume file) in the root folder of the C: drive. C: drive is called the *host* drive for this CVF.

If you make it using Windows 95, it'll be called DRVSPACE.000. Not that you'll *see* this file when in Windows. To Windows 95 and all your programs, it'll appear just as drive D:.

If you want to see the file, you'll have to turn off its setting as a hidden file. Don't bother. There is nothing useful you can do with a CVF. Don't delete it, attempt to change it, or anything else. *Only* approach a compressed drive through DriveSpace. If you want to remove compression, use DriveSpace to do it.

Compressing a Drive

You'll need at least 2MB of free space on your C: drive if that's the one being compressed. If it's another drive or floppy disk, you'll need 768K of free space before compression. Follow these steps:

1. Click on the Start button, then select Programs ➢ Accessories ➢ System Tools and then DriveSpace.

2. DriveSpace will check your system and report on what it finds (shown in Figure 17.11).

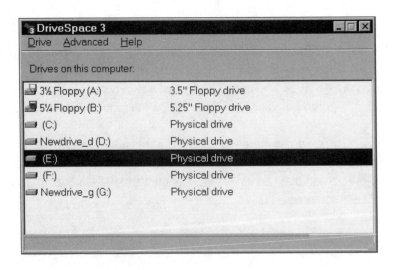

FIGURE 17.11: DriveSpace lists the drives on your machine.

3. Highlight the drive you want to compress and select Compress from the Drive menu.

4. The next window (Figure 17.12) shows the current status of the drive and what the status will be after compression.

5. Click on the Start button to compress files and free space on the drive.

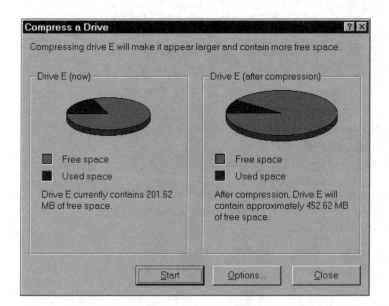

FIGURE 17.12:
This window shows what compression will gain you on the selected drive.

NOTE   **Compressed drives can't be larger than 512MB, unless you're using DriveSpace 3 from Plus! for Windows 95.**

At the end of the compression process, you'll see a window like the one in Figure 17.13 showing the amount of space you've gained by compressing.

Behind the Options Button

In Figure 17.12, you can see an Options button. Click on it and you can see how Windows is planning to proceed. In the above example, I told Windows 95 that I wanted to compress drive E:—free space and files included. Figure 17.14 shows that the new host drive will be J: and it will be hidden.

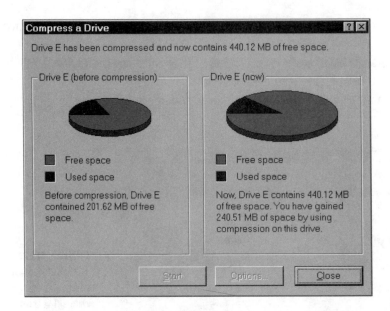

FIGURE 17.13:
The results after compressing a drive

There will still be a drive E: (what I'll see as drive E: will be the new CVF) and the 2MB left on the host drive won't be visible since it'll now be the hidden drive J:.

You can change these options: leaving more free space on J: and making it visible or changing the drive letter designation for the host drive.

TIP   You can change the designated drive letter for the drive that contains the Windows 95 folder.

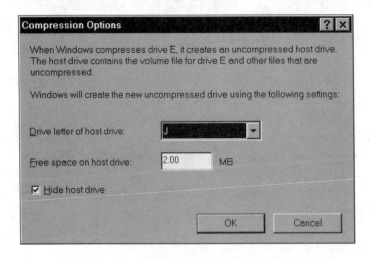

FIGURE 17.14:
If I had clicked on the Options button before compressing drive E:, this window would have provided additional information.

Compressing Free Space

To make a compressed volume from the free space on a drive, open DriveSpace and follow these steps:

1. Highlight an existing drive.
2. Select Create Empty from the Advanced menu.
3. Read the text surrounding the boxes (see Figure 17.15) and you'll see what's proposed. The text boxes with arrows next to them can be changed.

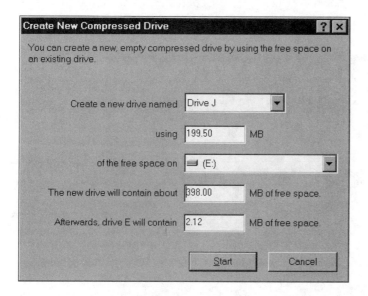

FIGURE 17.15:
Creating a compressed drive out of free space on a drive

Changing the Size of a Compressed Drive

If there's free space on your compressed drive, you can add free space to the host drive by making the compressed portion smaller. Likewise, if you have free space on the host drive, you can make the compressed portion larger—as long as you keep within the 512MB maximum size for compressed drives.

To change the size of a compressed file, follow these steps:

1. Start DriveSpace, then highlight an existing drive. Select Adjust Free Space from the Drive menu.
2. Move the slider bar to adjust the free space.

Removing a Compressed Drive

A compressed drive can be removed (that is, the drive returned to its pre-compression state) quite easily as long as there's enough space on the host drive for all the files once they're decompressed.

To remove a compressed drive, follow these steps:

1. Open DriveSpace and highlight the drive you want to uncompress.
2. Select Uncompress from the Drive menu.
3. The window shown in Figure 17.16 will open and show you the current state of the drive and what it will look like after being uncompressed.

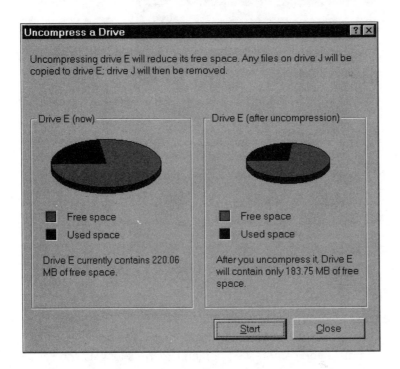

FIGURE 17.16: DriveSpace shows you the before and after views of a drive you've selected to uncompress.

4. You'll see a warning notice advising that your computer will be unusable during the uncompress cycle and also advising you to back up important files first. Click on Uncompress Now if you're ready to proceed.

A window with a progress bar will open so you can see how far along the process has gone. At the end you'll also get a window a lot like the one in Figure 17.16, except this one will show the final results.

Resource Meter

The Resource Meter is a handy little device if you're keeping track of resources on your computer. It's pretty hard to run out of resources in Windows 95 but you can get awfully low if you have enough windows open.

To put Resource Meter on the end of your Taskbar, take these steps:

1. Right-click on the Start button and select Open.
2. In the window that opens, double-click on Programs, then Accessories, and finally System Tools.
3. Right-click on Resource Meter and select Create Shortcut.
4. Right-click on the new shortcut and select Cut.
5. Next go to the Windows Startup folder. This can be done by using this icon on the toolbar at the top of the window.

    Click on it twice to move up two levels to Programs.

6. Double-click on Startup. When the Startup window opens, right-click in an empty area and select Paste from the pop-up menu.

The next time you start up your computer, a small icon will be placed on your Taskbar. Place your pointer on the icon and a flyover box will open showing available resources. Or right-click on the icon and select Details. A window like the one in Figure 17.17 will open.

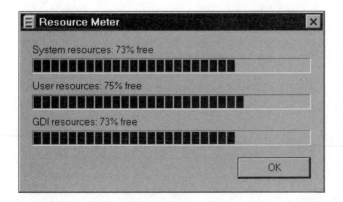

FIGURE 17.17:
The Resource Meter window

There's no point in trying to describe what the different resources mean because the explanation would involve terms like *memory heaps* and *device contexts*. Suffice it to say that if any of these numbers starts approaching zero, it's time to close some open programs to give yourself more maneuvering room.

Other System Tools

There are a couple of other system tools in the list but they're primarily for the use of technicians troubleshooting an iffy system. You can poke around in them if you wish, but it's doubtful you'll ever need to look at them twice.

Next Step

After this chapter, what remains is an appendix on installation and a glossary of computer terms you may encounter. Some of the terms aren't discussed elsewhere in this book but knowing their definitions can be helpful.

There's also a super-duper index, so you won't have any trouble locating sections you dimly remember seeing (but don't remember where)! That way, the book can continue to serve as a handy reference as you progress in your exploration of Windows 95.

Appendix

INSTALLATION

Installation of Windows 95 is easier than you might expect. There are quite a few steps, but none of them are especially difficult and the help screens as you go are excellent.

Before you start, it's important to do the preparatory work necessary to ensure a safe installation. There's a strong temptation to just jump in and get started. But as so many other chores, taking a few minutes to think out what you're doing will go a long way toward preventing having to do the installation twice.

Over Windows 3.x

The recommended-by-Microsoft approach is to install Windows 95 right on top of your existing Windows 3.x. The advantages to this approach include:

- You'll keep all your programs and their settings.
- If you have problems, you can use the uninstall program to automatically remove Windows 95 and get your original DOS and Windows 3.x back intact.
- You won't be able to boot into your previous version of DOS, but you will have the DOS mode of Windows 95, which works *better*.

From Plain DOS to Glorious Windows

If you've been true to your DOS all this time and now want to add Windows 95 to your computing life, the installation is fairly straightforward. You'll need to make sure you have the full version of Windows 95 (not the one designed to be installed on a system with some version of Windows already present).

You'll still need to review the checklist later in this appendix and do all the tasks that apply to your setup.

Starting with a Clean Slate

The cleanest install is done with a clean hard drive. You back up all your data files and reformat the drive (getting rid of everything on it), putting only the system files on the drive. The advantage of this approach is that there'll be none of those pesky files from previous versions of Windows and you won't have to clean up your AUTOEXEC.BAT and CONFIG.SYS files because they won't exist after the format.

The disadvantages are that you'll have to reinstall all your programs and therefore lose any special setting up that you've done. And no matter how carefully you back up your data files, you'll probably overlook something and it'll be lost.

This kind of install is ideal in many ways, but it's not practical for many people.

> **TIP**
>
> You can use the upgrade version of Windows 95 to do a clean install, providing you have the first disk from your previous version of Windows. When the Windows 95 installation can't find a previous installation, you'll be prompted for its location. Just put the setup disk from Windows 3.1 in the floppy drive and use the drop-down list in the dialog box to point Windows 95 to that drive.

Before You Install

Windows 95 is so smart about some things, it's scary. At the same time, it's pretty dumb about other things. And since there's no way to tell in advance how smart Windows 95 is going to be about your particular system, we recommend a fail-safe approach to installation (also known as the belt-and-suspenders school of thought).

Do yourself a favor and read all the items in this section carefully. Some may not apply to you but most will.

Do Some Housecleaning

Now's the perfect time to ponder which programs on your system you really need and to clean up some of the clutter and detritus that build up on your hard drive. Windows 95 is going to use more hard disk space than the combination of DOS and Windows you now have, so this is an even better reason to clean house.

The first step is to take a look at installed programs you haven't used in the last year or two. Time to get rid of them. If they're DOS programs, just delete them. If they're Windows programs, you have to delete them and find all the files they've stuck in your Windows directories without telling you.

Your best bet here is to get one of the ingenious programs designed to remove all traces of ill-behaved Windows applications like Uninstaller2 and Remove-It. Both do a good job of finding all the pieces of the programs they know about and removing them.

> **TIP**
>
> If you have any doubts about removing a program from your hard drive, just save any data files to a floppy. You can always reinstall the program from the original disks if you suddenly need it.

Make Enough Hard Drive Space

Free up as much hard drive space as you can: 50MB is not too much and more is even better. Windows 95 does its own memory management dynamically—that is, it makes adjustments constantly to meet the needs of the operations going on. If you make use of virtual memory (see Chapter 1) and we all do at one time or another, the more free disk space, the happier you and Windows 95 will be.

During the installation, if you don't have enough vacant space, Windows 95 will let you exit from the setup to clear more room. This is a pain and a needless waste of time, of course, so get as close to that 50MB mark as you can.

> **NOTE**
>
> You might look at this as a good excuse to get a bigger hard drive. The new Windows 95 programs that will be coming out are going to need a lot of space and the prices for hard drives have plummeted.

Defragment Your Hard Drive

Once you have all the extraneous files cleaned off your hard drive, you should do a complete disk defragmentation. This will consolidate your existing files on the disk, creating the maximum possible room for Windows 95 to do its thing.

> **TIP**
>
> If you have a permanent swap file in your current Windows con-figuration, change it to a temporary one before you defragment, so Windows 95 can make its own swap file.

Any defragmentation program will do. I used SpeedDisk in Norton Utilities, but DEFRAG, provided in MS-DOS 6.x is perfectly adequate for the job. If you're using Stacker or another third-party disk compression program, make sure you also run their disk defragmentation utility. If you're using SpeedDisk from version 7 or later of the Norton Utilities, you won't need to run the Stac defrag utility separately, since Norton understands Stacker.

Clean Out AUTOEXEC.BAT and CONFIG.SYS

During installation, Windows 95 will review your AUTOEXEC.BAT and CONFIG.SYS files and remove drivers and settings that aren't necessary. It places a REM at the beginning of any line that loads a device program or settings that Windows 95 doesn't need. But how-ever clever the install routine is, it still can miss some items and end up trying to execute commands that cause Windows 95 to choke. You're much better off doing a preemptive strike of your own.

Here's how to make it simple:

- Disable any third-party memory managers like QEMM. Type REM at the beginning of every line that loads a memory manager. Replace these lines with DEVICE= lines that point to HIMEM.SYS and EMM386.EXE.
- Disable any virus protection programs that run at startup. Check your BIOS to see if you have boot sector virus protection and disable that too. Windows 95 is going to make changes to your boot sector that will give the anti-virus utility fits if it's loaded, and in most cases will cause the installation to fail.
- REM out any fancy footwork in your AUTOEXEC.BAT such as calls, branches, or conditional executions.
- Disable hardware drivers except those for hardware you need to boot up and start Windows 3.x. If you're installing from a CD, leave the drivers for your CD-ROM drive, otherwise disable it. If you have a SCSI hard drive, leave those drivers too. Other candidates for REMing out include drivers for your:
  - Sound card
  - Scanner
  - Mouse
  - Tape back up

The idea is to let Windows 95 recognize and supply its own 32-bit drivers for as much of the hardware as possible. If it happens that Windows 95 doesn't have a driver for your scanner or other piece of hardware, for example, you can always reinstate your 16-bit drivers until such time as a 32-bit driver is available.

Why Disable a Memory Manager?

A good memory manager, such as QEMM or NetRoom, can use areas of memory that would not normally be available. It does this by tricking DOS and Windows into believing that certain addresses are not being used when they are.

Such stealth features are essential in DOS if you're to circumvent the problem of inadequate room to load everything you need into DOS's limited memory space. It's unnecessary in Windows 95, however, and can interfere with Windows 95's ability to correctly sense what hardware is on your machine.

New Windows 95-compatible versions of the good memory managers are now available, but they're certainly not required.

WARNING If someone tries to sell you a software product that will "double" or greatly increase your available memory, be extremely skeptical. Some released right after the launch of Windows 95 either didn't work or crashed your machine. Compressing RAM is possible, but for technical reasons it's very, very hard to do it in such a way that it actually makes your machine faster.

Do a Backup

Please, make a backup of your system before you start this upgrade. I can't stress this enough. While the installation program of Windows 95 is remarkably good, and the number of systems that fail is small, you should never, *never* do changes to your operating system without doing a backup. Going from any version of DOS to Windows 95 is about as significant a change as can be imagined.

Choosing a Backup Program

If you haven't invested in a third-party program, the backup program included with MS-DOS versions 6 and above is excellent. It's based on the Norton Backup program and is safe, easy to use, and reasonably fast. If you have another backup program you prefer, and are more comfortable with, by all means use it.

What to Back Up

Back up at least the root directory of your boot drive (C:) and your DOS and Windows directories, along with any files you simply could not live without or easily re-create. What this includes is really a personal decision, but obviously, if you're a business, the answer is different than if you use your computer primarily to run DOOM.

Take your time and review all the directories and even subdirectories on your hard drive. If you have any doubts about whether you should back up a particular file or group of files, it's best to err on the side of caution. What you don't need to back up are program files, because you can, in the worst case, re-install them from the original disks.

Installing with CD or Disks?

As long as your system has a CD-ROM, use it! Windows 95 comes on a several-inch-high stack of floppy disks. Installing from floppies is painfully slow, and if you change your hardware or add additional features, Windows 95 will likely ask you for the one original disk you won't be able to find. With a CD-ROM, there's only one disk. Either you have it, or you don't.

> **TIP**
>
> If circumstances make it impossible to use a CD-ROM for your installation, consider this trick. Copy all the files from the original Windows 95 floppies to a subdirectory of your hard drive. (Call it something like Win95src—for Windows 95 source directory.) Run your setup from that subdirectory to make the installation go considerably faster. Of course, this method also ties up about 35MB of disk space, but if you've got the room, go for it!

The CD version is better for another reason. Because CDs can hold so much data, this version includes the entire Windows 95 Resource Kit from Microsoft (just about everything *anyone* would want to know about Windows 95), plus other goodies such as video clips.

Starting the Installation

After you've done the prep work above, reboot your system and start Windows 3.*x*. Insert the Windows 95 Setup Disk 1 or the CD in the appropriate drive, select that drive in File Manager, and double-click on the SETUP.EXE file.

NOTE If you're not installing over a previous version of Windows, run SETUP.EXE from the DOS prompt.

You'll get a Welcome screen with an estimate of the time it'll take to do the installation (30 to 60 minutes depending on how much you install and the speed of your system). Windows 95 then performs a quick survey of your system and asks you to read and consent to the license agreement.

At every step, Windows 95 tells you what it plans to do and, after you click on Next, does it. Almost all the dialog boxes in the installation routine have a Back button as well as a Next button, so you can retrace your steps if you find you've made a wrong choice.

NOTE If you cancel the procedure before the Copying Windows Files to Your Computer screen, there's no harm done and your system won't have changed. However, if you stop after the copying of files has begun, you'll be warned that your previous version of Windows may not run correctly and instructions on how to restart Setup will be displayed.

Choose a Directory

You'll be asked to choose a directory for installation—the default is WINDOWS on your C: drive (or whatever directory your current version of Windows is in), but you can choose another location or a different name for the directory.

TIP It's not necessary for Windows 95 to be on the boot drive or even to be in a directory called Windows, but if you're installing Windows 95 as an upgrade over Windows 3.*x*, make sure you choose the directory that contains 3.*x*.

Save System Files

The next dialog box asks if you want the install program to save your Windows 3.*x* and DOS system files. These files (which occupy about 6MB of hard drive space) make it possible to uninstall Windows 95 in about five minutes should you run into trouble. So it's a good idea to select Yes. If you don't save these files, uninstalling later is a much messier affair where you have to seek out and delete individual Windows 95 files.

Setup Options

The next choice you have to make is about how much of the operating system you want to install. You can select:

Typical The major components (as defined by the installation program) are installed.

Portable Installs power management and PCMCIA support. You can choose the components you want to install or let the system install the major components (as in the Typical install).

Compact Selects a minimum configuration–for situations where space is tight.

Custom Lets you make selections at every step. Don't be put off by the designation of this choice as for "experts." Even a reasonably competent beginner can handle this installation.

> **NOTE** After any type of installation, you can use the Add/Remove Programs function in the Control Panel to easily add or remove any components.

Name and CD Key

Next is a dialog box asking for your name (and company, if any). If you're installing from a CD, you'll also be asked for a 10-digit CD key. The number is on a sticker on the back of the CD jewel case.

Analyzing the Computer

In the next step, you'll be asked about hardware that Windows 95 suspects you might have but hasn't found yet. The most common devices being sought are CD-ROM drives, network cards, and sound cards. Click on the check box for items that are actually on your computer, and Windows 95 will conduct a hardware search that can go on for several minutes.

Making the Connections

The Setup Wizard then inquires about the Windows 95 communication tools you want to use.

Microsoft Network This is the online service with the software built right into Windows 95. It offers e-mail, news, real-time chats, bulletin boards, and special interests of every kind.

Microsoft Mail If you're on a network, this mini-version of Microsoft Mail can be used to send, receive, and manage messages.

Microsoft Fax Install Microsoft Fax and you can send and receive faxes on your fax modem without any other special fax software.

Selecting Components

If you selected Custom install, you choose the components you want. For a Typical, Compact, or Portable installation, you can choose the components you want or let Windows 95 choose what to install based on the type of installation selected.

The main categories of components are listed in the window. Click on Details to see the total items that make up the category. Check the ones you want installed. A click of the mouse will remove check marks in front of items you don't want.

Making a Startup Disk

The setup program asks if you want to create a startup disk so you can boot your computer in case of trouble. The answer is definitely, positively YES!

The Startup Disk contains several programs that will enable you to boot your system and edit important files in case something gets horribly mangled. It also contains the invaluable UNINSTAL.EXE, which enables you to get rid of all of Windows 95 and start over in case things are severe enough to require re-installation.

NOTE Like the seat belts in your car or the smoke detector in your home, you'll only need a startup disk if things go very badly indeed. If you do need it, however, nothing else will do.

After the startup disk is made, there's a long pause while Setup copies files. If you have a CD-ROM, you can go get a cup of tea. If you're installing from floppies, you'll have to stick around and keep swapping.

The Finishing Touches

After all the copying, the Setup Wizard now needs to restart your computer and finish up. Your system might not be able to restart by itself. Wait five minutes or so and if nothing appears to be happening, hit the Reset button. This won't harm your installation and is not a sign of installation failure.

Setting Up the Control Panel

After the restart, Windows 95 still has a few chores—including setting up the Control Panel and putting your programs on the Start menu. There'll be a pause at the Day/Time settings for you to verify your time zone.

Setting Up the Exchange

If you chose to install the Microsoft Network or the Fax or Mail communications options, you'll now be stepped through setting up the Exchange, which is a central organizer for all your mail and fax messaging. (See Chapter 15 for help on Exchange setup.)

Installing Additional Hardware

If a piece of your hardware wasn't detected during the install, use the Add New Hardware function in the Control Panel to tell Windows 95 about it.

> **TIP**
>
> **If you installed over Windows 3.1, and your program groups don't appear under Programs on the Start menu, open a DOS window and run GRPCONV.EXE /s to restore them.**

Deleting Unnecessary Files

After Windows 95 is installed and you feel safe and secure with the new system, you can delete WIN95UNDO.DAT and WIN95UNDO.INI. This frees up the approximately 6MB of space occupied when you chose to Save System Files early in the installation. To see these hidden files, select Options from the View menu in the Explorer and click on Show All Files.

Glossary

GLOSSARY

16-bit, 32-bit

Refers to how certain programs address memory and other technical details. In general, 16-bit programs refer to those written for DOS or earlier versions of Windows. Windows 95 allows the use of 32-bit programs which can do true multi-tasking (as opposed to task switching). If designed correctly, 32-bit programs can be faster than 16-bit programs but they are not inherently so.

Active window

The window that keyboard or mouse movements act on. Many windows can be open, but only one is active at a time. You can spot the active window by its title bar, which is a different color than the title bar of other windows.

Application

An application is a collection of files that may include several programs. WordPerfect is an application that consists of any number of files constituting a single package. Applications are also grouped by type such as word processing applications, database applications, and so forth.

ASCII

Pronounced "AS-key." Stands for the American Standard Code for Information Interchange. Developed back in the '60s as a standard numerical code for characters used on all computers. Today, ASCII usually means normal text as opposed to code unreadable by regular folk.

Associate

To connect files having a particular extension to a specific program. When you double-click on a file with the extension, the associated program is opened and the file you clicked on is opened. In Windows 95, associated files are usually called regis-tered files.

Attribute

A bit of code in a file that determines an aspect of the file's status. The four file attributes are read-only, hidden, archive, and system. A file can have none or any number of the attributes. You can modify these but only if you have a good reason. (This is a noun, pronounced with the accent on the first syllable, not the second.)

Background

All the screen area behind the active window. Can also mean a process that is going on other than in the active window.

Baud

The speed at which data is transmitted over a communications line or cable. This is not *really* the same as BPS (bits per second) but the terms are used interchangeably.

Bit

Represents a single switch inside a computer set to 0 or 1. There are millions of them in every computer. Short for **b**inary dig**it**, 8 bits make up a byte, the basic unit of data storage.

Bitmaps

Picture or image files that are made up of pixels. Pictures made in Paint are automatically saved as bitmaps (with a .BMP extension).

Boot

A simple name for the complicated process your computer goes through when starting up.

Bootable disk

A disk containing the *system* files needed to start the computer. When your system starts up, it looks for a disk first in drive A:, if none is there it goes to drive C:. When a disk is found, the computer examines the disk to see if it contains the system files. When a disk with system files is found, the computer uses that disk's information to start the system running. If a disk with system files is in drive A:, information on that disk will be used to tell the computer about itself. Computers can normally be booted only from drive A: or drive C:.

BPS

Bits **p**er **s**econd. A unit of measurement for the communication speed of modems and fax modems.

Byte

The basic unit of data storage. A byte is 8 bits. For all intents and purposes, a byte equals a single character.

Configuration

A set of values in a program or for a device such as a printer. The values will be things such as how menu options work or a particular size of paper for a printer to use.

DDE

Stands for **D**ynamic **D**ata **E**xchange. An older standard for making information updated in one program available in another program. It's been replaced by OLE.

Default

The configuration settings that a device or program will have without any intervention from you. Usually you can change the default settings, but care should be taken.

Dialog box

A window that opens to ask you impertinent questions or request input. Windows and Windows 95 programs are knee-deep in dialog boxes.

DLL

Short for **D**ynamic **L**ink **L**ibrary. A file with information needed by one or more programs. Don't delete files with this extension willy-nilly because your programs will be dysfunctional without the DLL files they need.

Driver

A program made up of instructions to operate things that are added on to your computer such as a printer, modem, or mouse. Windows 95 includes most drivers you're likely to need, but there are rare times when you need to acquire a newer driver (and instructions on installing it) from the manufacturer of the device.

Folder

A means of organizing files. Each installed program will make its own folder and perhaps several subfolders. The user can likewise make folders to organize programs and files. Folders are analogous to Directories in Windows 3.1 and DOS.

Initialize

To prepare for use. With disks, this means to format the disk so it can be read. Programmers use this term to mean to get everything in the program to a known, beginning state.

Kilobyte

One thousand bytes (actually 1,024). Abbreviated as K and KB.

Landscape

A printer setting in which the characters are printed sideways along the length of the page. The opposite setting is "portrait."

Megabyte

One million bytes (or 1,048,576 bytes). Abbreviated as M or MB.

Modem

A contraction for **mo**dulator-**dem**odulator. A device that hooks up to phone lines so your computer can communicate with other computers, either individually or through an online service.

Multitasking

Using more than one application at a time. Most of the time in Windows 3.1, you were *task switching*, moving back and forth between applications, not actually using more than one at the same time. Windows 95 makes true multitasking possible, but to get the full effect you need to be running 32-bit programs.

OLE

Pronounced "O-lay." Short for **O**bject **L**inking and **E**mbedding. An automatic way for Windows programs to share data.

Online

To be in a state of readiness. A printer is said to be online when it's ready to print. These days, online is mostly used to mean being connected to another computer via modem. The connection can be to a commercial service, an Internet provider, and so forth.

Optimize

Computer jargon for "improve the performance of."

Parallel

A port on your computer usually used to connect a cable to a printer. Can also be used to connect other devices, such as an external drive or network adapter, to your computer. Information transmitted through a parallel port travels through multiple side-by-side paths inside the cable.

Peripheral

A device attached to the outside of your computer. This includes the monitor, keyboard, mouse, and printer.

Plug and Play

A recent standard for hardware. Hardware that adopts this standard can be installed on a Windows 95 computer with very little intervention by the user. The hardware will be detected and configured by Windows 95 to run properly. Manufacturers of disk drives, modems, network cards, and other devices have been rapidly adopting Plug and Play.

Port

A connecting point on your computer for plugging in external devices. At a minimum, most computers have two serial ports and one parallel (printer) port. Computers also have a specialized port for the keyboard; some have a special mouse port, too.

Portrait

The usual way a page of text is printed with lines running across the width of the sheet. The opposite setting is "landscape."

Protocol

A set of rules that determine the flow of data and how it's used. The modems at either end of a communication line have to be using the same protocol to talk to each other. Likewise, computers on a network need to be speaking the same protocol in order to connect.

RAM

Short for **R**andom **A**ccess **M**emory. In a nutshell, memory is where things happen in your computer. The processor (CPU) does the work but it can hold only so much information. Programs and files are retrieved from the hard disk and stored in RAM so that operations can proceed rapidly.

Register

To tell Windows 95 what program to use to open files of a certain type (that is, files with a particular extension). If a file type is registered, a double-click on a file of that type will start the necessary application and open the file. For example, a file with the .DOC extension will automatically be opened in Word. A .TXT extension will cause a file to be opened in Notepad. Same as *associate*.

Serial

A particular type of port that transmits information one bit at a time. Mostly used by a modem or a mouse, and occasionally by a scanner.

Shortcut

A tool that acts as a pointer to a file, folder, application, or device. Shortcuts are very small files that you can place almost anywhere. When you double-click on a shortcut, the object it points to will be opened. So you can have a shortcut to an object in various places without having to physically move or copy files.

Swap file

Space on the hard disk that Windows 95 uses to increase the amount of memory available to Windows programs. The swap file in Windows 95 is dynamic so it automatically grows larger or smaller based on current activity on the computer.

System resources

A finite portion of memory that is set aside for Windows to keep track of all the pieces of Windows. In Windows 3.1, running out of resources is common even if you have a lot of memory because the amount available for system resources cannot get larger or smaller. Windows 95 has more space for system resources and manages those resources much more intelligently, so you can have many more programs open at once.

Virtual memory

Simulated RAM that is created by taking advantage of free space on the hard drive, also called a swap file. If you start more programs or processes than your RAM has room for, the programs actively doing something will be placed in RAM while the less-active or inactive ones will be moved to the swap file space on the hard drive. Windows 95 will automatically swap programs back and forth as needed. The swap file is dynamic in Windows 95 which means it will also automatically grow and shrink as necessary.

Index

Note to the Reader: Throughout this index **boldface** page numbers indicate primary discussions of a topic. *Italic* page numbers indicate illustrations.

J

K

L

N

O

P

T

V

W

X

Y

Z

Meet tomorrow's deadlines today!

Sybex has just what you need...

Always Asking Colleagues and Friends for Help?

Use Sybex's new ABCs series instead. By skipping the long drawn-out introductions, you get right into the really useful information. With a task-oriented approach, these new ABCs help you maximize your effectiveness and save valuable time.

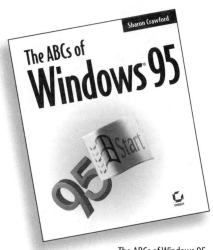
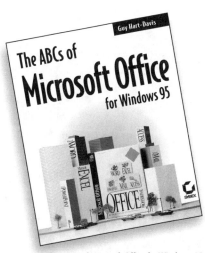